NEW FLAVOURS *of the*

JEWISH TABLE

DENISE PHILLIPS

NEW FLAVOURS *of the*

JEWISH
TABLE

DENISE
PHILLIPS

EBURY
PRESS

3 5 7 9 10 8 6 4 2

Published in 2008 by Ebury Press, an imprint of Ebury Publishing

A Random House Group Company

Text © Denise Phillips 2008

Denise Phillips has asserted her right to be identified as the author of this work
in accordance with the Copyright, Designs and Patents Act 1988

The Random House Group Limited Reg. No. 954009

Addresses for companies within the Random House Group can be found at
www.randomhouse.co.uk

A CIP catalogue record for this book is available from the British Library

The Random House Group Limited supports The Forest Stewardship
Council (FSC), the leading international forest certification organisation.
All our titles that are printed on Greenpeace approved FSC certified paper
carry the FSC logo. Our paper procurement policy can be found at
www.rbooks.co.uk/environment

To buy books by your favourite authors and register for offers visit
www.rbooks.co.uk

Designed and set by seagull.net

Printed and bound in UK by CPI Mackays, Chatham ME5 8TD

ISBN 9780091925352

Mixed Sources

Product group from well-managed
forests and other controlled sources
www.fsc.org Cert no. TT-COC-2139
© 1996 Forest Stewardship Council

FSC

Contents

Acknowledgements

WRITING THIS BOOK proved to be a very enjoyable challenge. The aim was to put together a delicious collection of modern recipes combined with some traditional ones from around the world. Visits to various destinations such as Prague, Marrakesh, Jerusalem, Vienna and New York were inspiring opportunities to enjoy Jewish cooking served the authentic way. Wherever I could, I would seek out and talk to the chefs in the restaurants to discuss the secret of the flavours in their dishes and their ways of cooking.

However, Jews have lived in a lot more countries than those that I had time to visit, so I am grateful to my various contacts in the food business, introductions from synagogues and e-mails to relatives abroad for ideas and contributions. 'Jewish geography' certainly proved useful, because whenever I spoke to one person invariably they would know someone else from another cultural background and with a different perspective on food. With help from so many sources, the backbone of the book emerged quite rapidly and is the comprehensive and practical collection of recipes that you now have in your hands – an authentic record of food from wherever Jews have established communities.

Compiling the recipes is just one aspect of writing a book. Cooking and testing each one is the other major part. So a special thank you goes to my most recent au pairs, Silvia and Zuzana, who helped me with this task and discussed the culinary delights of Eastern Europe that are so precious to them and their families.

The essence of a successful cookery book is to have recipes that work as a result of being tried and tested by cooks and not chefs. I would like to say a big thank you to the following people for taking part in the project of testing all of the recipes in book: Jane Joseph, Karin Hirsch, my sister Janice Fairfield, Caroline Shapiro, Debra Kasler, Elizabeth

Levenphal, Sue Soloway, Penny Grossman, Debbie Craig, Sue Morgan, Judy Jackson, mother Audrey Kostick, Jane Murad, Debbie Sands, Rachel Lipman, Susan Duboff, Danielle Gross, Lynne Misner, Marsha Schultz, Katrina Graham, Sharon Phillips, Jane Rome, sister Gilly Freed, Debbie Marks, Michelle Lubczanski, Tova Salaman, Karen Golanski, Rochelle Hope and Sharman Berwald.

A special thank you goes to my 'new' Auntie Nina from Newport, Gwent, who shared her early married culinary experiences in Singapore. Rabbi Simon Frances from Harrow, Middlesex, discussed his childhood culinary memories from Greece and his experiences of the Second World War. Thank you also to Michelle Ramdell, owner of Olive, the Persian kosher restaurant, for sharing some Persian Pesach traditions.

This book has numerous biblical references and I would like to thank Rabbi Nafatalie Brawer, Borehamwood United Synagogue, for his assistance as my rabbinical encyclopaedia. E-mails on various subjects were always acknowledged at '*toute vitesse*'!

I would like to thank Lesley Glassberg and Chaya Borden, my learned friends, for their regular Jewish studies lessons, which have broadened my Jewish knowledge on all aspects of the religion.

I am also very grateful to my friend Lynne Misner, who was always at the end of the phone for me to bounce ideas off, for her constant support and also to Marsha Schwarz for her time and inspiring contributions to the final editing of this book. One of the perks of the job was the various food samples that resulted from testing the recipes.

Family play a large part in writing a cookery book, and special thanks go to my twin sister, Sharon, for contacting her friends and neighbours in Florida for their festive specialities, and my Uncle Sidney from South Africa for sharing both South African and Lithuanian specialities. My uncle, Brian Redbart, is a keen genealogist and he retold the stories of my ancestors which I will always cherish.

Living in a house where up to five different recipes are cooked a day, it is only natural that my family have been involved in the creation of this book. My beloved children, Abbie, Samantha and Nicholas, and my stepdaughter Jessie, were always honest with their comments and supported me through late cooking sessions.

A special thank you goes to my mother Audrey Kostick, who has tested and tasted many of these recipes, for her help and advice, not just on this book but throughout my whole life.

Finally, thank you to my husband, Jeremy, for being so patient with me on those long nights of recipe creation and for learning to talk 'food' – a subject on which he is becoming increasingly knowledgeable. Enjoying food together from around the world on a regular basis has meant that meal times have become a lot more adventurous and extremely varied.

Introduction

WHAT WE EAT SAYS WHO WE ARE

It is said that the history of a country is visible 'on the plate'. In *New Flavours of the Jewish Table* I hope to show that the ancient, universal history of the Jewish people is just that – and that the Jewish plate is unique and eclectic.

For thousands of years, from biblical times until the creation of the state of Israel some 60 years ago, the Jewish people had no homeland. They were often exiled and, dispersed and wandering, were frequently forced to flee from persecution and hardship. There was one aspect of their lives, though, that benefited from their tribulations: Jewish cuisine. Wherever they settled for any length of time, Jews adapted the local food to fit their dietary laws and created a new culinary style that was all their own.

Jewish dietary requirements are known as kosher; the Hebrew word for fit or proper. *Kashrut* is the body of Jewish law that deals with what Jews can and can't eat, and how to prepare and eat what is allowed. The origins of these rules are found in the Torah, the first five books of the Jewish Bible. The reasons for these rules are not given and for thousands of years Jews have debated 'Why keep kosher?'. Possible explanations include health benefits, environmental considerations, to reach holiness through self-control, to practice religious ritual and to be separate from other groups. The debate is ongoing; the short answer for me is because the Torah says so. For an observant Jew no further reason is needed.

There are three categories of kosher food: meat, dairy and *parev*. In terms of meat, only animals that have split hooves and chew the cud are permitted. Cows and sheep are fine – pigs, horses and rabbits are not. Kosher poultry includes chicken, turkey, geese and duck. Animals that can be consumed are ritually slaughtered and no blood can be eaten. Dairy products from kosher animals are allowed, however these cannot be mixed with meat or poultry in the same recipe, at the same meal or even on the same dishes. So kosher households have two sets of everything to do with food preparation and delivery, from pans and plates to tea towels and dish cloths. Fish which have fins and scales such as tuna, salmon, cod and herring are kosher. Shellfish are forbidden. *Parev* is the Yiddish word for neutral and is used to describe kosher foods that contain neither meat nor dairy and therefore can be eaten with either. Eggs, fruits, grains and vegetables are all *parev* and may be served with meat or milk meals. Processed food is a complex issue in the Jewish world as it is often hard to know the source of ingredients and how they have been manufactured. So rabbinic authorities scrutinise products made for the Jewish and non-Jewish market and a system of certification exists to guide the shopper. Spirits and alcohol made from grains are kosher, however there are specific guidelines for wine and wine products such as brandy. To be kosher, wine has to be prepared from grape to bottle under rabbinic supervision.

Local influences on the Jewish style of cooking obviously included climate and lifestyle, as well as the ingredients that were available. And because Jews have at some time in their history been scattered in every part of the globe, these influences can still be recognised in their food today. This is particularly evident in the two main cultural threads that take us into the current tradition of Jewish classic cuisine.

Sephardi Jews have their roots in hot countries – Spain, North Africa, the Mediterranean region and the Middle East. Their food tends to be made quickly and is light, colourful and highly seasoned with a wide range of aromatic herbs and spices. Ashkenazi or western Jews hail from the much cooler climates of Eastern Europe. Their food is warming and filling; it often relies on a single flavouring and simple seasoning, and slow, lengthy cooking.

A major factor that influences Jewish cooking is celebration – not just the personal and family celebrations of birthdays, bar mitzvahs, weddings and more, but also the religious festivals. At these times food often becomes laden with symbolism and representation – its very colour, taste and texture has a wider meaning that involves a religious concept or historical event.

The Shabbat (Sabbath) begins at dusk on Friday and ends on Saturday night. It is a time for rest, prayer and contemplation, the family and food. We light candles, bless wine and eat *challah* bread to remember the manna God gave the Jews as sustenance while they wandered in the desert after fleeing from Egypt. Cooking is prohibited on the Sabbath so hot food is prepared in advance and kept warm. Guests have always been encouraged to share Shabbat and festival meals, and in times of poverty Jewish cooks used their skills to make a little go a long way – and ensure that the poorest ingredients were as tasty as possible.

While Shabbat takes precedence over the other festivals, all are important in the practice of Judaism – and they all have their special foods. Yom Tov is used to refer to all major and minor holidays and festivals and Jews greet each other with a 'Good Yom Tov' when they meet at these special times. Rosh Hashanah, the New Year, which falls in September or October is a time of hope. We eat apples, honey and sweet *challah* bread for a sweet year, and carrots for a prosperous one. (Carrot circles are golden and coin-shaped.) In contrast, Yom Kippur is a day set aside for fasting, depriving oneself of pleasures and repenting from the sins of the previous year. This always occurs ten days after Rosh Hashanah.

At Chanukah, the festival of lights in December, fried food is the order of the day – especially *latkes* and doughnuts. Food cooked in oil is a reminder of how, when the Temple in Jerusalem was rededicated after

Judah the Maccabee's victory over the Greek and Syrian occupiers of Israel, one day's supply of oil lasted, miraculously, for eight days.

Purim, the festival of lots, is a happy celebration, normally falling in March. It commemorates the time, 2500 years ago, when Esther, the Jewish queen of Ahasuerus, the king of Persia, foiled a plan to kill all the country's Jews. Foods with nuts and seeds are eaten to recall her vegetarian diet at the Persian court – they were among the few kosher foods she could obtain.

At Pesach (Passover) in March/April we eat *matzah* – unleavened bread. No food that rises is permitted for eight days and *matzah* meal is substituted for flour. Only foods that are Pesach-friendly (designated by a symbol at the beginning of the recipe) can be eaten over this period. This is in memory of the Jews' exodus from Egypt; they were in such a hurry to flee the pharoah's persecution that there wasn't enough time for their bread to rise. Seder refers to the festival meal eaten on the night of Pesach and means order in Yiddish, because what is eaten and the ceremonies performed at this meal follow a precise order.

For the harvest festival of Succot or Tabernacles in May we eat vegetables, strudels and other dishes filled with a variety of ingredients to celebrate the bounty and abundance of a successful crop. During the festival of Succot, it is a *mitzvah* (Hebrew for good deed) to sit in a *succah*, a temporary dwelling erected for the festival, and to eat all our meals there. Each day we also wave the Four Species of plants, in celebration of God's gift of the bounty.

Shavuot or Pentecost, the dairy festival, takes place in May or June, seven weeks after the festival of Passover and celebrates Moses receiving the Ten Commandments and other Jewish laws on Mount Sinai. The Jews knew the laws would include dietary ones, so until they were familiar with them they ate only dairy products. Cheesecake and cheese blintzes are year-round favourites but are particularly special at this time. Shavuot additionally commemorates the early wheat harvest in Palestine and hence homes and synagogues are decorated with flowers and greens. It is also known as the Festival of New Fruits, when each man brought the first of his barley, wheat, grapes, figs, olive oil, pomegranates and honey to the Temple in Jerusalem. There, everyone took part in the Bikkurim (First Fruits) ceremony, which has been revived in new dress in modern Israel.

The recipes in *New Flavours of the Jewish Table* include ones for festival food and come from all over Europe – Holland, Germany, Hungary, Poland, Italy – as well as from Morocco, Egypt, Syria and Iran. Researching and writing them has been thoroughly enjoyable and I have met and interviewed Jewish cooks from many different countries, and shared their recipes and food parcels. Persian rice cake, North African pitta bread salad and Egyptian fish balls are now regulars on my table along with my Ashkenazi roast chicken and potato *kugel*. In particular, I have become a great fan of Sephardi dishes and now use far more turmeric, cumin, coriander and lemons in my cooking than I did before.

Jewish people all over the world are passionate about food. The home is the focus of Judaism, and much of Judaism is based on nourishment – spiritual and physical. There is always an abundance of food in my house and my children say I could feed an army. Hospitality is a central principle of Jewish ethics: family and friends eating together creates community, continuity and tradition.

So, as they say in Yiddish: *Ess gezunterheit* – Eat in good health!

Notes on Recipes

- Always read through the recipe before you start cooking; it will enable you to understand the tasks more easily. Check the list of ingredients and possible substitutes, and locate everything you need before commencing. Having measured ingredients and the correct equipment to hand will make the whole experience faster and more efficient.
- Both metric and imperial measurements are given. Use either set of quantities but not a mixture.
- Standard level spoon measurements are given in all recipes:
  * 1 teaspoon = one 5 ml spoon
  * 1 tablespoon = 15 ml spoon
- Each recipe has approximate preparation and cooking times.
  * Preparation includes weighing, peeling, chopping and rolling out – in fact, anything that is 'hands on' or requires close attention before cooking.
  * Cooking is the length of time a dish (or part of a dish) is heated, or on the heat in the oven, under the grill or on the hob. Set a timer to remind yourself to check. During this time you may be able to prepare other parts of the dish or meal, which will speed up the total time taken to complete the recipe.
  * Multitasking in the kitchen takes concentration and planning at first, but will bring its own rewards.

- Where relevant, instructions for preparing dishes in advance are given in a note at the end of the recipe.
- The oven should be preheated to the specified temperature. If you are using a fan-assisted oven follow the manufacturer's instructions for adjusting the time and temperature.
- Cake tins vary in size. A cake in a deeper tin will take longer to cook. To check whether it is cooked, insert a skewer into the centre; if it comes out clean the cake is cooked.

FOOD

- All ingredients are kosher.
- Some 'milky' recipes may be made *parev* by substituting non-dairy products.
- Dishes suitable for Pesach are indicated and many others can be adapted by using kosher ingredients that are specifically for Passover, which are available prior to the festival.
- Where necessary, information is given about *kashrut*.
- Eggs are large unless otherwise stated.
- Breadcrumbs are made from fresh white bread unless otherwise stated.
- Olive oil is light unless otherwise stated.
- Sugar is caster unless otherwise stated.
- Vegetables such as potatoes, onions, carrots, etc. are peeled unless otherwise stated.
- Tomatoes are unpeeled unless otherwise stated.
- Only freeze dishes that are indicated by ❄.
- *Parev* recipes are indicated by Ⓟ.
- Pesach-friendly recipes are indicated by Ⓟ.
- Measurements for both herbs and spices are according to my preference; please adjust to your taste.

- Meat and poultry should be cooked thoroughly. To test whether poultry is cooked, pierce the thickest part of the flesh with a skewer or fork – the juices should run clear.
- To season, use sea salt and freshly ground black pepper.
- Both filo pastry and puff pastry vary in weight and size so adjustments to the recipe may be required.

Appetisers

A MEAL WITH a starter becomes more of a feast – so it is traditional at the Jewish table to offer a selection of appetisers to begin a Shabbat or Yom Tov meal. Popular Ashkenazi *vorspeise* (Yiddish for appetiser/ starter) include liver, egg and onion, and herring dishes, while Sephardi meze favour hummus, aubergine dips and salads made with tomatoes and cucumber. What they have in common is that they are all very tasty and full of flavour.

Baba Ganoush

THIS APPETISER FEATURES on most restaurant menus in Turkey, Israel and Morocco. It is an aubergine pâté that is eaten with pitta bread, bread sticks and a selection of crudités, as part of a meze. The special taste of this recipe is from the smoky flavour of the grilled aubergines. Jewish people have a particular liking for almonds, and they feature in many classic recipes including this one. It can be made in advance so it is ideal for Shabbat and Yom Tov. Many synagogues, including my own, use it as part of the Shabbat morning Kiddush, a selection of sweet and savoury snacks eaten at the end of service.

Try it with jacket potatoes, on toast or in a sandwich for a change, but do ensure that you add the garlic sparingly – because if it isn't cooked it can be quite strong.

Preparation: 10 minutes + cooling
Cooking: 40 minutes
Serves 6–8

2 large aubergines, halved lengthways
2–3 tablespoons olive oil
2 garlic cloves, crushed
4 tablespoons tahini
25 g (1 oz) ground almonds
Juice of ½ lemon
1 teaspoon ground cumin
Sea salt and freshly ground black pepper
Large handful of fresh mint leaves, roughly chopped

To serve:
Selection of crudités – fresh vegetables such as baby
artichokes, radishes, peppers, carrots and sugar snap peas

- Preheat the oven to 200°C/400°F/Gas Mark 6.
- Brush the cut sides of the aubergines with some of the oil and bake the aubergines for about 35 minutes or until soft. Meanwhile, heat the grill to its highest setting.
- Place the aubergines under the grill, cut sides up, and leave until they are black and blistered. This will take about 5 minutes. Remove and set aside to cool.

- Scoop out the flesh of the cooked aubergine and discard the skins. Put the flesh in a food processor. Add the garlic, tahini, almonds, lemon juice, cumin, and season with salt and pepper. Process to a smooth paste and check the seasoning.

- Spoon the mixture into a serving dish, drizzle with the remaining oil and scatter the mint leaves on top.

- Serve with a selection of crudités.

NOTE: *Baba ganoush* can be made up to two days in advance, and refrigerated, and will still taste delicious.

Fried Kibbeh Balls

FRIED *KIBBEH* (or *kube*) balls are the Lebanese equivalent of meat balls. They are a brilliant example of a recipe that has travelled far from its roots, as there are very few Jews still living in Lebanon. In 1948 there were an estimated 24,000; now there are less than a hundred as a result of mass emigration to Israel, France and North America.

You will find this dish in kosher restaurants all over the world. True *kibbeh* have an outer layer made of minced chicken and are filled with a finer, spiced mixture of lamb or beef cooked with pine nuts and onions. They are eaten hot with a sauce or warm with a selection of dips. Not only are they very popular; they are also filling.

As with chicken soup, every household has its own special recipe. I made these *kibbeh* three times using different ratios of semolina and bulghar wheat to get the best consistency, and decided to use semolina.

It is worth making a large batch as they freeze beautifully. The secret of their unique shape is to roll them with wet hands. To get the best flavour – over-season the filling.

You need to make two separate mixes – one for the outside shell and one for the filling.

❄

Preparation: 35 minutes
Cooking: 25 minutes
Makes 30 balls

For the outside shell:
2 onions, finely chopped
450 g (I lb) minced lean chicken
250 g (9 oz) semolina
2 tablespoons salt
I teaspoon freshly ground black pepper

For the filling:
2 tablespoons vegetable oil
50 g (2 oz) pine nuts
2 large onions, finely chopped
I tablespoon allspice
2 tablespoons ground cinnamon
225 g (8 oz) minced beef or lamb
2 tablespoons raisins
Salt and pepper

Vegetable oil, for deep-frying

To serve:
Hummus, aubergine dip, tahini and salad

- First make the outside shell. Place the onions and chicken in a food processor and whiz to form a very fine mixture. Stir in the semolina and the salt and pepper.

- Leave the mixture in the fridge for 10 minutes; this makes it easier to handle.

- To make the filling, heat 1 tablespoon of the oil in a frying pan and fry the pine nuts until light brown. Be careful not to burn them as they will taste bitter. Set aside.

- Sauté the onions until soft in the remaining oil. Add the allspice and cinnamon and cook for a further 2 minutes so that the flavour infuses. Stir in the meat and continue to cook until it is brown. Remove from the heat. Place in a food processor and whiz just briefly to combine the mixture. Add the pine nuts and the raisins and season with salt and pepper.

- The filling is now ready to be combined with the raw *kibbeh* mix that will form the outside shell.

- Heat the oil in a deep-fryer to 375°C/190°F *or* until it is hot enough to brown a cube of bread in 30 seconds.

- Take a walnut-size amount of the shell mixture and flatten it in the palm of your hand. Then take 1–2 teaspoons of the filling mixture and put it in the middle of the shell. Gently wrap the shell around the filling and, using wet hands, roll the *kibbeh* into an egg shape.

- Add the *kibbeh* to the oil in batches and fry for approximately 3 minutes or until golden brown. Remove, place on kitchen paper and keep warm in a low oven.

- Serve hot or warm with aubergine dip, hummus or tahini and a salad.

Herring Salad
in Soured Cream Sauce

SOUTH AFRICA HAS a long history of Jewish settlement, with immigrants coming from all over the world to escape persecution and poverty. In the late 1880s alone, over 40,000 Jews arrived there from Lithuania and today their descendents still form the majority of the Jewish community. One of the most Orthodox in the world, it is the largest in Africa although, with emigration to Israel and elsewhere averaging about 2000 people a year, it numbers only around 70,000 and is increasingly worried about a growth in anti-Semitism. The mainly Ashkenazi community continues to enjoy favourites such as herrings, *gefilte* fish and *kuchens.*

This particular recipe is a great favourite with South African Jews who eat it as a starter, as part of a Kiddush and to break religious fasts. Herring and soured cream are classic Jewish ingredients that are also widely used in Sweden and Holland where herrings are plentiful and popular.

Preparation: 20 minutes + 24 hours chilling
Cooking: None
Serves 4–6

1 x 300 g jar pickled herrings
1 shallot or small onion, finely chopped
1 red apple, cored and coarsely chopped
2 dill pickles, rinsed and roughly chopped
150 ml (¼ pint) soured cream
1 teaspoon sugar or to taste
Sprigs of fresh dill or fresh parsley, to garnish
Pumpernickel or rye bread, to serve

- Drain and rinse the herrings, scrape off any skin and/or membrane and cut into small pieces.

- In a medium bowl, combine the herrings, shallot or onion, apple, dill pickles, soured cream and sugar.

- Cover and refrigerate for at least 24 hours.

- Garnish with dill or parsley and serve with pumpernickel or rye bread.

Israeli Salad

WHEN I WAS 16 I was lucky enough to visit Israel for a month and work on a kibbutz. Discovering this salad at breakfast on the first day was a true delight for someone as keen on fresh foods as I am – although by the 30th day its appeal had begun to wane! Today this salad is still very popular, whether served at Shabbat lunch with *gefilte* fish, as part of a meze of salads with pitta breads, hummus and falafel, or as an accompaniment for just about every meal – both at home and in restaurants. Its enduring appeal comes from its abundant, inexpensive ingredients as well as the brief preparation time and delicious fresh taste.

The essential ingredients are tomatoes and cucumbers. I like to add red and green peppers to keep in tune with their colours, but whatever you use all the vegetables should be cut into 6 mm (¼ in) pieces.

To complete the authentic Israeli experience, I have garnished the salad with home-made *zaatar* (pronounced ZAH-tahr). *Zaatar* is a miz of spices used as a table condiment in Israel and the Middle East. Key ingredients include thyme, oregano, sesame seeds, sumac and salt but there are many variations. It is often mixed with olive oil and served with warm pitta bread, hummus and yoghurt. As a shortcut you can buy *zaatar* from kosher supermarkets.

Preparation: 10 minutes (for salad)
Cooking: None
Serves 6

3 beef tomatoes, or 6 salad tomatoes cut into cubes
1 cucumber, peeled, deseeded and cut into cubes
1 green pepper, halved, deseeded and cut into cubes
1 red pepper, halved, deseeded and cut into cubes
1 small red onion, roughly chopped
4 tablespoons finely chopped fresh parsley
3 tablespoons extra virgin olive oil
Juice of 1 lemon
Salt and freshly ground black pepper
Fresh mint leaves and *zaatar*, to garnish

For the zaatar:
1 tablespoon toasted sesame seeds
25 g (1 oz) sumac (Mediterranean spice)
2 tablespoons finely chopped fresh thyme
2 tablespoons finely chopped fresh marjoram
2 tablespoons finely chopped fresh oregano
1 teaspoon coarse salt

- First make the *zaatar*. Grind the sesame seeds in a food processor or with a pestle and mortar. Add all the remaining ingredients and mix well.

- If you have made the *zaatar* in advance, put it into a plastic bag or airtight container and store in a cool, dark place.

- To make the salad, mix the tomatoes, cucumber, peppers, onion and parsley together in a large mixing bowl. Sprinkle with the oil and lemon juice, season with salt and black pepper and mix again. Check and adjust the seasoning.

- Garnish with mint leaves and sprinkle with a little of the *zaatar*.

The Rise of Salmon

SMOKED SALMON IS undoubtedly one of the most popular types of fish with the Jewish community today, and is synonymous with being Jewish. For many, including my husband, the Sunday lunch-time ritual is smoked salmon and cream cheese bagels.

However, it was not always so. During the Middle Ages, herring was the most widely available fish in Central Europe and Germany. It was cheap, and with many Jews living in poverty, salt-cured herring became one of the staples of their diet, and a symbol of bad times and of being of a lesser class.

During the eighteenth and nineteenth centuries, as Jews began to prosper, they turned away from salted herring and its sad reminders and looked for foods that reflected their improved lives. Salmon was a more luxurious option and they soon applied the curing recipes that had been used for herring to this more lavish fish. The result was tender, delicate flesh with a smooth, silky texture and subtle salty taste and cured salmon immediately became a delicacy that is treasured to this day.

Americans call it lox, which is derived from *lachs*, the German word for salmon. However, true lox is not actually smoked salmon – it is cured in a salt/sugar/spice mixture. True smoked salmon, also called Nova-style salmon, is briefly cold-smoked at room temperature for a few hours in addition to being salt-/sugar-cured. This does not cook or preserve the salmon. Its sole purpose is to impart a slight smoky taste to it.

Today, the flavour varies according to the type of salmon used (wild or farmed, Atlantic or Pacific species, etc.), and the smoking technique. Cold-smoked salmon tends to be subtly smoky, and more oily and smooth than the hot-smoked variety, which is much more smoky and much drier. The popular Scottish smoked salmon uses wood chips from old whisky or sherry casks for a very distinctive flavour. Most salmon in supermarkets is typically cold-smoked farmed salmon.

Salmon Pâté on Melba Toast with Cucumber Relish

THIS RECIPE IS a scrumptious appetiser for any occasion – a wonderful combination of fresh and smoked salmon whizzed together with cream cheese. It is one of my favourites and I serve it frequently as it is so quick and easy to make.

I like to elevate the recipe and serve it as a canapé or offer larger portions as a light lunch. I am also particularly fond of the combination of fresh and pickled cucumbers and gherkins in the relish – a unique creation that enhances the delicate pâté.

Melba toast is a classic accompaniment to soups and starters.

P **P** (to be suitable for Pesach use non-dairy cream cheese and omit melba toast)
Preparation: 20 minutes
Cooking: 10 minutes
Serves 6

100 ml (4 fl oz) white wine
250 g (9 oz) fresh salmon, skinned and cut into bite-size
    pieces
110 g (4 oz) smoked salmon
2 tablespoons cream cheese or Toffutti non-dairy cream
    cheese
1 teaspoon lemon juice
2 tablespoons finely chopped fresh dill
Salt and freshly ground black pepper

For the cucumber relish:
2 pickled cucumbers, very finely chopped
3 gherkins, very finely chopped
5 cm (2 in) fresh cucumber, halved and seeds removed,
    finely chopped
1 spring onion, very finely chopped
1 tablespoon extra virgin olive oil
1 teaspoon lemon juice
2 tablespoons finely chopped fresh dill
Salt and freshly ground black pepper

For the Melba toast (omit for Pesach):
6 slices of white or brown soft-grain bread
1–2 tablespoons grated Parmesan cheese (optional)
Salt and freshly ground black pepper

- Pour the wine into a pan and bring it to the boil. Add the fresh salmon and reduce the heat to a simmer. Cook until the salmon is no longer bright pink – this will take about 5 minutes. Drain the salmon and discard the wine.

- Place the fresh salmon, smoked salmon, cream cheese, lemon juice and dill in a food processor and whiz gently so that the mixture is roughly combined. Season to taste with salt and pepper.

- To make the relish, combine all the ingredients. Check the seasoning just before serving.

- To make the Melba toast, preheat the grill to its highest setting and toast the slices of bread lightly on both sides. Quickly cut off the crusts and split each slice into two thin slices. Scrape any doughy bits off the untoasted sides and sprinkle with the Parmesan, if using, and salt and pepper.

- Place, untoasted sides up, on a baking sheet and grill for 2–3 minutes or until golden.

- To serve, place some salmon pâté on the sides of individual white plates, and dust with pepper. Garnish with the cucumber relish and Melba toast.

NOTE: The cucumber relish can be made a day in advance and refrigerated. The Melba toast can be made *up* to two days in advance. Allow it to cool and store it in an airtight tin. Warm through in *a low* oven just before serving. The pâté can be made up to two days in advance; store covered and refrigerated until required.

Chicken Liver Salad with Figs and Walnuts and a Soy Honey Dressing

THE FLAVOURS OF some recipes can develop at different stages of cooking and with the addition of different types of ingredients. This is an excellent example: the flavour is transformed by the final addition of the soy/honey dressing, which delicately picks up the sweetness of the figs. This warm, stylish, quick salad can be served as a substantial starter or as a main course.

The fig is one of the hugely symbolic fruits in the Jewish religion with a history that goes back to the first chapters of Genesis, and the story of Adam and Eve who covered their nakedness with fig leaves. In ancient Israel, fig trees were planted in gardens throughout the country and the fruit was eaten fresh or as a seasoning, and used to make honey and alcohol. Figs are best straight from the tree in the late afternoon after being baked naturally by the sun.

They are available in the summer season from most good supermarkets. Once the fruit is ripe, the skin splits easily so choose unblemished figs and do not try to keep them for more than a day or two in the fridge. Dried figs are available all year round and make for a reasonable alternative, but be careful because figs have the highest sugar content of all fruits – over 50 per cent.

Preparation: 15 minutes
Cooking: 5 minutes
Serves 6 as a starter, 4 as a main course

575 g (1¼ lb) chicken livers, koshered, washed and trimmed
1 egg, lightly beaten

**3 slices of white bread, made into breadcrumbs,
    or 6 tablespoons medium *matzah* meal
3 tablespoons vegetable oil
2 tablespoons fruity red wine
225 g (8 oz) rocket leaves
6 fresh figs, quartered
75 g (3 oz) chopped walnuts**

For the soy and honey dressing:
**I tablespoon soy sauce
I tablespoon honey
2 tablespoons sesame oil
2 tablespoons extra virgin olive oil
Salt and freshly ground black pepper**

- First make the dressing. Combine the soy sauce, honey and sesame and olive oils and season with salt and pepper. Set aside.

- Dip the chicken livers in the beaten egg and then coat in the breadcrumbs or *matzah* meal.

- Heat the oil in a large frying pan. Fry the chicken livers for 3 minutes then turn them over. Pour in the red wine and continue to fry the livers for a further 2 minutes. (Chicken livers taste better if they are slightly undercooked otherwise they become tough and leathery.) Cut the livers into small pieces.

- Arrange the individual plates with the rocket leaves, figs and walnuts. Mix in the livers and drizzle with the dressing.

- Serve immediately or at room temperature.

NOTE: The dressing can be made up to two days in advance and refrigerated.

HOW TO KOSHER CHICKEN LIVERS:

Even if sold by a kosher butcher, the livers may need to be koshered at home – by roasting them over an open flame to ensure that all possible traces of blood are removed.

- Score each liver with a knife kept especially for this purpose. Rinse the livers well under cold running water and sprinkle with salt.

- Place the livers on a wire grid so that the blood can drip freely into a pan or other container. (Both utensils will be non-kosher and should be kept for this purpose only.)

- Roast the livers over a naked flame or under a high grill or in an oven until they are cooked and their outer surfaces are dry.

- Wash the livers. They are now ready for use.

Pickled Cucumbers

ALTHOUGH DIFFERENT PICKLES and relishes are regular features on Jewish dining tables, none is held in such high regard, or flavoured or eaten in so many ways, as the humble pickled cucumber.

The Sephardi community likes them salty and sharp. Ashkenazis prefer them sweeter and crunchy. But you can also have them sweet and sour, with dill, new green, with garlic, sweet, sliced, whole, spears, chunks, crunchy, soft, hot or mild. And, of course, they go with everything from salt beef to schnitzel, from cream cheese to roast chicken – and are even good on their own.

They are found on most Friday-night tables as a matter of routine, and in my household they are enjoyed while we munch on the egg and onion, and chopped liver, the classic appetisers for the Shabbat meal.

The joy of making your own pickled cucumbers is that you can flavour them to your personal taste. Have them sweet or sour – it's your choice. And it's great fun to make them with children as the cucumbers miraculously turn from plain bright green to a pickled, dark relish colour.

Preparation: 5 minutes + 2 days chilling
Cooking: 2 minutes

1 large (30 cm/12 in) cucumber or 2 smaller cucumbers, unpeeled
340 ml (12 fl oz) cider or white wine vinegar (use kosher for Passover)
2 teaspoons salt
6–8 tablespoons sugar or to taste
10 black peppercorns
2 garlic cloves, sliced
5 bay leaves (fresh or dried)

- Wipe the sides of the cucumbers with a damp cloth and cut them into 5 mm (¼ in) slices.

- Place the vinegar, salt, sugar and peppercorns in a pan with 120 ml (4½ fl oz) water. Bring to the boil, then reduce the heat and simmer for 2 minutes or until the sugar has dissolved.

- Allow the liquor to cool, then add the garlic and bay leaves.

- Pour the liquor over the cucumbers and place in a 2 litre (3½ pint) sterilised jar.

- Store in the refrigerator for two days before using.
- Serve at room temperature.

NOTE: Radishes, sliced baby carrots and sliced fennel can be pickled in the same way. Add 1 tablespoon capers to the pickling liquor and garnish with sprigs of coriander before serving.

The Russian Influence

THE VAST TERRITORIES of the Russian Empire at one time hosted the largest Jewish population in the world. Russia was also where many of today's most distinctive theological and cultural traditions developed and leading rabbis grew up there. However, by the late nineteenth century Jews were facing anti-Semitic discriminatory policies and were being persecuted, most notably in 1881 in southern Russia, where there were large-scale anti-Jewish pogroms (or riots) in 166 towns, when the Jews were wrongly blamed for the assassination of Alexander II. Thousands of Jewish homes were destroyed and many Jews were killed or injured; most of the survivors were reduced to extreme poverty with many emigrating, either voluntarily or through force – as portrayed so well in the film *Fiddler on the Roof*.

My own great-grandparents came from Kroby in Russia and fled the country because of the pogroms and persecution. They had ten children, of whom five came to the United Kingdom and five went to the United States. The ones who arrived in the UK created a new home in Club Row, Bethnal Green, where my grandfather started his trade as a cabinetmaker and, together with his sons, built up a business in Hackney Road.

The Second World War resulted in further horrors for the Jews of Russia and in the late 1980s and early 1990s, with a more liberal emigration policy, over half the Jewish population left Russia, mainly for Israel and the United States.

Russian Salad

IT IS INEVITABLE that Jewish cooking has become imbued with a slightly Russian flavour, and nowhere is this more apparent than in this recipe, which has been passed down through generations of my family. I have adapted it slightly for modern tastes.

Classic Russian salad consists of very finely diced vegetables, cooked and combined with mayonnaise. Garnished with radishes, olives and parsley, it looks as amazing as it tastes. It is popular for Shabbat lunch, with herring, smoked fish or cold chicken.

🔷 Ⓟ (to be suitable for Pesach use kosher capers and mayonnaise)
Preparation: 25 minutes
Cooking: 40 minutes
Serves 8

5 medium-size potatoes, unpeeled and very finely diced
6 medium carrots, very finely diced
2 tablespoons olive oil
6 gherkins, finely diced
3 tablespoons capers, rinsed (use kosher for Pesach)
4 tablespoons mayonnaise (more if preferred) (use kosher for Pesach)
Salt and freshly ground black pepper

To garnish:
10 radishes, finely chopped
4 tablespoons stoned, finely chopped black olives
1 large bunch fresh parsley, finely chopped

- Preheat the oven to 200°C/400°F/Gas Mark 6.

- Cook the potatoes in boiling water for 8–10 minutes until just soft. Drain.

- Cook the carrots in boiling water, using another pan, until soft but not mushy. This will take about 15–20 minutes. Leave to cool for 10 minutes.

- Heat the oil in a large frying pan and fry the potatoes for 10 minutes or until golden. Leave to cool for 10 minutes.

- Mix the potatoes, carrots, gherkins, capers and mayonnaise together. Season well with salt and pepper, transfer to a large serving plate and garnish with rows of the radishes, olives and parsley.

- Serve at room temperature.

Date and Rocket Salad with Goats' Cheese Dressing and Garlic Croutons

THE TORAH TELLS us we should protect our trees as they are an important part of our environment. So every year on the 15th day of the Jewish month of Shevat, Jews around the world, especially in Israel, celebrate the New Year for Trees, or Tu B'Shevat. I like to mark this festival by using ingredients indigenous to Israel. Dates are a favourite of mine as they are so versatile and can be used in both sweet and savoury recipes.

Some people refer to dates as the 'candy' that grows on trees because of their sweetness, but as well as being full of sugar they are also a good source of vitamins A and B, and calcium. Medjool dates are great to snack on with cheese and biscuits, while some of the dried varieties are better for cooking cakes, biscuits and pies.

This impressive salad is light and tasty, and is perfect as a starter, light lunch or even as an accompaniment with fish. Although I have used goats' cheese, feta cheese is a good alternative should you prefer it. The rocket can be replaced with baby spinach.

Preparation: 10 minutes
Cooking: 10 minutes
Serves 4

110 g (4 oz) rocket leaves
6 spring onions, finely sliced
75 g (3 oz) pitted dates (fresh if available), roughly
   chopped

For the goats' cheese dressing:
110 g (4 oz) goats' cheese (soft variety without a rind),
   crumbled
1–2 teaspoons lemon juice
1 tablespoon mayonnaise
4 tablespoons olive oil
Salt and freshly ground black pepper

For the garlic croutons:
6 thick slices of white or brown bread, crusts removed
3 garlic cloves, finely chopped
Extra virgin olive oil, for drizzling
Salt and freshly ground black pepper

- First make the croutons. Preheat the oven to 200°C/400°F/Gas Mark 6 and cut the bread into cubes. Place the cubes on a baking sheet. Scatter with the garlic, drizzle with the oil and season with salt and pepper. Place in the oven for 10 minutes or until golden. Put a timer on as the croutons will taste bitter if they burn! Remove and set aside to cool.

- To make the dressing, place the goats' cheese, lemon juice and mayonnaise in a food processor with 1–2 tablespoons water and whiz until smooth. With the motor running, gradually add the oil and blend until emulsified. Taste and adjust the seasoning with salt and pepper.

- In a large salad bowl, toss together the rocket, spring onions and dates.

- To serve, garnish the salad with the dressing and sprinkle with the croutons. Serve immediately.

The Falafel Story

FALAFEL MAY NOW be considered Israel's national vegetarian dish, but it was originally Arabic (various versions hail from Egypt and Iraq). Made from ground chick-peas, then shaped into patties and fried, it became popular in the early days of the Israeli state when easy-to-eat street foods lent themselves to the busy lifestyles of the settlers. With a general shortage of meat, falafel made a cheap, protein-rich meal – and people liked it!

As with all popular dishes, every restaurant and chef has their own personal recipe. I have vivid memories of devouring some amazing falafel packed within a pitta bread overflowing with fresh salad from a bar in Ben Yehudah Street, Jerusalem, during a family holiday there in 2006.

The Israelis may not have invented falafel, but they have certainly adapted it to their tastes, with most bars offering a dizzying array of accompaniments: pickles, North African harissa (hot sauce), chopped peppers, onions, cucumbers, coleslaw, red cabbage salad, aubergine dip, tomato salad and many, many more. Portions are generous and will certainly satisfy a healthy appetite.

Yemenite Jews and the Arabs of Jerusalem make falafel with chick-peas alone but in Egypt and other Arab countries it is made with a mixture of broad beans and chick-peas.

Israel celebrated its 60th anniversary in 2008 and there were festivities all over the world to mark the occasion. My community in Northwood, in north-west London, celebrated Yom Ha'Atzmaut (Israel Independence Day) with a group of Israeli teenagers who, as part of the Magic Moments project, were invited to find out more about Jewish life in Britain. The Magic Moments programme takes 14–15-year-olds from the UK to visit the region of the Galil, northern Israel. The UK teenagers stay with local families where they experience true Israeli hospitality. They learn about this area of Israel, culture, visit schools and historical cities like Safed, and enjoy fun activities such as hiking and kayaking. The Israeli teenagers in turn come to the UK where they are shown around and are looked after in Jewish homes. Falafel, salad and pitta breads were served on the anniversary to cement the link between the Israelis and our community – and to make them feel truly at home.

Falafel with Chick-peas

THIS RECIPE REQUIRES some forward planning, because it works best with dried chick-peas which need to be soaked overnight. Canned ones are too wet and the result is not as good. In addition, the recipe uses quite a number of ingredients, including herbs and spices, to give it a strong aromatic flavour, so it is best eaten fresh, straight out of the fryer.

Preparation: 30 minutes + soaking time (overnight or at least 4 hours)
Cooking: 55 minutes
Makes 40 patties

250 g (9 oz) dried chick-peas
3–4 tablespoons bulghar wheat
I large onion
5 garlic cloves
5 tablespoons finely chopped fresh parsley
5 tablespoons finely chopped fresh coriander leaves
3 tablespoons ground cumin
I tablespoon ground coriander
2 teaspoons baking powder
I teaspoon salt
Pinch of cayenne pepper
Freshly ground black pepper
I egg
3–4 tablespoons gram flour
Vegetable oil, for deep-frying

To serve:

Pitta breads, pickles, olives, shredded cabbage, Israeli salad (see page 15), hummus (see page 34) and tahini

- Place the chick-peas in a large bowl and cover with water. Leave to soak for at least 4 hours or overnight. Drain and rinse.

- Put the chick-peas in a medium-size pan and cover with about 1 litre (1¾ pints) water. Bring to the boil then reduce the heat and simmer for 45 minutes, adding more water if required. Drain.

- Grind the chick-peas in a food processor. Put the ground chick-peas in a bowl and stir in the bulghar wheat.

- Put the onion, garlic, parsley, fresh coriander, ground cumin, ground coriander, baking powder, salt and cayenne in the food processor and season with pepper. Process to form a spicy paste. Add this to the chick-pea mixture in the bowl.

- Add 100 ml (4 fl oz) water and the egg to the bowl. Stir in the flour, adding a little more water if the mixture is too dry or more flour if it is too wet. Using wet hands, shape the mixture into about 40 walnut-size patties.

- Heat the oil in a deep-fryer until it is hot enough to brown a cube of bread in 30 seconds. Add the falafel patties to the oil in batches and cook for 3–4 minutes until golden brown. Remove with a slotted spoon and drain on kitchen paper.

- To serve, tuck the falafel into warm pitta breads along with a spoonful of hummus and some shredded cabbage. Accompany with olives, pickles, Israeli salad and tahini.

A Middle Eastern Tradition

A CREAMY GOLDEN purée of chick-peas, hummus is a speciality of Middle Eastern Jews but has become popular worldwide with Jews and non-Jews alike.

It is eaten throughout the Middle East and the Mediterranean, as well as in many parts of India. Although chick-peas were used as food by our hunter-gatherer ancestors, and were cultivated around 7000 years ago in the Middle East, the history of hummus is unknown and there is no way of knowing where it originated – though this is presumed to be somewhere in the Middle East. We do know that many versions have existed for many thousands of years.

Hummus is traditionally scooped with flatbreads such as pitta, but outside the Middle East it is increasingly popular as a dip for tortilla chips. It is also used as an appetiser to accompany main courses, as part of a meze and as a dressing (for example with falafel, Israeli salad, grilled chicken and aubergine dip). In Israel and many parts of the world densely populated with Jewish people, a hummus sandwich is a popular snack for children.

It can be garnished in numerous ways, including with chopped parsley, paprika, cumin (popular in Egypt), pine nuts (traditional with Palestinian hummus), tomatoes, cucumber, pickled turnips (traditional in Lebanon), thinly sliced onions, sautéed mushrooms or whole chick-peas before being drizzled with olive oil.

On a health note, hummus contains large amounts of the nutrients iron and vitamin C, and is a good source of protein and dietary fibre. Depending on the recipe, it contains varying amounts of monounsaturated fat. It is especially suitable for vegetarian and vegan diets. When eaten with pitta bread, the combination provides all the essential amino acids for humans.

Hummus

I HAVE CHOSEN to use canned chick-peas for this recipe to speed it up, but traditionally the dried variety was used; these need to be soaked overnight and then cooked for 2 hours or until soft.

Preparation: 10 minutes
Cooking: None
Serves 8

2 x 400 g cans chick-peas, drained and rinsed
Juice of ½ lemon
3 tablespoons tahini
2 garlic cloves, crushed
4–6 tablespoons olive oil
Salt and cayenne pepper
Chopped fresh parsley and olives, to garnish
Hot pitta breads, to serve

- Place the chick-peas in a food processor with the lemon juice and work to a smooth purée. Add the tahini, garlic and all but 2 teaspoons of the oil, and season with salt and cayenne. Blend until smooth.
- Check the seasoning and adjust accordingly, then spoon into a serving dish.
- Garnish with parsley and olives and drizzle the reserved oil over the top. Serve with hot pitta breads.

NOTE: To provide a vibrant colour and unusual flavour, add cooked beetroot to the mixture.

Jews in North Africa

THE JEWISH COMMUNITIES in Morocco, Algeria, Tunisia, Libya and Egypt date back several thousand years and prospered over the last few centuries despite the growth of other religions. However, the effect of the Second World War and the anti- Jewish riots in most parts of North Africa and the Middle East that followed the creation of the State of Israel in 1948, left virtually no Jew in this part of the world untouched. Mass expulsions and mass emigration mean that today there are only a few small pockets of Jewish life in North Africa.

Several thousand Jews remain in Morocco, most of them in Casablanca but some in cities like Fez, Rabat and Marrakech, and there is a continued Berber Jewish presence in small villages like Inezgane. Today, Moroccan Judaism is a blend of oriental, Berber, Arab and Spanish customs, resulting in a variety of practices that combine rabbinical teachings with a devotion to spiritualism unfamiliar to most Western Jews.

Chick-pea, Feta and Olive Salad with Harissa Dressing

I RECENTLY SPENT a week in Marrakech, and was astonished by the vitality of the place, the spices with their amazing aromas, and the abundance of poultry, dried pulses, fruits, nuts and fresh herbs. This recipe is an adaptation of a salad I had during my visit, that is found all over Turkey, Morocco and Spain, and has all the flavours of the Med in one dish. It is popular for Shabbat and over Shavuot.

Preparation: 20 minutes
Cooking: 30 seconds
Serves 4

1 x 400 g can chick-peas, drained and rinsed
250 g (9 oz) cherry tomatoes, halved
200 g (7 oz) feta cheese, cut into cubes
150 g (5 oz) stoned black olives
4 tablespoons finely chopped fresh flatleaf parsley
Green salad leaves, to serve

For the harissa dressing:
1 tablespoon coriander seeds
2 teaspoons cumin seeds
2 fresh red chillies
2 garlic cloves
1 tablespoon lemon juice
6 tablespoons extra virgin olive oil
½ teaspoon salt
Freshly ground black pepper

- First make the dressing. Put the coriander seeds and cumin seeds in a frying pan and place over a medium heat for 30 seconds or until the seeds smell aromatic.

- Remove the seeds and veins from the chillies. Place them in a food processor together with the coriander and cumin seeds, garlic and lemon juice. Gradually add the oil and whiz until smooth. Add the salt and some pepper to taste.

- For the salad, mix the chick-peas with the tomatoes, feta and olives. Stir in the parsley.

- To serve, arrange the salad leaves on individual plates. Add the salad and drizzle with the dressing.

Red Pepper Potato Tortilla

THIS IS A classic Spanish dish that is similar to an omelette, but it is made with thinly sliced potatoes and onions, and other store cupboard ingredients. I like to add chopped red pepper for both colour and flavour. Using a food processor to ease the task of slicing the potatoes speeds up the preparation. This dish is *parev* and is also suitable for Passover, so keep it for then.

The tortilla can be served for breakfast, lunch or dinner – an excuse to make it is not required. If you are preparing it as part of a tapas meal, cut it into wedges and serve it hot from the frying pan. With salad it is also a tasty vegetarian option for Shabbat lunch. It slices up beautifully when cold and can be warmed on a hot plate without going dry.

Preparation: 15 minutes
Cooking: 25 minutes approx.
Serves 2–3

1 Spanish onion
450 g (1 lb) baby new potatoes, thinly sliced
2 tablespoons olive oil
1 red pepper, halved, deseeded and roughly chopped
4 eggs, well beaten
Salt and freshly ground black pepper
Sprigs of fresh flatleaf parsley, to garnish

- Slice the onion into rings. Boil the potatoes until they are just cooked. This will take about 5–8 minutes.

- Heat the oil in a 20 cm (8 in) heavy-based frying pan. Add the onion and cook over a low heat for about 5 minutes until just coloured. Stir in the potatoes and the red pepper.

- Season the eggs with salt and pepper, pour them over the vegetables and swirl to cover. Cook over a medium heat until the eggs are set.

- Using a knife, loosen the sides of the tortilla. Place a large plate upside down over the pan, invert the tortilla on to the plate and then slide it back into the pan. Cook for a final 2–3 minutes until the underside of the tortilla is golden brown.

- Slide the tortilla out of the pan on to a chopping board and cut it into wedges.

- Serve warm, garnished with sprigs of parsley.

Salmon and Ginger Fish Balls

WE TEND TO make special dishes for Pesach even though they can be enjoyed at any time of the year. Boiled fish balls are a popular choice and I thought I would ring the changes and, instead of making them with a mixture of white fish, use fresh salmon with ginger. It is a delicious combination, flavoured with spring onions and fresh dill. In addition, this is an extremely healthy recipe, as there is no added fat and the fish balls are very low in cholesterol – only egg white is used to combine the mixture.

They can be eaten hot, warm or cold so they won't spoil if they have been made in advance or left in warm water and the Seder service goes on for a little longer than anticipated. You can vary the size from cocktail to larger main-course portions. However, I recommend that you keep them to the same size when cooking so that they are all ready at the same time.

I like to serve them cold with *chrain*, a Yiddish grated horseradish and beetroot sauce, or beetroot relish or mayonnaise and a salad, or even hot with vegetables.

Preparation: 20 minutes
Cooking: 30 minutes
Serves 6

800 g (1¾ lb) fresh salmon, skinned and cut into cubes
5 cm (2 in) piece of fresh root ginger, peeled and finely
    chopped
3 tablespoons finely chopped fresh herbs (dill, parsley,
    tarragon or coriander)
8 spring onions, trimmed to include green and white parts
4 teaspoons salt
Freshly ground black pepper
1 small egg white
1 bay leaf
2 black peppercorns

To garnish:
Sprigs of fresh dill
2 lemons, sliced

- Place the salmon, ginger, fresh herbs and spring onions in a food processor and whiz until smooth. Season very well with 2 teaspoons of the salt, and pepper to taste, as the mixture needs plenty of flavour – the addition of the egg white weakens the seasoning.

- While the food processor is running, slowly add the egg white. Remove the mixture and place it in a dish. Using wet hands, take 1–2 tablespoons of mixture and roll it into balls. Set aside the balls to chill in the fridge whilst the stock is made.

- Now make the stock for boiling the fish balls. Place the bay leaf, peppercorns and remaining salt in a large deep pan with 570 ml (1 pint) water or enough to cover the fish. Bring to the boil, then reduce the heat to a simmer for 20 minutes.

- Carefully drop the fish balls into the simmering stock, cover the pan with a lid and cook for about 10 minutes. The balls are cooked when they rise to the surface. Use a slotted spoon to remove them and transfer them to a warmed serving plate.

- Garnish with dill and slices of lemon before serving.

Soups

SOUPS HAVE BEEN a staple of the Jewish table throughout time as they are economical and nutritious. In hot Sephardi lands a spicy, meaty soup helped diners to keep cool. Ashkenazi soups tend to be thicker and more stew-like to provide winter warmth. The most famous Jewish soup, with its claim to promote good health and banish sickness, is made from chicken. While scientists continue to debate its value as a cure, I suggest you just enjoy it!

A JEWISH TRADITION

The first chicken soup was probably made in the poor communities of Russia where for centuries poultry was the only affordable meat. Families found uses for the whole bird, so a three-course traditional meal might be chopped chicken liver, followed by a broth-like soup, with the rest of the fowl for an entrée. Today, chicken soup is still served as part of a Shabbat meal in most Jewish homes, at festivals and weddings, and as a general cold weather pick-me-up. Additional 'extras' can include cooked *lokshen* (vermicelli or egg noodles), *kreplach* (three-cornered 'Jewish ravioli' filled with onion and minced beef or chicken), or *knaidlach* (*matzah* balls).

Chicken soup is well known for its health-giving properties. At the University of Nebraska Medical Center in the United States, researchers found that (even when diluted with water) it has anti-inflammatory properties that help soothe cold-ridden stuffy noses and sore throats.

And it's widely believed that, beyond being rich in protein and vegetables, it acts as a placebo because it is generally prepared as a comfort food that warms one's insides. But you don't have to be Jewish to make and enjoy chicken soup.

Vermicelli Chicken Soup

THE BASIS OF good soup is a good stock and in my recipe I use a varied combination of vegetables that produces an excellent flavour. The more ingredients in a soup, the longer it needs to cook. Simmering for 3 hours or more extracts the best flavour from the vegetables and chicken carcasses. If you are planning to have roast chicken on Friday night, remove the giblets and add them to the soup along with the carcass or carcasses left over from the meal.

The quantity here is generous, to allow for 'seconds'. It is a good idea to leave the skins on the onions as they give more flavour and I add a few threads of saffron to enhance the soup's golden appearance. Regular skimming helps to keep it clear and I suggest that this is done frequently throughout the 3 hours. The soup must be prepared in advance as you need to refrigerate it overnight.

Preparation: 20 minutes + overnight chilling
Cooking: 3 hours
Serves 12–15

2 chicken carcasses and giblets or 2 turkey necks
4 tablespoons chicken stock powder or 3 chicken stock
cubes
4 carrots, sliced
5 sticks celery, sliced
2 turnips, sliced
I leek, sliced
2 onions, unpeeled, washed and halved
2 small tomatoes, halved
2 tablespoons salt
3 bay leaves (fresh or dried)
3 black peppercorns
I swede, sliced
A few saffron threads, to taste
Croutons or *knaidlach* (see page 67), selection of
vegetables (carrots, celery and onions) and vermicelli
***lokshen*, to serve**

- Place the carcasses and giblets in a large deep pan and add all the remaining ingredients. Pour in 6 litres (10½ pints) water and bring to the boil, then reduce the heat and simmer for 3 hours. From time to time skim off any scum or fat that rises to the surface.

- Allow to cool then strain the soup into a bowl. Add a selection of the vegetables that are still intact. Leaving them in the soup allows the chicken flavours to continue to infuse. Some soups benefit from time and this is one of them.

- Refrigerate overnight. Remove the fat from the top and use to make *knaidlach*.

- Reheat the soup until it starts to boil.

- Put a generous helping of piping hot soup into each bowl and add a selection of vegetables, I like to use carrots, a little celery and some onion. Sprinkle with croutons, or add some *knaidlach* and vermicelli *lokshen*.

NOTE: The simpler a soup, i.e. the fewer the ingredients, the better it is to eat it fresh, but chicken soup actually improves with time – it can be kept in the fridge for a maximum of three days before deterioration starts to take place.

Mushroom and Barley Soup (Krupnik)

BARLEY IS ONE of the seven types of food specifically mentioned in the Bible. In biblical times, it was the poor man's staple food and could be eaten at any meal, whether as a porridge, a type of cake or as the main ingredient of bread. It was also fed to cattle and other livestock. Barley is *seòrah* in Hebrew and is the first grain to ripen in Israel. Because of this, gathering it marked the start of the spring harvest season and the counting of the *omer* (a measure of barley) connected the holiday of Passover to the holiday of Shavuot. Today, the grain has become a culinary ingredient used in soups and stews.

This is a really tasty soup that has more variations than you can begin to imagine. This recipe is my version of a classic Polish soup that has been updated by the addition of dried porcini and some Kiddush wine or sherry. It makes a pleasant change to traditional chicken soup for a family Rosh Hashanah gathering. Adding chicken or turkey meat or giblets subtly incorporates natural flavour without salt. It is a nutritious filling soup, so keep it for cold winter days when only the best warming broth will do.

❄ Ⓟ

Preparation: 15 minutes + soaking (1 hour or overnight)
Cooking: 1 hour 5 minutes
Serves 10–12

2 tablespoons vegetable oil
2 onions, roughly chopped
2 garlic cloves, finely chopped
2 potatoes, cut into cubes
3 sticks celery, roughly chopped
4 chicken wings or 2 turkey or chicken necks and hearts or
a mix of giblets
3 litres (5¼ pints) water plus 3 tablespoons vegetable or
chicken stock or 2 stock cubes
200 g (7 oz) barley, soaked in hot water for 1 hour or in
cold water overnight
200 g (7 oz) mushrooms, sliced
3 carrots, grated
20 g (¾ oz) dried porcini, soaked in hot water to cover for
10 minutes
2 tablespoons Kiddush wine or sherry
Salt and freshly ground black pepper
Sprigs of fresh flatleaf parsley, to garnish

- Heat the oil in a very large deep pan. Add the onions, garlic, potatoes and celery and sauté on a medium heat for 5 minutes until slightly softened. Add the chicken or turkey meat or giblets, chicken or vegetable stock and barley. Bring to the boil, then reduce the heat and simmer for 30 minutes. From time to time, remove any scum that rises to the surface.

- Add the mushrooms, carrots and the porcini with their soaking liquid. Continue to simmer for a further 30 minutes. Remove the chicken or turkey meat or giblets. Add the Kiddush wine or sherry and season with salt and pepper.

- Garnish with sprigs of parsley and serve.

The Jews of Spain

ONE OF THE great privileges I have enjoyed while writing this book has been to explore how recipes originate and migrate around the world to become traditionally Jewish.

The Jews of Spain used to be one of the largest and most prosperous Jewish communities in the world, and lived in peace under both Muslim and Christian rule until the Spanish Inquisition in 1492 when all Jews were expelled (or forced to convert to Christianity). Nowadays there is only a small Jewish population in Spain, but their descendants, the Sephardic Jews, make up around a fifth of the global Jewish population. Some of the more traditional Spanish Jews speak Ladino, derived from Old Castilian (Spanish) and Hebrew, in the same way that Yiddish is linked to German.

Spanish Onion and Almond Soup

THIS IS A delicious fresh-tasting soup with all the flavours of Spain captured in one ladle. The recipe works particularly well for a busy cook as I have made sure that all the ingredients are readily available and the method of cooking simple. It is ideal for entertaining as it can be made in advance.

I have used Spanish onions, which are some of the mildest, largest, best-looking onions available. They are easy to handle and have a longer shelf life than regular onions. Another feature of the soup is the use of ground almonds, which is a typical Spanish way of thickening soups.

Preparation: 15 minutes
Cooking: 25 minutes
Serves 6

2 tablespoons olive oil
2 Spanish onions, thinly sliced
4 garlic cloves, finely chopped
2 large leeks, trimmed and thinly sliced
1.2 litres (2 pints) vegetable stock
50 g (2 oz) ground almonds
3 tablespoons Kiddush wine or sherry
Salt and freshly ground black pepper

To garnish:
25 g (1 oz) toasted almonds
1 bunch fresh parsley, roughly chopped

- Heat the oil in a large pan. Add the onions, garlic and leeks and sauté on a medium heat for 10 minutes or until softened. Add the stock, ground almonds and Kiddush wine or sherry. Bring to the boil, then reduce the heat and simmer for 10 minutes.

- Liquidise 4 ladles of the soup in a food processor and return them to the pan. Season well with salt and freshly ground black pepper.

- Serve in individual warmed bowls with a scattering of the toasted almonds and a dusting of freshly chopped parsley.

NOTE: The soup can be made up to two days in advance and refrigerated.

Sephardi Red Lentil Vegetable Soup

RED LENTILS FEATURE strongly in Genesis (chapter of Toldot) where we are told about red lentil stew both in the scene where Jacob acquires his brother's birthright (*b'chorah*) and in the final scene where he steals Esau's blessing (*brachah*). (Note the Hebrew play on words.)

Also, on the day that Abraham died, Jacob boiled lentils to provide the customary first meal for the immediate mourners. It is thought that this tradition developed because lentils are round like a wheel and mourning (sorrow) is a wheel that touches every spot in turn. Another reason is that just as lentils have no serrated edge, mourners have no mouths because they are forbidden to greet anyone.

In more recent times, lentils have become a poor person's food and are rarely served on the Sabbath, a day when only the best will do.

This recipe is a great family favourite; it is very colourful and, like many Sephardi dishes, it smells fantastic while it cooks. I have used canned chick-peas but if you prefer, and plan ahead, you can use the dried variety and cook them according to the packet instructions.

Like other legumes, lentils are low in fat and high in protein and fibre, but they have the added advantage of cooking quickly. They have a mild, often earthy, flavour and are best combined with assertive flavourings like ginger, garlic, cinnamon, turmeric and coriander – as in this soup.

Red lentils have a slightly sweeter taste than brown and take a little less time to cook; they tend to become somewhat mushy and are therefore more suitable for soups and stews.

Preparation: 10 minutes
Cooking: 1 hour 10 minutes
Serves 6

1 tablespoon olive oil
1 onion, sliced
2 sticks celery, roughly chopped
4 garlic cloves, thinly sliced
1 red pepper, deseeded and roughly chopped
1 teaspoon ground cinnamon
4 cm (1½ in) piece of fresh root ginger, peeled and very
    finely chopped
1 teaspoon turmeric
1.4 litres (2½ pints) vegetable stock
250 g (9 oz) red lentils
2 x 400 g cans chick-peas, rinsed
1 x 400 g can chopped tomatoes
Juice of 2 lemons

50 g (2 oz) fresh coriander leaves, finely chopped
Sea salt and freshly ground black pepper
Sprigs of fresh flatleaf parsley, to garnish

- Heat the oil in a large pan. Add the onion, celery, garlic and red pepper and sauté over a medium heat for 5 minutes until soft. Add the cinnamon, ginger and turmeric and mix thoroughly, then add the stock and lentils.

- Bring to the boil, then reduce the heat, cover and simmer for 45 minutes. Add the chick-peas and tomatoes. Cook for another 15 minutes, then stir in the lemon juice and coriander. Taste and season with salt and pepper.

- Garnish with flatleaf parsley and serve.

Jews in Syria

SYRIAN JEWS TRACE their ancestry back to two groups: those who have lived in Syria since ancient times and those who fled there from Spain in 1492. The main centres of settlement were Aleppo, Damascus and Beirut. The opening of the Suez Canal in 1869 changed the major trade routes in the area and Jewish Syrian merchants suffered as the country declined in commercial importance. Many left for Egypt, and later for Great Britain, the United States, Mexico and Argentina.

Life for the remaining Syrian Jews was relatively harmonious until 1947 when anti-Jewish riots were widespread. For several decades times were difficult as state regulations prevented Jews emigrating, but in the early 1990s the movement ban was lifted and the final 4000 or so were allowed to leave Syria for the United States. Only a handful of Jews remain in Damascus.

Syrian Jewish food is similar to Syrian food, partly because of similarities between *kashrut* and Islamic food laws. Popular dishes include *kibbeh*, *sambusaks* (see page 187), *adafina* (see page 162) and *mejadera* (see page 217).

Golden Potato Soup

THIS GOLDEN SYRIAN soup is delicate yet filling, and just what you need when eating a large pre-fast meal in a hurry. Cooking the potatoes separately and adding them to the vegetable base produces an interesting texture – the soup seems to be thick and thin at the same time.

However, take care with the seasoning if you are serving this soup before a fast. While it should be tasty, too much salt or pepper will spoil its delicacy and make you thirsty. I have used lemon and turmeric to give it a beautiful colour and flavour. The soup freezes well and doubling the quantity will not affect the success of the recipe.

Preparation: 20 minutes
Cooking: 35 minutes
Serves 6

1 tablespoon olive oil
2 large carrots, sliced
3 garlic cloves, finely chopped

1 onion, sliced
3 sticks celery, with leaves, sliced
1.75 litres (3 pints) chicken stock
900 g (2 lb) potatoes, sliced
Juice of 1 lemon
½ teaspoon turmeric
Salt and freshly ground black pepper
Sprigs of fresh flatleaf parsley, to garnish
200 g (7 oz) freshly cooked rice, to serve

- Heat the oil in a deep pan and add the carrots, garlic, onion and celery and sauté over a medium heat for 5 minutes. Add 500 ml (18 fl oz) of the stock, bring to the boil, then reduce the heat and simmer covered for 15 minutes or until the vegetables are soft. Transfer to a food processor and whiz to form a purée. Return the puréed vegetables to the pan.

- In a separate pan, boil the potatoes for 10 minutes or until soft, drain, then mash them using a potato ricer or fork.

- Add the potatoes to the soup pan. Add the lemon juice, remaining stock and the turmeric. Cook for a final 10 minutes, stirring from time to time to prevent the potatoes sticking to the bottom of the pan. Season with salt and pepper.

- Garnish the hot soup with sprigs of parsley and serve with freshly cooked rice added to the soup.

Sweet Potato and Carrot Soup with Pistou

A TASTY VEGETABLE SOUP is always welcome for Rosh Hashanah, the Jewish New Year, when there is a need for a family-friendly dish. However, this recipe also has an interesting connection with the festival. Carrots are one of the significant special foods that Jews are encouraged to eat at this time. This is because the Yiddish word for carrots is *mehren*, which means to increase. So by eating carrots at this time we are wishing for more good things in the year ahead.

In this soup the sweet potatoes and carrots combine well and produce a vibrant orange-coloured broth. Full of goodness, sweet potatoes contain huge amounts of beta-carotene, vitamin C and vitamin E, making them one of the best anti-cancer foods.

This particular recipe has no 'bits', making it ideal for fussy eaters, but with its twist of delicious *pistou* dressing it is also suitable for more adventurous ones. *Pistou* is a purée of basil, garlic and olive oil, very similar to pesto but without the toasted pine nuts. Parmesan cheese is an optional addition unless, of course, you want to keep the soup *parev*.

Preparation: 20 minutes
Cooking: 35 minutes
Serves 8–10

3 tablespoons vegetable oil
3 onions, sliced
1 teaspoon ground cinnamon
1.5 kg (3½ lb) carrots, sliced
1 kg (2¼ lb) sweet potatoes, sliced

1 litre (1¾ pints) vegetable or *parev* chicken stock
Salt and freshly ground black pepper

For the pistou:
25 g (1 oz) fresh basil leaves
8 garlic cloves, roughly chopped
Salt and freshly ground black pepper
120 ml (4½ fl oz) olive oil

- Heat the vegetable oil in a deep pan. Add the onions and cinnamon and sauté over a medium heat for 5 minutes until slightly softened. Add the carrots and sweet potatoes and pour in the stock. Bring to the boil, then cover the pan and reduce the heat to a simmer for 30 minutes.

- To make the *pistou*, place the basil and garlic in a food processor, season with salt and pepper and whiz to combine. With the motor running, gradually add the olive oil to make a purée. Taste and adjust the seasoning if necessary.

- Blend the soup in a food processor until it is smooth. For a more textured effect, only process half the quantity, return it to the pan containing the remaining soup and reheat gently if necessary.

- Divide the hot soup between individual warmed bowls, season and drizzle with the *pistou* dressing.

Borscht: A Staple Food

DURING THE Second World War Poland's Jewish population of over three million was totally decimated by the Holocaust and less than 300,000 Jews survived. Poland was the only country where the Nazis imposed the death penalty on anybody found sheltering or helping Jews. The situation was made worse by the severe food rationing that was imposed on the local population and high black market prices for food, which made it very difficult for sympathetic Poles to even consider hiding or feeding their Jewish friends. However, despite these issues, Poland has the greatest number of Righteous Among the Nations awards, given to those who risked their lives to help Jews during the Second World War and who are honoured at the Yad Vashem Holocaust Museum in Israel.

Beetroot soup or *borscht* originated in Poland and Russia. In the nineteenth and twentieth centuries political and social persecution was rife and finding adequate nutrition was a constant challenge, especially during the long freezing winters. *Borscht* became a staple meal and at times was the only food available. Beets stored well and were not damaged by exposure to frost, as well as being abundant and relatively cheap.

Original recipes vary from a simple water and beetroot stock to more affluent *borschts* which include meat or chicken, beaten raw eggs or chopped hard-boiled eggs, soured cream or boiled potatoes. In recent years the dish has become popular once again. This is for several reasons including the interest in peasant or rustic foods, and a 'beetroot revival' stemming from an awareness of the vegetable's nutritional value and the realisation of how delicious it can be when it is not just pickled.

Hot Borscht

MY RECIPE IS a complete healthy meal in one bowl. Serve on the coldest days with good bread, for a sustaining supper. Remember to wear gloves when handling the beetroot as the colour stains easily.

(P)

Preparation: 15 minutes
Cooking: 2 hours 25 minutes
Serves 8

3 marrow bones or 200 g (7 oz) chicken giblets
450 g (1 lb) beetroot, ready cooked without vinegar
3 onions, roughly chopped
250 g (9 oz) green cabbage, shredded
4 salad tomatoes, peeled and sliced
2 apples, peeled and sliced
1 tablespoon salt
Freshly ground black pepper
Juice of 2 lemons
3 tablespoons sugar

To serve:
450 g (1 lb) boiled potatoes

- Place the marrow bones or giblets in a deep pan with 3 litres (5¼ pints) water and simmer gently for 1½ hours.

- Grate the beetroot. Add the beetroot to the broth along with the onions, cabbage, tomatoes and apples. Season with the salt and with pepper to taste. Cover and simmer for 45 minutes. Add the lemon juice and sugar and simmer for a further 10 minutes.

- Remove the marrow bones or giblets. Taste and adjust the seasoning accordingly.
- Serve in individual warmed bowls with the boiled potatoes floating on top.

Jews in Yemen

YEMENITE JEWS ARE those whose ancestry can be found in Yemen on the southern tip of the Arabian peninsula. The earliest Jewish settlements in this area can be traced back to the time of King Solomon. With the rise of Islam in the seventh century the status of Yemenite Jews was relegated to second-class citizenship. At the beginning of the nineteenth century their population numbered 30,000.

From the 1880s Yemenite Jews were encouraged to emigrate to Palestine and this continued in waves, culminating in the famous Operation Magic Carpet mass airlift in 1949, which moved the remaining population to the newly established state of Israel. This was one of the most amazing mass exoduses since Moses. With the establishment of the State of Israel, the situation for Jews in the Yemen had become very difficult. Anti-Semitism was growing and the population of 46,000 Jews in the Yemen felt increasingly threatened. In a highly dangerous and secret operation, during May 1949 Israel chartered every available passenger and cargo plane and in over 380 flights evacuated over 45,000 civilians from all over the country to a new life in Israel. In total in 1949, over 250,000 immigrants arrived in Israel, putting a huge strain on the state budgets and resources, and adding almost 15 per cent to the population.

Distinct Yemenite religious rituals that are well established and still practiced today include reading the Torah in Hebrew and Aramaic, and decoration with henna as a pre-wedding ceremony. These henna rituals are among the lengthy wedding rituals practiced among Jews of Yemen and are held for the bride and groom during the wedding week, in which the palms of their hands and feet are covered with a material extracted from the henna plant. The bride's henna ritual is the principal rite of passage for women. This ritual is an important stage in preparing the bride for her new life, as she changes from a girl-youth into a man's wife, becomes separated from her family and goes to live in her husband's home.

Yemenite Lamb and Tomato Soup

SMALL CUBES OF lamb are tenderised for this hearty tomato soup. It is an ideal first course for Friday night or Yom Tov and, unlike the more traditional chicken soup, it can be made on the day it is eaten rather than the day before.

Adding rice to soup is a Sephardi practice that works particularly well with tomatoes.

Preparation: 20 minutes
Cooking: 1 hour 10 minutes
Serves 8–10

2 tablespoons vegetable oil
2 medium-size onions, finely chopped
225 g (8 oz) lamb, fat removed, cut into 5 cm (2 in) cubes
2 teaspoons ground coriander
4 garlic cloves, crushed
I teaspoon sugar
3 large carrots, finely chopped
2 x 400 g cans chopped tomatoes
2 litres (3½ pints) beef stock
Salt and freshly ground black pepper
150 g (5 oz) long grain rice
Sprigs of fresh coriander, to garnish

- Heat the oil in a large pan. Add the onions, lamb, coriander, garlic, sugar and carrots and sauté over a medium heat for 10 minutes until the onions and lamb start to brown. Add the tomatoes and stock and season well with salt and pepper. Bring to the boil, then reduce the heat and simmer, covered, for 1 hour.

- Cook the rice according to the instructions on the packet.

- To give the soup a semi-smooth consistency put half the quantity in a food processor and blend until smooth. Return it to the pan and add the rice. Check the seasoning and add more salt and pepper if necessary.

- Divide the soup between individual warmed bowls and garnish each with a sprig of coriander.

Lemon Split-pea Soup

SAFFRON, LEMON, ground cumin, ground coriander and turmeric are all distinctive flavours used particularly in abundance in Syrian, Moroccan and Tunisian Jewish recipes. Cooked together their colours produce a vibrant yellow soup – and, as with all complex soups, the longer you cook it, the more intense the flavour.

Tunisia used to have a thriving Jewish community of over 50,000, but as a result of the Nazi invasion during the Second World War and anti-Jewish riots in the 1950s, most of its members emigrated, mainly to France or Israel. Today the 1300 Jews who remain are the country's largest indigenous religious minority, but the suffering continues. In 2002, a gas tanker exploded outside the ancient Ghriba synagogue on the resort island of Djerba, killing 20 people and almost destroying the oldest synagogue in Africa.

Yellow ingredients are dominant in Sephardi cooking and they come together wonderfully in this fragrant traditional dish. Eat it with torn strips of warm pitta bread – make plenty because this is a very popular soup. It can be served hot or cold.

❄ Ⓟ (omit soured cream)
Preparation: 25 minutes + 2 hours soaking
Cooking: 1 hour 40 minutes
Serves 6

200 g (7 oz) yellow split peas, rinsed
2 tablespoons olive oil
2 courgettes, roughly chopped (yellow if available)
1 yellow pepper, deseeded and roughly chopped
1 onion, finely chopped

3 garlic cloves, finely chopped
3 cm (1¼ in) piece of fresh root ginger, peeled and very
finely chopped
2 teaspoons turmeric
1 tablespoon ground cumin
1 tablespoon ground coriander
6 saffron threads
1.2 litres (2 pints) vegetable stock
2 tablespoons brown sugar
1 lemon, cut into wedges
1 x 200 g can chopped tomatoes
¼ teaspoon cayenne pepper
2 tablespoons chopped fresh coriander leaves
Salt and pepper to taste

To garnish:
Fresh coriander sprigs
150 ml (¼ pint) soured cream (omit for a *parev* option)

- Soak the split peas in water for 2 hours, then drain and set aside. This can be done the previous day and the peas can be kept in the fridge overnight.

- Heat the oil in a large pan. Add the courgettes, yellow pepper and onion and sauté for 5 minutes or until softened but not brown. Add the garlic, ginger, turmeric, cumin, ground coriander and saffron. Cook for 2 minutes to bring out the flavour. Stir in the stock, sugar, lemon wedges, tomatoes and cayenne.

- Bring to the boil, then reduce the heat and add the peas, simmering for 1½ hours or until they are soft. Add the coriander leaves, and taste and adjust the seasoning.

- Remove the lemon wedges, pour the soup into a food processor and blend until smooth. Return the soup to the pan and reheat it if you wish to serve it hot.
- Garnish each serving with sprigs of coriander and a dollop of soured cream.

Butternut Squash and Chestnut Soup

SQUASH IS A particularly popular vegetable for serving during the week-long festival of Succot. Also known as the 'Festival of the Harvest', this begins on the fifth day after Yom Kippur and is a time of celebrating the goodness of life and all that the earth can offer. The word *succot* means 'booths' and refers to the makeshift huts that the Jews lived in during their 40 years of wandering in the desert after their exodus from Egypt. Today, it is customary to build something similar in the garden and decorate it with fruits and vegetables of the season; these temporary dwellings are known as *succah*. Naturally, food and sharing a meal with family and friends under the stars in the *succah* plays an important role in this harvest festival.

I first came across butternut squash about 15 years ago when I was weaning my daughter on to solids. Nowadays the vegetable is commonly available in most supermarkets and, like all squash, it is extremely versatile. Low in fat and high in vitamins, it is quickly finding its place in the family weekly diet. It blends well with herbs, spices and flavourings, producing delicious dishes of all types from entrées, casseroles and salads to soups.

This is a wonderful warming soup with a great combination of flavours. It also freezes well so make double the quantity and keep one batch for another time. Although roasting chestnuts is a fun way of spending a Sunday afternoon and they taste delicious hot off the pan, for this recipe you can buy them ready-peeled, vacuum-packed or frozen to save time. I have left the chestnuts roughly chopped as my personal preference is for a 'textured' soup. However, creating a smooth, puréed soup will not diminish the sensational flavour.

Preparation: 15 minutes
Cooking: 30 minutes
Serves 6–8

2 tablespoons olive oil
1.3 kg (3 lb) butternut squash, peeled and chopped into
   small pieces
2 red onions, roughly chopped
2 teaspoons ground cinnamon
1 teaspoon ground cumin
4 garlic cloves, finely chopped
1.2 litres (2 pints) vegetable or chicken stock
Salt and freshly ground black pepper
200 g (7 oz) chestnuts (vacuum-packed or frozen are
   ideal), roughly chopped
Finely chopped fresh parsley, to garnish

- Heat the oil in a large pan. Add the butternut squash, red onions, cinnamon, cumin and garlic and sauté over a medium heat for 5 minutes until the vegetables start to soften. Add the stock. Bring to the boil, then reduce the heat and simmer for 20 minutes. Season with salt and pepper.

- Transfer half the soup to a food processor and whiz until smooth. Return the soup to the pan and add the chestnuts. Reheat when ready to serve.

- Serve the soup in individual warmed bowls and garnish with sprigs of parsley.

Moroccan Chick-pea Soup

I RECENTLY TRAVELLED to Marrakech where I tried a traditional Moroccan version of minestrone. It was delicious and this is my take on that recipe, made with spices bought from the souk and still full of flavour. It made me realise that our supermarket spices are far inferior to those obtained in the markets of exotic countries – where they make the air aromatic and pungent. They cost next to nothing, so bring lots home, but always remember to wrap them well as turmeric does stain.

This is a warming thick vegetable soup, most comforting during the cold winter months. The combination of chick-peas and tomatoes in Middle Eastern cuisine is very common and this 'Moorish' soup is a great midweek starter.

When fresh broad beans are in season, substitute them for the frozen variety. Remove the pods and blanch the beans in boiling water before removing the skins. A slightly laborious task, but well worth it.

To make it authentic, enjoy the soup with warm flatbreads or pitta breads.

Preparation: 15 minutes
Cooking: 20 minutes
Serves 8

2 tablespoons olive oil
2 onions, chopped
4 sticks celery, chopped
2 teaspoons ground cumin
2 teaspoons ground cinnamon
1.2 litres (2 pints) hot vegetable stock
2 x 400 g cans chopped tomatoes with herbs
2 x 400 g cans chick-peas, rinsed and drained
Salt and freshly ground black pepper
200 g (7 oz) frozen broad beans
225 g (8 oz) baby spinach leaves
Juice of 1 lemon

To garnish:
Grated zest of 1 lemon
1 large bunch fresh flatleaf parsley or 1 large handful of
    fresh coriander leaves, finely chopped

- Heat the oil in a large deep pan. Add the onions and celery and cook gently over a medium heat for 5 minutes until the vegetables start to colour. Stir in the cumin and cinnamon and fry for a further minute until the spices start to release their flavour. Add the stock, tomatoes and chick-peas and season well with salt and pepper. Bring to the boil, then reduce the heat and simmer for 10 minutes.

- Meanwhile, place the broad beans in a pan of simmering water. Cook for 3 minutes, then drain. Remove the skins and set aside.

- When the soup has simmered for 10 minutes, stir in the broad beans, spinach and lemon juice. The spinach leaves will wilt in the heat of the hot soup.

- Pour the soup into individual warmed bowls and garnish with a sprinkling of lemon zest and chopped parsley or coriander.

Soup Extras and Dumplings

ACCOMPANYING JEWISH SOUP is a cuisine in itself. Jewish cooks go well beyond a slice of crusty bread. Ashkenazi Jews favour the addition of a starch such as *knaidlach* directly into the soup. Historically this made the soup more substantial in times of cold and hunger. Sephardi soups differ in that whilst the accompaniment is also added to the soup, it tends to be a spicy dip. This increases flavour and promotes thirst and perspiration – both essential in hot climates.

Hilbeh

THIS SPICY SAUCE is made from fenugreek seeds, which are available from Middle Eastern and Indian supermarkets and other specialist shops. Recipes for *hilbeh* are passed down through the generations and it is a popular starter, traditionally eaten with pitta bread and as a dip to go with falafel.

If you want to be more adventurous, you can add cardamom seeds, ground coriander and various types of chilli and hot pepper sauces.

Preparation: 10 minutes, plus 12 hours to soak seeds
Cooking: None
Serves 8–10

3 teaspoons fenugreek seeds
1 tablespoon lemon juice

3 garlic cloves, finely chopped
2 tablespoons finely chopped fresh coriander leaves
½ teaspoon cayenne pepper
I teaspoon *zhug* (see page 69)
Salt

- Put the fenugreek seeds into a small bowl, add 225 ml (9 fl oz) water and soak the seeds for 12 hours or overnight. Drain well.

- Put the fenugreek seeds, lemon juice, garlic, coriander and cayenne in a food processor and whiz until the mixture is smooth.

- Remove from the processor and put into a glass dish. Stir in the *zhug* and season with salt.

NOTE: The *hilbeh* can be stored, covered, in the fridge for up to one month.

Knaidlach

KNAIDLACH (also known as *matzah* balls) and chicken soup are the two most familiar Jewish dishes. They are small round dumplings. Add them to your soup after you have cooked it and taken the fat off the top. Uncooked *knaidlach* can be frozen.

These *knaidlach* are light and fluffy as I have used fine *matzah* meal, but for a heavier version replace it with the medium variety. The other little secret of their success is to make sure the soup is hot before adding them.

Preparation: 10 minutes + 15 minutes chilling
Cooking: 15 minutes
Serves 6

For the knaidlach:
1–2 tablespoons ground almonds
250 g (9 oz) fine *matzah* meal
2 tablespoons *schmaltz* (fat from chicken soup) or
vegetable oil
1 egg
Salt and freshly ground black pepper
250 ml (10 fl oz) hot chicken soup (see pages 42–4)

- Combine all the ingredients for the *knaidlach* in a bowl, then refrigerate the mixture for 30 minutes.

- Using wet hands, make small balls with the mixture. Cover and refrigerate until you are ready to cook them.

- Cook the balls in hot chicken soup for approximately 15 minutes. They are cooked when they rise to the surface.

NOTE: The *knaidlach* can be frozen after they have been shaped into balls. They can be stored, covered, in the fridge for two days.

Zhug

THIS TASTY, spicy sauce or dip was very popular in the ancient Middle East. But be warned – it can be very hot indeed, depending on the heat of the chillies, so use it sparingly. It will keep in the fridge for up to three months if covered with olive oil. *Zhug* is often part of the Yemenite chicken soup experience and is swirled onto the soup when serving, or dipped into with pitta bread, or served chilled with eggs, meat, poultry, falafel etc.

Preparation: 5 minutes
Cooking: None
Serves 6–8

1 teaspoon black peppercorns
2 teaspoons caraway seeds
4 hot red chillies
25 g (1 oz) fresh coriander leaves
6 garlic cloves
Salt
Olive oil, to cover

- Place the peppercorns, caraway seeds, chillies, coriander and garlic in a food processor and whiz to form a paste. Taste and season with salt.

- Transfer to a glass jar, cover with olive oil and store in the fridge for up to three months.

Kreplach

KREPLACH **ARE THE** Jewish equivalent of Italian ravioli or Chinese wontons. Chicken-filled ones are traditionally served in chicken soup on Rosh Hashanah for Kol Nidre night (the meal before the fast of Yom Kippur). For Shavuot they are filled with cheese and at Purim with fruit and served as part of the meal.

Many foods have a symbolic connection with a particular Jewish festival and one explanation for the link with Purim is that the *kreplach's* triangular shape symbolises the three Jewish patriarchs: Abraham, Isaac and Jacob.

My grandmother always made *kreplach* for Rosh Hashanah and I have vivid memories of watching her as she carefully and meticulously rolled them out, to be put into the chicken soup. They were always a special treat as they are quite time-consuming to make, but the rewards are great. I recommend using a pasta machine to guarantee that the dough is not too thick. Try not to overfill the *kreplach* and make sure they are sealed properly to ensure perfect results.

I like to cook my chicken soup with turkey necks, giblets and chicken carcasses. I then take the meat from these to make the filling.

❄

Preparation: 40 minutes + 1½ hours resting
Cooking: 5 minutes
Serves 10–12 (makes about 80 kreplach)

For the dough:
225 g (8 oz) plain flour, plus extra for tossing
Pinch of salt
2 large eggs

For the filling:
I tablespoon *schmaltz* (fat from chicken soup) or vegetable
oil
I small onion, very finely chopped or minced
I10 g (4 oz) cooked beef or chicken mince or meat from a
turkey neck
I teaspoon finely chopped fresh parsley
Salt and freshly ground black pepper

- First make the dough. Place the flour, salt, eggs and 4 tablespoons water in a food processor and use the dough blade to work them together until smooth. Alternatively, work the ingredients by hand. Cover with cling film or wrap in a plastic food bag and leave for I hour to rest.

- While the dough is resting, make the filling. Melt the *schmaltz* or oil in a frying pan. Sauté the onion over a medium heat for 5 minutes until it starts to soften, then add the beef or chicken. Add the parsley and season with salt and pepper. Place in a food processor and whiz until smooth. Remove and refrigerate until ready to use.

- After I hour, the dough is ready to roll. Divide it into six portions and press each one through a pasta machine, rolling it through all the settings until it is on the thinnest. Alternatively, do this by hand with a rolling pin.

- Using a 5 cm (2 in) round cutter, cut out circles of dough. Put ½ teaspoon of the filling into the centre of each circle. Dampen the sides and fold them over to make a three-point triangle. (This is like a *Hamanstchen* triangle, or pyramid shape.) Toss the circle in flour to prevent sticking. Continue adding the filling until all the dough has been used. Leave the *kreplach* to stand for 30 minutes before cooking them.

- Cook the *kreplach*, in batches, in a pan of simmering salty water for

about 5 minutes or until they are just tender. They will rise to the
surface when they are cooked.

- To serve, drop two or three *kreplach* into individual warmed bowls of
hot chicken soup (see pages 42–4).

NOTE: Once they have been tossed in flour, uncooked *kreplach* can be
kept in the fridge for one week or frozen.

Breads

BREAD MAKES A Jewish meal complete in that according to Jewish law it must be eaten at the start of the meal after the HaMotzi blessing has been recited over it: *Baruch atah Adonai, Eloheinu Melech ha'olam, hamotzi lechem min ha'aretz* (Blessed are you, Lord our God, King of the universe, who brings forth bread from the earth). If this is done, Birkat Hamazon – grace after the meal – can be recited. Without these blessings a meal has only the status of a snack.

Jewish breads vary from the heavy rye and black loaves of German origin to light and fluffy Middle Eastern pittas. *Challah* – a slightly sweet plaited loaf – is the best loved and no Friday night is complete without it.

Challah and its Traditions

THREE MEALS HAVE to be eaten on Shabbat, and as they must include bread, observant Jews eat *challah* at the beginning of each one. As the meals tend to be meat-based, classic *challah* is made without the addition of dairy products. This distinguishes it from brioche and other enriched European breads, which often contain butter, milk or both.

Two loaves of *challah* (*challot* is the word for two loaves) are placed on the Sabbath or holiday table. They are always covered with an embroidered cloth so that, symbolically, when the blessing is said over the wine the bread does not get jealous. The bread is blessed separately as part of the Kiddush ceremony.

The two loaves are in memory of the double portion of manna that was provided on Friday to the Israelites in the desert after the exodus from Egypt. Work such as gathering food is, of course, banned on the Sabbath, so God cleverly arranged an extra-large delivery the day before.

The term *challah* also refers to a small piece of dough that is traditionally separated from the rest of the dough before baking. This is a reminder of the portion that was set aside as a tithe for the Jewish priests (*kohanim*) in the Temple and is burnt in the oven when the *challah* is baked. The *mitzvah* (good deed) of separating the *challah* is one of the three performed especially by women (the others are lighting the Shabbat candles and guarding family purity).

The Torah says that when you offer up a sacrifice to God you should sprinkle it with salt; a dining table is symbolic of an altar. The significance of salt is that it completes other foods, enhances their taste and is also a preservative. And on Friday nights when the blessing for the *challah* is recited in my Ashkenazi household, we sprinkle salt on the bread before eating it. However, like so many customs and traditions in the Jewish way of life, there are always different opinions – three in the case of the *challah* and salt.

Some say that because there is no Temple today sprinkling the *challah* with salt – as we do in my family – reminds us that it was destroyed. According to others, since we have no Temple, and no longer perform sacrifices, the *challah* should not be sprinkled with salt but should be dipped into it. Finally, there is the third view that since there is no Temple there are no sacrifices, and we should not use salt at all. The choice is yours.

There are as many recipes for *challah* as there are Jewish cooks and cookery books. Different ethnic traditions call for differences in the recipes. One distinctive addition is sprinkling sesame seeds or poppy seeds on the top of the dough before baking (usually after glazing it with an egg wash, to help the seeds stick).

Festival Sweet Challah

THERE ARE MANY special customs for Rosh Hashanah, but one of the most enjoyable is to eat sweet *challah* in a bid to ensure that the coming year will be sweet and prosperous. In many homes, including my own, we go further and between Rosh Hashanah and Simchat Torah we dip our portions of *challah* in honey.

This is one of my favourite recipes. I have added an apple so that all the symbolic ingredients of Rosh Hashanah are included. Festival *challah* is cooked in a spiral shape to signify the circle of life, unlike the regular Friday night *challah* that is plaited.

Preparation: 10 minutes + 1½ hours rising
Cooking: 30 minutes
Makes 2 round loaves

600 g (1 lb 5 oz) strong white flour
1 x 7 g sachet dried yeast (1 tablespoon)
2 teaspoons salt
1 egg
1 heaped tablespoon clear honey
25 g (1 oz) raisins

2 teaspoons ground cinnamon
I apple, peeled, cored and cut into chunks (optional)
100 ml (4 fl oz) vegetable oil
150 ml (¼ pint) warm water
Olive oil, for greasing
I egg yolk, lightly beaten
2 tablespoons sesame seeds, for sprinkling
Honey and ground cinnamon, to serve

- Combine the flour, yeast, salt, egg, honey, raisins and cinnamon in a large mixing bowl. Mix the ingredients together using a dough hook, if available.

- Place the apple, if using, in a food processor and whiz to a semi-purée. Add this to the mixture in the bowl, together with the vegetable oil and warm water.

- Continue to mix the dough for 2–3 minutes with the dough hook, or 10 minutes by hand, until it is smooth and the mixing bowl is clean. Remove the dough from the bowl and lightly grease the bowl with olive oil.

- Knead the dough lightly and return it to the mixing bowl. Turn the dough so that it is coated with oil, cover with cling film and leave in a warm place to rise for 1½ hours or until the dough has doubled in size.

- Meanwhile preheat the oven to 200°C/400°F/Gas Mark 6 and line a baking sheet with baking parchment.

- Knock back the dough. Remove a small piece, the size of an olive, as the *challah* tithe and place it on a baking sheet. Cut the remaining dough in half and knead each half into a long sausage. Curl each sausage into a spiral shape and place on the prepared baking sheet. Brush with the egg yolk and sprinkle with the sesame seeds.

- Bake for 30 minutes or until the *challahs* are golden. They should feel light when you turn them over and sound hollow when you tap the undersides.

- Brush with honey, dust them with ground cinnamon and serve slightly warm – if possible.

Home-made Bagels

BAGELS ARE PROBABLY the best known of all Jewish breads, although few people will recognise their Jewish heritage as they have been fully adopted by our cousins in the United States, where they are as popular as hot dogs, burgers and pizzas. The word bagel is German for bracelet or ring, and because they are round with no beginning and no end they were considered to be full of God-given luck. Bagels were said to ward off demons and evil spirits – the *ayin hora* – or evil eye and to bless whoever ate them with prosperity. Today Jews still eat bagels with hard-boiled eggs after funerals because the shapes of both are said to symbolise the eternal cycle of life.

When I first went to New York I could hardly believe the variety of flavours in which bagels were available, such as blueberry, toasted onion, garlic, etc., in addition to the popular bagel bites – thin slices of toasted bagel. These used to be on my shopping list for every trip to the United States but are today found in many United Kingdom supermarkets.

Now, as you discover how to make bagels, you can create your own varieties of texture and flavour – and the amazing aroma that fills your kitchen will ensure that you want to make them time and time again.

Unlike most other breads, bagels need to be boiled before they are baked. This gives them their unique chewy and crispy texture, and great fresh taste. However, they do go stale quickly, so if you have extras cut them into thin slices and toast them for a great snack any time (apart from Passover).

Preparation: 10 minutes + 1–1½ hours rising and 1 hour proving
Cooking: 30 minutes
Makes 12 bagels

1 tablespoon sugar
1 x 7 g sachet dried yeast (1 tablespoon)
1 tablespoon salt
200 ml (8 fl oz) warm water
500 g (1 lb 2 oz) strong white flour, plus extra for dusting
1 egg, lightly beaten
2 tablespoons vegetable oil, plus extra for greasing
1 egg white
2 tablespoons (approx.) poppy seeds or sesame seeds, for sprinkling

- Mix 1 teaspoon of the sugar with the yeast, salt and warm water. Set aside for 10 minutes until frothy.

- In a large mixing bowl, combine the flour, remaining sugar, beaten egg, oil and yeast mixture. Using a dough hook, if available, knead the dough 5 minutes until it is smooth and spongy. Alternatively, work the dough by hand, which will take about 10 minutes.

- Grease a bowl with oil. Place the dough in the bowl, turn it so that it is coated with oil and cover with cling film. Leave to rise for 1–1½ hours or until the dough has doubled in size.

- Knock back the dough and knead it again until all the air is pressed out and it is smooth. Divide the dough into 12 pieces and roll each piece on a floured surface into a strip 18 cm (7 in) long and 1.25 cm (½ in) thick. Join the ends together to form a circle.

- Line a baking sheet with baking parchment and place the bagels on it. Cover with a damp cloth and leave to rise again (prove) for 1 hour.

- Preheat the oven to 220°C/425°F/Gas Mark 7. Bring a large pan of water to the boil, then reduce the heat to a simmer and add four of the bagels. When they pop to the surface – about 2–3 minutes – remove them with a slotted spoon and return to the baking sheet. Repeat with all the bagels.

- Lightly whisk the egg white with 1 tablespoon water, brush the bagels with the mixture and sprinkle them with poppy seeds or sesame seeds. Bake for 20 minutes or until golden brown.

- Allow the bagels to cool slightly before cutting them in half.

Wholewheat Pitta Breads

PITTAS ARE THE classic breads to go with falafel, hummus and many Sephardi soups, dips and stews. The bread's flat shape with its pocket opening makes it perfect for filling, and when it is sliced or torn it is ideal for scooping up a dip or relish. It is traditional in many Middle Eastern and Mediterranean cuisines and is believed to have originated in ancient Greece.

Nothing beats a warm toasted pitta bread filled with Israeli salad and all the trimmings. This recipe uses wholemeal flour and so the pittas are slightly heavier than ones made with white flour. If you have any leftovers you can use them to make North African Pitta Bread Salad (see page 232).

Preparation: 30 minutes + 1¾ hours rising and 30 minutes
proving
Cooking: 3 minutes
Makes 8 pitta breads

1 x 7 g sachet dried yeast (1 tablespoon)
1 teaspoon clear honey
300 ml (½ pint) warm water
110 g (4 oz) wholemeal flour
200 g (7 oz) strong white flour
4 tablespoons extra virgin olive oil, plus extra for greasing
1 teaspoon salt
2 tablespoons cornmeal

- In a large bowl, mix the yeast and honey with 120 ml (4½ fl oz) of the warm water. Leave for 5 minutes until the yeast starts to froth.

- Mix the wholemeal and white flours together in another bowl. Whisk 50 g (2 oz) of the mixed flours into the yeast mixture until smooth. Cover with cling film and leave to rise for 45 minutes.

- Stir in the oil, salt, the remaining mixed flours and the remaining warm water and mix until a firm dough forms. Using a dough hook, if available, knead the dough for 5 minutes until it is smooth and elastic. Alternatively, work the dough with your hands for about 10 minutes. Form the dough into a ball.

- Grease a large bowl with oil. Put the dough in the bowl and turn it so that it is coated with oil. Cover with cling film and leave to rise in a warm place for 1 hour.

- Meanwhile, preheat the oven to 240°C/475°F/Gas Mark 9 (or its highest setting). Line two baking sheets with baking parchment and sprinkle with cornmeal to prevent the pitta breads sticking.

- Knock back the dough and cut it into eight pieces. Form each piece into a ball, then flatten it and roll it out into a 15 cm (6 in) round. Place the rounds on the baking sheets, cover loosely with cling film and leave to rise (prove) for 30 minutes.

- Bake for 2 minutes or until the pittas are just puffed up and pale golden. Turn them over with tongs and bake for a further 1 minute.

- The pittas are best served straightaway.

Rye Bread

SLICED RYE BREAD is very popular, especially when enjoyed with herring, smoked salmon or egg and onion. Rye was traditionally the most important grain crop in Germany and it was not long before the many Jews resident there in the eighteenth and nineteenth centuries became master bakers of this now classic bread, which is made around the world in whichever place Jews call home.

This particular combination of rye flour and white flour produces a soft, light texture, but if you prefer a denser loaf use wholemeal flour in place of white. The authentic finish to rye bread is achieved by glazing the loaf with a boiled cornflour mixture. This creates a shiny, glossy finish.

You can't beat baking your own bread – bought loaves from kosher delis are a second-best option. In fact, I never really enjoyed rye bread until I made this recipe. I like to put the loaf in the oven at 180°C/350°F/Gas Mark 4 for 10 minutes before slicing it, for a great authentic flavour.

Preparation: 10 minutes + 1½ hours rising and 30 minutes proving
Cooking: 25–30 minutes
Makes 1 large loaf

1 x 7 g sachet dried yeast (1 tablespoon)
Pinch of sugar
300 ml (½ pint) warm water
200 g (7 oz) strong white flour
400 g (14 oz) rye flour
2 tablespoons caraway seeds, plus 1 teaspoon for sprinkling
1 teaspoon salt
2 tablespoons vegetable oil, plus extra for greasing
1 tablespoon clear honey
1–2 egg yolks, lightly whisked
1 tablespoon cornflour

- Mix the yeast and sugar with 100 ml (4 fl oz) of the warm water. Leave for 10 minutes until the yeast starts frothing.

- Place the flours, 2 tablespoons caraway seeds and salt in a large mixing bowl. Add the yeast mixture, oil and honey. Mix together, using a dough hook if available, for 2–3 minutes, gradually adding the remaining warm water so that the dough is soft and well kneaded but not too wet. Alternatively, work the dough with your hands for about 10 minutes. The dough has been kneaded enough when it springs back as you touch it.

- Lightly grease a large bowl with the oil, and turn the dough in it so that it is coated. Cover with cling film and leave in a warm place to rise for 1½ hours or until the dough has doubled in size.

- Meanwhile, preheat the oven to 200°C/400°F/Gas Mark 6. Line a baking sheet with baking parchment.

- Punch the dough down and shape it into a 20 cm (8 in) oval loaf. Brush the loaf with the egg yolk/s and sprinkle it with the remaining caraway seeds. Using a sharp knife, make five slashes across the top. Place the loaf on the prepared baking sheet and leave in a warm place to rise again (prove) for 30 minutes or until the dough has risen significantly.

- Bake for 25–30 minutes. Place a tray of boiling water on the base of the oven and remove it after 10 minutes. The steam will help to develop a crispy crust. The bread is cooked when it is deep golden and sounds hollow when tapped on the underside.

- Meanwhile, in a small pan, mix the cornflour with 100 ml (4 fl oz) water and boil until the liquid is clear. Brush this over the baked loaf as soon as it comes out of the oven.

- Cool on a wire rack before slicing or freezing.

Potato Challah (Berches)

BERCHES IS POSSIBLY a corruption of *b'rachah*, the Hebrew word for blessing, and is a savoury German-Jewish Sabbath loaf that consists of two layers of plaited strands. Unusually, it is made with old, dry potatoes; in fact, the drier the better, as if they are too wet the dough will be difficult to knead. The dough will not rise as much as usual during proving due to the denseness of the potatoes. However, once it is placed in a hot oven the moisture in the potatoes will cause the loaf to expand dramatically.

The unique difference between this *challah* and others is that it is plaited in two sections. The large one acts as a base for the top layer and the whole loaf is glazed with poppy seeds. An impressive *challah* for the Shabbat table!

If you need this *challah* for Friday evening, you can start the dough at about eight o'clock on Thursday night and let it rise slowly overnight, then complete the recipe on Friday morning.

***Preparation: 20 minutes + 2–3 hours rising and 1 hour
    proving***
Cooking: 55 minutes
Makes 2 loaves

500 g (1 lb 2 oz) floury potatoes, cut into chunks
1 x 7 g sachet dried yeast (1 tablespoon)
150 ml (¼ pint) warm water
500 g (1 lb 2 oz) strong white flour, plus extra for dusting
1 teaspoon sugar
2 teaspoons salt

1 tablespoon vegetable oil
1–2 egg yolks
2 tablespoons poppy seeds

- Boil the potatoes in a pan of water for about 15 minutes until soft, then drain and mash with a potato ricer or fork.

- In a large mixing bowl, dissolve the yeast in 120 ml (4½ fl oz) of the warm water. Leave for 5 minutes.

- Combine the flour, sugar and salt in another bowl, then mix 3 tablespoons of this mixture into the yeast mixture. Leave the yeast mixture covered for 20 minutes. Add the remaining flour mixture and the mashed potato, then gradually add the remaining warm water, if needed, until a firm dough has formed.

- Knead the dough for 5 minutes if using a dough hook, or 10 minutes by hand. It must be firm, so add more flour if it is too wet.

- Grease a bowl with the oil. Put the dough in the bowl and turn it so that it is coated with oil. Cover with cling film and leave to rise in a warm place for 2–3 hours until the dough has doubled in size.

- Knock back the dough, place it on a lightly floured work surface and divide it into two equal pieces. Set aside one half.

- Divide the remaining half into one two-thirds portion and one one-third portion. Use the two-thirds portion to make a four-plait loaf – the base. Use the one-third portion to make a three-plait loaf – the top layer. Repeat with the set aside dough.

- Line a baking sheet with baking parchment.

- Lightly whisk the egg yolk/s with 1 teaspoon water. Place the *challahs* on the prepared baking sheet, brush them with the egg yolk and water mixture and sprinkle them with the poppy seeds. Leave in a warm place to rise again (prove) for 1 hour.

- Meanwhile, preheat the oven to 200°C/400°F/Gas Mark 6.
- Bake the *challahs* for 45 minutes until golden. They should sound hollow when their undersides are tapped.
- Cool on a wire rack.

Pretzels

PRETZELS ORIGINATED IN Germany but are now found all over the world. Interestingly, crunchy-hard pretzels evolved from a mistake made by a baker who put some in the oven without giving them time to prove and forgot about them. Baked too long and unrisen, the pretzels became dark, hard and crunchy – and turned out to be a wild success. Nowadays they can be bought pre-packed, and are found fresh on streets from Hamburg to New York – a truly universal Jewish snack.

You can flavour these twisted, ring-shaped rolls with sesame seeds, poppy seeds or sea salt. There are two main types of pretzel: hard and crisp, and light and chewy. If you prefer your pretzels hard and crisp omit the final rising (proving) after the dough has been shaped. The same dough can be made into bread sticks.

Preparation: 15 minutes + 2 hours rising and 45 minutes proving
Cooking: 15–20 minutes
Makes 15 pretzels

1 x 7 g sachet dried yeast (1 tablespoon)
300 ml (½ pint) warm water

500 g (1 lb 2 oz) strong white flour
1½ teaspoons salt
Vegetable oil, for greasing
1 egg yolk
Sea salt, poppy seeds or sesame seeds, for sprinkling

- Dissolve the yeast in 120 ml (4½ fl oz) of the warm water. Mix together and leave for 5 minutes.

- Put 110 g (4 oz) of the flour, the salt and the yeast mixture in a large mixing bowl. Using a dough hook, if available, knead the ingredients to form a paste. Cover and leave for 20 minutes until the mixture is frothy and has risen.

- Mix in the remaining flour and gradually add the remaining warm water to form a stiff, sticky dough. Knead for 5 minutes with a dough hook or 10 minutes by hand, until the dough is smooth and elastic.

- Grease a bowl with oil. Put the dough in the bowl and turn it so that it is coated in oil. Cover with cling film and leave to rise in a warm place for 2 hours.

- Preheat the oven to 220°C/425°F/Gas Mark 7.

- Knock back the dough and divide it into 15 pieces, each approximately 50 g (2 oz). Shape each piece into a round roll and then into an oval. Roll each oval backwards and forwards, moving your fingers along the dough to form a strip about 40 cm (16 in) long and 2.5 cm (1 in) thick in the middle and 5 mm (¼ in) thick at each end. Form the shaped dough into pretzels.

- Line a baking sheet with baking parchment. Place the pretzels on the baking sheet and leave to rise again (prove) for 45 minutes or until they have doubled in size if you want them to be light and chewy.

- Lightly whisk the egg yolk with 1 teaspoon water, brush the pretzels with the mixture and sprinkle them with sea salt, poppy seeds or sesame seeds.
- Bake for 15–20 minutes until golden brown.
- Cool on a wire rack.

New Year for Trees

IN RECENT YEARS my synagogue has held a Seder for Tu B'Shvat (the Jewish festival for the New Year for Trees). This follows the tradition of the Kabbalists of the sixteenth century in Safed, northern Israel, who began the custom of holding an evening meal, loosely based on the Pesach Seder, at this time of the year. It involves a special meal and four cups of wine, and the recitation of 13 biblical verses that relate to the vegetation of Israel. Many different foods are blessed and eaten. The aim is to show our respect for God's work and to appreciate the produce of the land.

We ask and discuss four questions that are designed to help us understand the significance of this day, for example:

- Our other holidays honour events and people. Why does this holiday honour trees?
- Ordinarily, we eat whatever fruit is in season. Why, today, do we specifically eat fruit that is grown in Israel?
- We usually take the environment for granted. Why, today, do we focus on conservation?

- It's winter. Why are we thinking about planting when spring is several months away?

The four cups of wine are symbolic of the seasons and their associated fruits:

White wine represents winter when fruits are covered by a shell – as the ground is covered in snow – and symbolises most types of nuts, such as almonds, hazelnuts and walnuts.

Rosé wine – red wine mixed with a greater volume of white wine – represents spring. The fruits that it symbolises have hard inedible pips or stones; peaches, plums, nectarines, apricots, etc. are examples.

Rosé wine – white wine mixed with a greater volume of red wine – represents summer and fruits like apples, grapes, pears, raspberries, blueberries, strawberries, etc. that can be eaten in their entirety.

Red wine is blood-red wine that represents harvest time. No fruit is symbolised; we rely on the power of scent from herbs and spices like rosemary, mint, cinnamon, thyme, sage, etc.

Peanut and Fruit Bread

AMONG THE FOODS served at the Seder are olives, dates, grapes, figs, pomegranates, apples, walnuts, carob fruit, pears, cherries, sunflower seeds and peanuts. So to mark this occasion, I decided to write a recipe specifically for Tu B'shvat that would include several of these ingredients and would enhance the ceremony.

This delicious tea bread is ideal for picnics, lunch boxes and whenever you fancy a slice of cake with a cup of tea or coffee. It combines a tasty blend of many of the nuts and fruits that grow in the land of Israel.

Preparation: 20 minutes + 1 hour soaking
Cooking: 1 hour
Serves 8–10

110 g (4 oz) dried figs, roughly chopped
110 g (4 oz) dried apricots, halved
75 g (3 oz) raisins
125 g (4½ oz) unsalted butter or margarine
200 g (7 oz) caster sugar
½ teaspoon bicarbonate of soda
75 g (3 oz) roasted unsalted peanuts
2 tablespoons brandy or calvados
2 eggs
125 g (4½ oz) self-raising wholemeal flour
125 g (4½ oz) plain wholemeal flour
110 g (4 oz) raw peanuts
Icing sugar, to serve

- Place the figs, apricots, raisins, butter or margarine, sugar and 180 ml (6 fl oz) water in a large pan. Bring to the boil, then reduce the heat and simmer for 3 minutes. Add the bicarbonate of soda, roasted peanuts and brandy or calvados and mix well. Leave to stand at room temperature for 1 hour.

- Meanwhile, preheat the oven to 180°C/350°F/Gas Mark 4 and line a 900-g (2-lb) – 12 x 21 cm (4½ x 8½ in) loaf tin with baking parchment.

- Whisk the eggs and flours together and stir the mixture into the fruit batter. Pour the mixture into the prepared loaf tin. Smooth the surface of the mixture. Sprinkle with the raw peanuts and press them lightly into the batter.

- Bake for I hour or until a skewer inserted in the centre of the bread comes out clean.

- To serve, invert the bread on to a rectangular plate, slice and dust with icing sugar.

Sephardi Almond and Raisin Bread

I LOVE THIS delicious Sephardi bread. It can be made at any time of the year but I like to make it for Purim when nuts and raisins are popular. At Purim we tell the story of Esther, the Jewish wife of the king of Persia. She had to keep her religion a secret and worked hard to keep the laws of *kashrut*, which dictate what Jews can and can't eat and how to prepare and eat what is allowed, so she tended to eat a lot of nuts and seeds. This bread is ideal for the special Purim *seudah* (meal); it can be enjoyed with butter and jam or served instead of a traditional *challah*.

Ideally start making it the night before it is required and let it rise slowly in the fridge; it has a high sugar content and the dough needs a minimum of 3 hours to rise.

Preparation: 20 minutes + 3 hours rising and 30 minutes proving
Cooking: 20 minutes
Makes 20 small rolls

2 x 7 g sachets dried yeast (2 tablespoons)
180 ml (7 fl oz) warm water
50 g (2 oz) whole skinned almonds
600 g (1 lb 5 oz) strong white flour
110 g (4 oz) sugar
Grated zest of 1 lemon
5 tablespoons vegetable oil
50 g (2 oz) raisins
1 egg
1 egg yolk

- Mix the yeast with 120 ml (4½ fl oz) of the warm water. Leave for 5 minutes until the yeast starts to froth.

- Toast the almonds in a dry frying pan over a high heat. Cook for 2–3 minutes until golden brown then immediately remove the almonds from the pan and chop them roughly.

- Put the flour, yeast mixture, sugar, lemon zest, 4 tablespoons of the oil, almonds, raisins and whole egg in a large mixing bowl. Using a dough hook, if available, knead them together, gradually adding the remaining water. Continue to knead the dough until it is smooth. This will take a total of 5–8 minutes. Alternatively, work the dough by hand for 10–12 minutes.

- Grease a bowl with the remaining oil. Place the dough in the bowl and turn it so that it is coated in oil. Cover with cling film and leave to rise for a minimum of 3 hours in a warm place or in the fridge overnight.

- Preheat the oven to 200°C/400° F/Gas Mark 6. Line a baking sheet with baking parchment.

- Knock back the dough and divide it into 20 equal pieces. Roll the pieces into balls or shape them as desired. Place the rolls on the baking sheet. Lightly whisk the egg yolk with 1 teaspoon water and brush the rolls with the mixture. Leave in a warm place to rise again (prove) for 30 minutes.

- Bake for 20 minutes or until golden.
- Cool on a wire tray.

Sesame Seed Grissini

THESE CRUNCHY ITALIAN bread sticks are particularly delicious when home-made. I like to vary the toppings – poppy seeds, finely chopped herbs or even ground cinnamon or cumin. Italians serve *grissini* before meals to keep their guests occupied without filling them up too much. They are great on their own as snacks, used with dips and salads, or even broken up and eaten with soup.

At the start of the Second World War, Italy took in many Jewish refugees from Germany who were seeking to avoid the Holocaust. Later, however, although the Nazi-backed puppet government of the Italian Social Republic had initially refused to assist with deportations, it was forced to obey the Nazis and the country's Jewish population was decimated; many Jews were sent to death camps and the rest fled Italy – taking their food traditions with them to other parts of the world. Today only a small community of around 40,000 Jews remains in Italy.

Preparation: 10 minutes + 15 minutes rising
Cooking: 15–18 minutes
Makes 30 grissini

1 x 7 g sachet dried yeast (1 tablespoon)
150 ml (¼ pint) warm water

Pinch of sugar
I teaspoon salt
200 g (7 oz) strong white flour
2 tablespoons sesame seeds

- Preheat the oven to 200°C/400°F/Gas Mark 6.

- Put the yeast, warm water and sugar in a mixing bowl. Mix well and leave to stand for 5–10 minutes or until the yeast starts to froth.

- Add the salt and flour to the yeast mixture. Using a dough hook, if available, knead for 5 minutes until the dough is smooth and elastic. Alternatively, work the dough with your hands for 10 minutes.

- Remove the dough from the bowl and form it into a large ball. Tear a walnut-size lump of dough from the ball and roll it lightly into a small sausage shape. Repeat until all the dough is used up. There should be approximately 30 pieces.

- Line a large baking sheet with baking parchment and sprinkle the sesame seeds over a large plate.

- Roll out a piece of dough into a long shape about I cm (½ in) thick and roll it in the sesame seeds. Transfer to the baking sheet. Repeat with the remaining pieces of dough, taking care that the *grissini* are all about the same thickness and length.

- Cover the *grissini* with a damp cloth and leave to rise in a warm place for 15 minutes.

- Bake for 8–10 minutes. Turn the *grissini* over and return them to the oven for a further 7–8 minutes.

- Cool on a wire rack.

NOTE: If you freeze the *grissini*, then reheat them straight from frozen at 200°C/400°F/Gas Mark 6 for approximately 10 minutes or until crisp.

Aniseed Bread

THIS DELICIOUS MOROCCAN *challah* is flavoured with aromatic aniseeds and sesame seeds, and was popular among the Jews in North Africa in the nineteenth century. Many of them were poor and did not have their own ovens, so they would put their risen loaves on a tray, cover them with a white cloth and take them to the local baker and use his oven for a fraction of the price of a bought loaf.

For Shabbat this bread is plaited in intricate delicate designs, but for Rosh Hashanah it is an ascending spiral circle. Try this recipe on Yom Kippur to break the fast, but add blanched almonds and raisins.

Preparation: 20 minutes + 2 hours rising and 1 hour proving
Cooking: 30–35 minutes
Makes 2 loaves

1 x 7 g sachet dried yeast (1 tablespoon)
2 tablespoons sugar
300 ml (½ pint) warm water
600 g (1 lb 5 oz) strong white flour
2 tablespoons aniseeds
1 tablespoon sesame seeds
1 teaspoon salt
5 tablespoons vegetable oil
2 eggs
1–2 egg yolks

- Mix the yeast and sugar with 125 ml (4½ fl oz) of the warm water. Leave for 5 minutes until it starts to froth.

- In a large mixing bowl, combine the flour, aniseeds, sesame seeds, salt, 4 tablespoons of the oil and the whole eggs. Stir in the yeast mixture and gradually add the remaining warm water. Using a dough hook, if available, knead the dough for 5–8 minutes or until it is very smooth and elastic. Alternatively, work the dough with your hands for 10 minutes.

- Grease a bowl with the remaining oil. Form the dough into a ball, put it in the bowl and turn it so that it is coated with oil. Cover and leave to rise for 2 hours or until the dough has doubled in size.

- Knock back the dough and divide it in half. Knead each half for 2 minutes. Shape the halves into rounds, or roll each one out into a long strip and twist it into a spiral with the end of the dough at the high point in the centre.

- Line a baking sheet with baking parchment and place the loaves on it.

- Lightly whisk the egg yolk/s with 1 teaspoon water, brush the loaves with the mixture and leave them to rise again (prove) for 1 hour.

- Meanwhile, preheat the oven to 200°C/400°F/Gas Mark 6.

- Bake the loaves for 30–35 minutes or until golden brown. They should feel light when you turn them over and sound hollow when you tap the undersides.

- Cool on a wire rack.

Onion Platzels

BREAD IS A symbolic food in the Jewish religion and is eaten at most meals. However, as a special treat keep this recipe for after Pesach. It's the smell and texture of fresh bread that I miss most during Passover (when no leavened food is allowed) and this recipe satisfies on both counts.

These tasty savoury rolls are great with most soups and delicious combined with Cheddar cheese and pickles. The onions can be red or white although white ones are most commonly used.

Preparation: 15 minutes + 1½–2 hours rising and 25 minutes proving
Cooking: 20 minutes
Makes approximately 15 small rolls

1 x 7 g sachet dried yeast (1 tablespoon)
300 ml (½ pint) warm water
500 g (1 lb 2 oz) strong white flour, plus extra for dusting
2 teaspoons salt
1 egg
1 tablespoon olive oil
1 onion, finely chopped
1–2 egg yolks, lightly whisked
1 tablespoon poppy seeds or black onion seeds

- Sprinkle the yeast into 100 ml (4 fl oz) of the warm water and leave for 5 minutes to dissolve.

- In a large mixing bowl, using a dough hook, combine the flour, salt, whole egg and yeast mixture. Gradually add the remaining water as needed until a moist dough is formed. Turn the dough out on to a lightly floured work surface and knead gently for a final 2 minutes until the dough is smooth.

- Grease a bowl with oil. Put the dough in the bowl and turn it so that it is coated with oil. Cover with cling film and leave to rise in a warm room for 1½–2 hours or until the dough has doubled in size.

- Meanwhile, preheat the oven to 200°C/400°F/Gas Mark 6. Line a baking sheet with baking parchment.

- Knock back the dough and divide it into 15 small rolls, each approximately 50 g (2 oz). Make a small indentation in the top of each roll and add about 1 teaspoon of the onion. Place on the baking sheet and leave to rise again (prove) for 25 minutes.

- Brush the rolls with the egg yolk/s, and sprinkle them with the poppy seeds or black onion seeds.

- Bake for 20 minutes or until golden. They should sound hollow when their undersides are tapped.

- Cool on a wire rack.

NOTE: The dough can be used to make a loaf, with the onion seeds sprinkled on top just before cooking for 40–45 minutes.

Fish

FISH IS IMPORTANT to the Jewish table for several reasons. It is *parev*, it is versatile, lending itself to plain and also more complex cooking and happy as part of a dish or as the main feature. The symbol of the fish in Judaism is interesting – it represents fertility and can be seen in art, architecture and jewellery. The head of a fish graces some Rosh Hashanah tables, to signify the head of the year and our wish to lead from the front and not come behind like the tail. The Hebrew word for fish is *dag* and its numerical value is seven. There are seven days in a week, with the Sabbath (Shabbat) falling on the seventh day, so fish is often eaten as part of the Shabbat meal.

Aromatic Stuffed Sea Bass

THIS IS A classic Turkish/Algerian dish, eaten on the coast where sea bass are plentiful and can be bought fresh at the local ports. Today, Turkey's total Jewish population is around 26,000 and it is the second largest Jewish community in a Muslim country (the largest is in Iran). The majority live in Istanbul and in 1992 they celebrated the 500th anniversary of the arrival of Jews in Turkey. Most came from Granada in Spain when, following the country's capture from the Moors, Ferdinand

and Isabella of Spain expelled all the Jews from their lands and ended the largest Jewish settlement in Europe.

Although this recipe has quite a list of ingredients, the blended flavours produce the most amazingly aromatic fish. I have wrapped the sea bass in parcels of baking parchment and baked them with orange juice and white wine. If you are planning a barbecue, wrap an outer layer of foil around the parcel so that the paper does not burn. The secret of a perfect result is a low cooking temperature.

Preparation: 35 minutes + 1 hour marinating
Cooking: 40 minutes
Serves 4

4 x 675 g (1½ lb) sea bass, gutted, cleaned and de-scaled
8 tablespoons fresh orange juice
8 tablespoons white wine
Salt and freshly ground black pepper
Rice mixed with broad beans and dill, to serve

For the stuffing:
4 saffron threads
1 tablespoon hot water
2 tablespoons olive oil
6 spring onions, roughly chopped
50 g (2 oz) ready-to-eat dried apricots, roughly chopped
25 g (1 oz) breadcrumbs
1 tablespoon ground almonds
Juice of 1 orange
50 g (2 oz) chopped walnuts
½ teaspoon ground cardamom
Salt and freshly ground black pepper

For the marinade:
Grated zest of 1 orange
1 teaspoon ground cumin
1 red chilli, deseeded and finely chopped
4 tablespoons extra virgin olive oil
1 garlic clove, crushed
Salt and freshly ground black pepper

- First make the marinade. In a small bowl, mix together all the ingredients.

- Cut three diagonal slits in each side of each sea bass and rub in the marinade. Cover and refrigerate for 1 hour.

- To make the stuffing, place the saffron in a small bowl with the hot water.

- Heat the oil in a frying pan and sauté the spring onions over a medium heat for 2 minutes until the onions start to soften. Stir in the apricots, breadcrumbs, ground almonds, orange juice, walnuts and ground cardamom and season well with salt and pepper. Add the saffron and cook for 1 minute, stirring from time to time.

- Preheat the oven to 350°C/180°F/Gas Mark 4.

- Fill the cavities of the sea bass with the stuffing. Place each fish on enough baking parchment to make a parcel. For each parcel pour in 2 tablespoons of the orange juice, 2 tablespoons of the white wine, a quarter of any remaining marinade and season with salt and pepper. Roll up the parcels and secure each one with a safety pin. Wrap each parcel in foil if you are barbecuing the fish.

- Bake in the oven for 40 minutes or until the fish flakes easily.

- Serve with rice mixed with broad beans and dill.

Easy Fish Plait with Leek and Pea Purée

TWISTING OR PLAITING is a stylish way of presenting fish and one that Jews have mastered over the years, perhaps because of their experience with making *challah*.

For this recipe I have combined cod with salmon, which is a popular fish in both Ashkenazi and Sephardi cuisines. The delicate flavours of the salmon and cod require only the simplest of accompaniments to make a delightful meal. I like to serve the fish with a potato salad made with lemon mayonnaise. This dish is easy as well as being most impressive; if you wish, you can ask your fishmonger to cut the fish into strips for you. You will need 12 cocktail sticks to secure the plaits.

Preparation: 15 minutes
Cooking: 20 minutes
Serves 6

1.8 kg (4 lb) cod, skinned and filleted
1.8 kg (4 lb) salmon, skinned and filleted
250 ml (9 fl oz) white wine
Juice and grated zest of 1 lemon
Salt and freshly ground black pepper
300 g (11 oz) fresh or frozen peas
500 g (1 lb 2 oz) leeks, sliced
2 lemons, cut into wedges, to garnish

- Preheat the oven to 200°C/400°F/Gas Mark 6.

- Cut the fish into strips 20 cm (8 in) long and 1 cm (½ in) wide. Take two strips of salmon and one of cod and plait them together, securing each end of the plait with a cocktail stick. Repeat with two strips of cod and one of salmon. Continue until all the fish is plaited.

- Lay the plaits in an ovenproof dish. Make sure they do not touch; if they do they will stick together and removing them whole might be difficult. Pour over the wine, lemon juice and zest, and enough water to cover. Season well with salt and pepper.

- Cover and bake for 20 minutes, then carefully remove the cocktail sticks.

- Meanwhile, boil the peas and leeks together until soft. Drain and place in a food processor then whiz to a purée. Season well.

- To serve, line individual warmed plates with some hot pea and leek purée. Put a fish plait in the centre of each and garnish with a lemon wedge.

NOTE: The fish plait can be made in 2-3 hours advance and refrigerated.

Saffron Salmon Couscous

THIS IS A delicious dish that fuses all the flavours of Middle Eastern cuisine. Cinnamon, ginger, garlic, saffron and the zest of an orange work very well together, and although I have given specific quantities don't be afraid to increase one particular seasoning if you want a stronger taste.

Cooking this combination of salmon with couscous is a real pleasure as it makes a little piece of fish go a long way. A plain green salad is all that is needed to accompany this dish. I like to cook the couscous in vegetable or *parev* chicken stock for a richer flavour.

Preparation: 15 minutes
Cooking: 30 minutes
Serves 4

2 tablespoons olive oil
2 red onions, thinly sliced
5 cm (2 in) piece of fresh root ginger, peeled and finely chopped
2 teaspoons ground cinnamon
2 garlic cloves, finely chopped
50 g (2 oz) raisins
Juice and grated zest of 1 orange
1 teaspoon saffron threads
750 ml (1¼ pints) vegetable stock
300 g (11 oz) couscous
575 g (1¼ lb) salmon fillet, skinned and cut into large cubes
Salt and freshly ground black pepper

To garnish:
4 tablespoons pine nuts
4 tablespoons roughly chopped fresh mint, to garnish

- First toast the pine nuts for the garnish. Place them in a dry pan and heat gently until golden. Remove and set aside.

- Heat the oil in the same pan. Add the onions, ginger, cinnamon and garlic and sauté over a medium heat for about 10 minutes until softened.

- Add the raisins, orange juice and zest and saffron. Pour in 150 ml (¼ pint) of the stock. Bring to the boil, then reduce the heat and simmer, covered, for a further 5 minutes.

- Pour the remaining stock over the couscous. Cover with cling film and leave for 5 minutes.

- Stir the salmon into the saffron and vegetable mixture in the pan and simmer for a further 5–8 minutes or until the salmon is cooked. Season with salt and pepper.

- To serve, pour the saffron salmon over the couscous and garnish with the pine nuts and mint.

Red Paella

AN AUTHENTIC PAELLA is made with Valencia rice and with seafood such as prawns, which is an obvious problem for Jews as seafood is prohibited under the laws of *kashrut*. So I have adapted this traditional Spanish dish to produce a kosher version that has all the flavours of the classic one; it is made with red mullet, red tomatoes, red peppers and red snapper.

Smoked paprika, made in Spain from smoked ground pimiento peppers, can be found in varying intensities: sweet and mild (*dulce*), medium hot (*agridulce*) and hot (*picante*). It adds the absolutely perfect taste of real paella and gives the dish a striking deep-red colour. It has an intoxicating smoky aroma as a result of slow oak smoking, and a silky texture from being ground between stones.

Keep this smoked paprika for barbecues and for roast potatoes –

Sephardi Jews often use it to flavour them, as well as adding it to sauces, stews, chicken, roast meats and grills.

Preparation: 15 minutes
Cooking: 35 minutes
Serves 6

4 tablespoons olive oil
1 red onion, roughly chopped
2 red peppers, deseeded and roughly chopped
3 garlic cloves, chopped
1 x 900 g (2 lb) red snapper, skinned, filleted and cut into
   6 pieces
2 red mullets, skinned, filleted and cut into 6 pieces
340 g (12 oz) Valencia (Spanish) rice or risotto rice
1 tablespoon smoked paprika
900 ml (1½ pints) hot vegetable stock
300 ml (½ pint) dry white wine
1 teaspoon saffron threads
225 g (8 oz) frozen peas
2 x 170 g (6 oz) tuna steaks, cut into 2.5 cm (1 in) cubes
225 g (8 oz) cherry tomatoes, halved
Juice and grated zest of 1 lemon
Salt and freshly ground black pepper

To garnish:
12 sprigs of fresh flatleaf parsley, chopped
2 tablespoons stoned black olives, halved
2 lemons, cut into wedges

- Heat the oil in a deep pan. Add the onion, peppers, garlic, red snapper and red mullet and sauté gently for about 5 minutes until softened. Add the rice and paprika and cook for about 2 minutes or until the rice has become transparent.

- Place the stock, wine, saffron and peas in a different pan. Bring to the boil, then reduce the heat and simmer for 2 minutes.

- Add the stock mixture to the rice, fish and vegetables and simmer, covered, for about 15 minutes. Add the tuna and continue cooking, covered, for a further 5 minutes or until the tuna is just cooked. (Overcooked tuna is tough and leathery.) Add the tomatoes and the lemon juice and zest, and mix them into the paella. Season with salt and pepper.

- Serve immediately on individual warmed plates, garnished with the parsley, olives and lemon wedges.

Salmon Salad with Apple and Honey Dressing

APPLES AND HONEY are enjoyed at Rosh Hashanah as a symbol of our wish for a sweet year. Our sages tell us that on this very day, celebrated on the first and second of the Jewish month of Tishrei (mid-September to October), Adam violated the commandment that God gave him: the prohibition to eat from the Tree of Life. On this day God said to Adam: 'As you were judged before me this day and emerged forgiven, so will your children be judged before me on this day and emerge forgiven.'

Thus, from the beginning of our history, Rosh Hashanah has been associated with judgement and forgiveness.

In biblical times Israel was known as 'a land flowing with milk and honey'; honey represents sweetness, goodness, fertility and wealth.

For the high holy days I am always looking for recipes that can be easily prepared in advance and served either cold or at room temperature, for those times when you return home hungry after synagogue. I also try to use honey and apples in my cooking at this time of the year. This dish meets both my goals and can be served as a small starter or larger main course. Drizzle the dressing over the salad just before serving to keep the ingredients crisp.

I like to use a strong honey, such as Australian eucalyptus that gives a rich toffee flavour to the salmon. Keep all types of honey in a dry, cool place at room temperature.

Preparation: 15 minutes
Cooking: 20 minutes
Serves 6

6 x 150–175 g (5–6 oz) salmon fillets, skinned
Salt and freshly ground black pepper
3 tablespoons olive oil
2 teaspoons clear honey
250 g (9 oz) mixed salad leaves
3 ripe nectarines, stones removed, sliced into thick
   segments
100 g (3½ oz) blueberries
3 tablespoons chopped fresh chives, to garnish

For the honey and apple dressing:
6 tablespoons olive oil
3 teaspoons clear honey
Juice and grated zest of 1 orange
1 teaspoon balsamic vinegar
Salt and freshly ground black pepper
1 apple, cored and roughly chopped

- Preheat the oven to 200°C/400°F/Gas Mark 6.

- Place the salmon in an ovenproof dish and season with salt and pepper. Mix the oil and honey with 3 tablespoons water and pour over the salmon. Cover and bake for 20 minutes. Remove the salmon from the dish and leave it to cool on a clean plate.

- For the dressing, combine all the ingredients except the apple. Set aside and refrigerate until ready to use. Add the apple just before serving.

- To serve, line a serving platter with the mixed salad leaves. Add the nectarine slices and blueberries. Place the cooled salmon fillets on top, pour over the dressing and garnish with the chives. Serve immediately.

NOTE: The dressing will keep for up to three days in the fridge.

Poached Trout in a Pomegranate Sauce

FISH AND POMEGRANATES are eaten at Rosh Hashanah for several reasons. The custom of eating specific foods at festivals is based on the teachings of the Talmud and the desire to celebrate in more ways than just through prayer. So at this time we taste foods that represent a sweet year, an abundant year and, hopefully, an end to our sins and troubles with our enemies.

The multiseed pomegranate represents our wish to increase our goodness and merits. Allegedly it contains 613 seeds – the same number as the Torah's *mitzvot* (commandments) – but I have never counted to check! We also need a 'new' fruit to bless and pomegranates come into season just in time to fulfil this requirement.

In addition, pomegranates (*rimonim* in Hebrew) are mentioned in the Old Testament as one of the fruits found in Israel as proof of God's promise to give the Israelites a fertile homeland. They are frequently pictured in Jewish artworks as well as being cast in silver or carved in wood and used to decorate the holy Torah scrolls.

My fishmonger de-bones the trout leaving the whole fish intact (like kippers). The fish skin can be left on and eaten, or removed once cooked – it's up to you. If trout are unavailable, replace them with red snapper or sea bass or salmon. I like to serve this dish with fried aubergine slices.

Preparation: 15 minutes
Cooking: 40 minutes
Serves 6

6 x 450 g (1 lb) trout, centre bones removed
Salt and freshly ground black pepper
6 tablespoons olive oil

To garnish:
6 tablespoons pomegranate seeds
3 tablespoons roughly chopped fresh parsley

For the pomegranate sauce:
3 x 225 g (8 oz) pomegranates
1 x 570 ml (1 pint) carton pomegranate juice
1 tablespoon cornflour
1 onion, minced
2 tablespoons roughly chopped fresh basil
2 tablespoons roughly chopped fresh coriander leaves
1 garlic clove, crushed

- Preheat the oven to 190°C/375°F/Gas Mark 5.

- Sprinkle the trout with salt and pepper and place them in a single layer in an ovenproof dish. Drizzle with the oil and add enough water to almost cover the fish. Place in the oven and poach, basting from time to time, until tender – approximately 35 minutes.

- Meanwhile, make the sauce. Cut the pomegranates in half, squeeze out the juice and strain it into a bowl. Discard the skins. In a separate bowl mix 2 tablespoons of the carton juice with the cornflour.

- Boil the strained juice and remaining carton juice with the onion until reduced by half. Stir in the cornflour and juice mixture and simmer for a further 3 minutes, or until the sauce has thickened. Add the basil, coriander and garlic.

- To serve, transfer the cooked trout to a warmed serving platter and drizzle with the pomegranate sauce. Garnish with the pomegranate seeds and parsley.

Jews in Italy

THE JEWS IN Italy were once a prosperous and accepted part of Italian society – albeit with some restrictions, as anyone who is familiar with *The Merchant of Venice* will know. Visitors to modern Venice should not miss out on one of the great attractions of this magical city – a visit to the Jewish ghetto area, where you can almost smell and feel former Jewish life. In Italy today there is a small but well-established Jewish community of about 40,000, mainly living in Milan and Rome. However, most Italian Jews either perished in the Second World War or took flight to other European countries and later to Israel; some hoped to find shelter in the Alps, local villages and convents or monasteries, while others joined the partisans. Mussolini had initially been supportive of the Jews, but by 1943 orders had been given to ransack Jewish areas and deport their residents. After the war Jews were reinstated as first-class citizens.

Italian Fish Casserole

FISH FEATURES FREQUENTLY in Italian Jewish cooking – it is a major ingredient in all Mediterranean diets and Jews who had moved to Italy from other countries combined the flavours of their homelands with regional specialities to create Jewish Italian fusion cooking.

This casserole is easy and versatile. Fillets of white fish, such as sea bass, cod, haddock, plaice or sea bream are best but mullet or salmon can be used. The bread soaks up all the flavours and juices of the fish and is added at the very end. I like to serve it with a mixed leaf salad.

Should you have a problem buying fish stock, you can make it by placing a selection of fish bones in a pan of simmering water together with 1 chopped onion, 1 bay leaf, 2 sticks celery, 3 carrots, 1 fennel bulb, 1 bunch fresh parsley, fresh thyme and a pinch of salt. Simmer for 30 minutes and strain. The stock can be frozen once cooled, or refrigerated and used within three days.

Preparation: 15 minutes
Cooking: 30 minutes
Serves 6

2 tablespoons extra virgin olive oil
12 thin slices of ciabatta
6 garlic cloves, roughly chopped
Salt and freshly ground black pepper
4 tablespoons olive oil
4 tablespoons finely chopped fresh parsley, plus extra for serving
1.8 kg (4 lb) white fish fillets (sea bass, cod, haddock, plaice or sea bream)
200 ml (8 fl oz) fish stock
2 lemons, cut into wedges, to serve

- Preheat the oven to 200°C/400°F/Gas Mark 6.

- Drizzle the 2 tablespoons extra virgin olive oil over the ciabatta and sprinkle with one-third of the garlic and some salt and pepper. Bake for 10 minutes.

- Heat the 4 tablespoons olive oil in a wide, deep frying pan with a lid. Add the remaining garlic and the parsley and fry over a medium heat for 2 minutes until the garlic starts to cook and soften. Add the fish and continue to fry for a further 5 minutes. Add the fish stock, cover and simmer very gently for 15 minutes.

- To serve, arrange the bread on a large warmed serving platter. Carefully remove the fish from the frying pan and place on top of the bread. Pour some of the cooking liquor into a gravy boat.

- Sprinkle the fish with parsley and serve with the lemon wedges; squeeze some juice from the wedges over the fish first. Serve the cooking liquor separately.

Salmon Provençale

WHEN YOU THINK of the flavours of Provence, garlic, rosemary, peppers and red wine come to mind – and this is what this recipe is all about. Jews first settled in Provence in the sixth century and formed important communities in Arles and Marseilles.

This recipe has become a signature dish of mine that has done the dinner party circuit. It is easy to make, perfect for large numbers and never fails to impress. I like to serve it with mashed potatoes, rice or just some crusty bread to soak up the delicious juices, together with shredded green cabbage. For some variety, try making it with cubed lamb.

Preparation: 20 minutes
Cooking: 25 minutes
Serves 6

2 tablespoons olive oil
6 x 150 g (5 oz) salmon fillets, skinned
4 large red onions, roughly chopped
6 garlic cloves, roughly chopped
2 red peppers, deseeded and roughly chopped
2 tablespoons plain flour (potato flour for Pesach)
450 ml (¾ pint) vegetable stock
300 ml (½ pint) red wine
I bunch fresh rosemary, leaves stripped from stems
200 g (7 oz) black olives, stoned
Salt and freshly ground black pepper
Sprigs of fresh rosemary, to garnish

- Heat the oil in a large frying pan and sauté the salmon fillets, in batches, over a medium heat for 5–7 minutes until slightly brown. Remove and set aside.

- Add the onions, garlic and peppers to the pan and fry for 3 minutes, stirring from time to time. Add the flour and cook for 2 minutes, stirring. Pour in the stock and wine and add the rosemary and olives.

- Bring to the boil, then reduce the heat, return the salmon to the pan and simmer, covered, for 15 minutes. Season with salt and pepper.

- To serve, spoon generous helpings of the salmon on to individual warmed plates and garnish with sprigs of rosemary.

Tunisian Fish

THIS RECIPE IS a great favourite among Tunisian Jews. It is simple to prepare and makes a perfect main course for Passover. The dish is flavoured with caraway seeds and chilli powder, which fuse well with delicate fish such as red snapper and sea bream. Caraway seeds have a pungent aroma and a distinctly sweet but tangy flavour. They are actually the fruit of a biennial herb of the parsley family and are a common flavouring for many kinds of rye bread. They are also used to flavour sauerkraut, sausages, cheese, cabbage and soups – recipes that feature frequently on the Jewish menu, especially in Eastern Europe.

I like the simplicity and speed of this recipe – at the same time, it is impressive to serve. Accompany it with rice, couscous or chunky bread to soak up the delicious juices.

Preparation: 5 minutes
Cooking: 15 minutes
Serves 6

2 tablespoons olive oil
3 garlic cloves, finely chopped
2 teaspoons caraway seeds
2 teaspoons red chilli powder
½ teaspoon salt
¼ teaspoon black pepper
1 tablespoon tomato purée
100 ml (4 fl oz) vegetable stock
Juice of 1 lemon
6 x 150 g (5 oz) red snapper or sea bream fillets, skinned

- Heat the oil in a large frying pan. Add the garlic, caraway seeds, chilli powder, salt and pepper and sauté over a medium heat for 2 minutes to bring out the flavours of the spices. Add the tomato purée, stock and lemon juice and stir to mix with the seasonings.

- Add the fish fillets and simmer, covered, for 10 minutes or until the fish is cooked through.

- Serve immediately.

Lime Tuna with Spring Vegetables

JEWISH PEOPLE LOVE fish, and tuna is definitely high on the popularity scale when it comes to my family. It is delicious cold and an ideal option for Shabbat lunch when guests tend to be around.

This recipe is a tasty main-course summer salad, one of those dishes that is always welcome when you want to avoid spending hours over a hot stove. The ingredients combine well to produce a light but satisfying meal that is very low in fat and will impress anyone who is watching their weight. The tuna can be grilled, barbecued or fried, but slightly undercooking it is the secret of its culinary success.

I like using lime juice with tuna as it has a subtle taste that does not spoil the true flavour of the fish. To maximise the amount of juice in a lime, place it in a microwave for 1 minute before juicing and you will get every last drop – this works for all citrus fruits.

◆P

Preparation: 10 minutes + 15 minutes marinating
Cooking: 15 minutes
Serves 6

6 x 170g (6 oz) tuna steaks
Juice and grated zest of 2 limes
2 tablespoons extra virgin olive oil
1 red chilli, halved, deseeded and finely chopped
150g (5 oz) fresh peas
2 tablespoons olive oil
3 courgettes, sliced
2 red peppers, quartered and deseeded
1 bulb fennel, roughly chopped
Sprigs of basil, to garnish
Lime wedges, to serve

- Place the tuna steaks in a large casserole dish. Pour over the lime juice and zest and the 2 tablespoons extra virgin olive oil, and sprinkle with the chilli. Cover and leave to marinate for 15 minutes.

- Cook the peas in boiling water for 5 minutes until they are just soft. Drain and refresh under cold water.

- Heat the 2 tablespoons olive oil in a frying pan. Add the courgettes, peppers and fennel and sauté gently for 5 minutes until they are just cooked. Set aside.

- Cook the tuna steaks – the healthiest way is to either barbecue or grill them. Sear their sides to give them a lined effect. Let the steaks cook for 3 minutes without touching them, then turn them over for a final 2 minutes to complete cooking. Of course, if the steaks are particularly thick the initial cooking could take slightly longer.

- To serve, place the vegetables on a warmed serving platter. Put the tuna steaks on top with sprigs of basil. Complete the dish with a dusting of pepper and serve with lime wedges.

Jews in Egypt

UNTIL COMPARATIVELY RECENTLY Egypt was home to the oldest Jewish community in the world, one that was perhaps even related to the Jews of biblical times. Its members lived at one with their Arab neighbours, although they generally kept a low profile. However, with the establishment of the state of Israel in 1948, Jews in all Arab lands faced increasing threats to their lives and property – both officially sanctioned and in the form of ad hoc attacks and riots. In Egypt, this culminated on 23 November 1956 when the Egyptian government issued a proclamation stating that 'all Jews are Zionists and enemies of the state'. This was followed by the expulsion of almost 25,000 indigenous Jews, who were forced to sign declarations that they were leaving voluntarily and had to allow their property to be confiscated. Foreign observers reported the taking of hostages and in total over 1000 Jews were imprisoned. After 1967, more confiscations took place and bombings of Jewish areas killed 70 Jews and wounded nearly 200, while riots claimed many more lives. The result was the almost complete disappearance of Jews from Egypt but their traditions and great recipes live on in disparate communities all over the world.

Egyptian Fish Balls
with Tomato Sauce

FISH BALLS OR *gefilte* fish are the epitome of Jewish cooking, whether they are fried or boiled, and my recipe is associated with the Jews of Egypt. It is made with minced fish – a combination of cod, haddock and bream – flavoured with cumin, garlic and minced onion. Cooked in a tomato sauce and served with rice or couscous, it makes a delicious meal any time.

The original recipe for *gefilte* fish was carp stuffed with minced fish. Over many decades, and many miles travelled, while purist versions can still be found, *gefilte* fish and fish balls have metamorphosed into one recipe – albeit one based on family preference and local tradition.

Preparation: 20 minutes
Cooking: 40 minutes
Serves 6–8
Makes 36 balls

675 g (1½ lb) minced white fish (cod, haddock and bream)
2 onions, minced
2 teaspoons salt
Grated zest of 1 lemon
2 garlic cloves, finely chopped
2 tablespoons finely chopped parsley
2 teaspoons ground cumin
3 tablespoons fine *matzah* meal
1 egg, lightly beaten
Plain flour, for dusting
1 litre (1¾ pints) vegetable oil, for deep-frying
Couscous or rice, to serve

For the tomato sauce:
2 tablespoons vegetable oil
I onion, finely chopped
3 garlic cloves, finely chopped
I kg (2¼ lb) fresh tomatoes, peeled and roughly chopped,
     or 2 x 400 g cans chopped tomatoes
2 tablespoons tomato purée
120 ml (4½ fl oz) red wine
450 ml (¾ pint) vegetable stock
Salt and freshly ground black pepper

- Place the minced fish, onions, salt, lemon zest, garlic, parsley and cumin in a food processor and whiz to form a stiff mixture. Remove the mixture from the processor and stir in the *matzah* meal and egg.

- With wet hands, make a ball with about I tablespoon of the mixture and place it on a lightly floured plate. Repeat until all the mixture is used up.

- Heat the oil to 190°C/375°F in a deep-fryer. Test the oil by adding a cube of bread. If it starts to cook fast then the oil is ready. Fry the fish balls, in batches, for 3–4 minutes or until golden brown. Remove and place on kitchen paper to drain.

- For the tomato sauce, heat the oil in a medium-size pan and sauté the onion and garlic over a medium heat for 2 minutes until the onions and garlic start to soften. Add the tomatoes, tomato purée, wine and stock and season well with salt and pepper. Bring to the boil, then reduce the heat and simmer for 35 minutes.

- Add the fried fish balls to the tomato sauce and cook for a final 10 minutes.

- Serve with couscous or rice.

NOTE: For a spicy option add ¹/₂ teaspoon harissa.

Smoked Salmon Latkes

JEWISH PEOPLE LOVE their smoked salmon and *latkes* – and in this recipe for *latke* with a smoked salmon and poached egg topping I have brought the two together to create the perfect brunch or tea recipe.

Latkes have a special affiliation with Chanukah, the joyous festival celebrated on the Hebrew date of 25th Kislev (generally late December). We remember the story of Judah the Maccabee and his followers who won a military victory by overthrowing the mighty Greeks and Syrians who were occupying Israel. When the Jews reclaimed and rededicated the Holy Temple in Jerusalem there was only enough oil to last for one day but then a miracle occurred, and the oil burnt for eight days until more could be found.

It is this connection with oil that has made it a tradition to have fried foods on this festival, with *latkes* at the top of the list. The secret of great *latkes* is to extract as much water as possible from the potatoes. This will give a crisp texture to the pancakes. Also, to avoid greasy *latkes* it is essential to use hot oil so that when they are fried they absorb very little oil.

❄ *(latkes only)* Ⓟ
Preparation: 30 minutes
Cooking: 40 minutes
Serves 6

I kg (2¼ lb) new potatoes
I onion
2 eggs, lightly beaten
2 tablespoons finely chopped fresh chives
I tablespoon lemon juice

6 tablespoons plain flour
I teaspoon baking powder
Salt and freshly ground black pepper
Vegetable oil, for frying

For the topping:
6 eggs
450 g (I lb) smoked salmon slices
I bunch fresh chives
Freshly ground black pepper

- Grate the potatoes and onion, using a food processor if available. Squeeze out as much excess water as possible, using kitchen paper. Add the eggs, chives, lemon juice, flour and baking powder, season with salt and pepper and mix well.

- Heat I cm (½ in) oil in a large frying pan.

- Put I tablespoon of the potato and onion mixture into the hot oil, and flatten it with the back of the spoon. Repeat with the remaining mixture and cook the *latkes*, in batches, over a steady moderate heat, for 5 minutes on each side until they are rich brown. (You will have to change the oil if it becomes burnt.)

- Drain the *latkes* on absorbent paper and keep them hot in an oven heated to 180°C/350°F/Gas Mark 4.

- For the topping, break each egg into a wide shallow pan of simmering water. Immediately turn the heat up so that the bubbles in the water draw the white around the yolk and prevent it sticking to the bottom of the pan. Once the white turns opaque, reduce the heat.

- Poach the eggs gently for 2–3 minutes. Lift the eggs out of the water with a perforated spoon and trim off the ragged edges with scissors.

- To serve, place the hot *latkes* on individual warmed plates and top with slices of smoked salmon and a poached egg. Use scissors to snip some of the chives over each serving, dust with a sprinkling of pepper and serve immediately.

NOTES: The *latkes* can be made up to two days in advance and refrigerated. The poached eggs can be made an hour in advance and kept in cold water. Reheat them in simmering water for 30 seconds. Cooled *latkes* can be frozen between layers of baking parchment.

Fish Tagine

TODAY, THERE ARE fewer than 5000 Jews living in Morocco compared to 300,000 in 1950, and much of Jewish Morocco is hidden from view. However, on a recent trip to Marrakech we found a guide who gave us a rich understanding not only of the role of Jews in Moroccan society, but also of the fascinating role of Moroccan Jews in the Jewish world. The synagogue there is slightly off the beaten track but well worth a visit.

A tagine is a conical clay pot that is placed on top of a gas hob or put in the oven, but the word is also used to describe the stew cooked within it. In Morocco, tagines of all varieties are eaten for lunch. Fish, chicken, beef and lamb – everyone has their own special recipe. The unexpected addition of sugar gives the dish a shine and a hint of sweetness.

My visit confirmed that the secret of a great tagine is its spices. Purchased fresh from the market, the vibrant mix of turmeric, saffron and cinnamon adds a truly authentic flavour without heat. Another secret is to use a mix called *ras el hanout*: this combination of up to 27 different spices is rather like the Indian garam masala.

The tagine method of cooking follows the pattern of S, B, S – seal, boil and, finally, simmer. The dish is often completed with a garnish of cooked dried fruits such as dates, figs or apricots and/or a sprinkling of almonds, walnuts or pistachios. The saffron and turmeric slightly colour the fish and successfully enhance its flavour. This tagine is straightforward to make and is low in fat.

Preparation: 25 minutes
Cooking: 25 minutes
Serves 6

3 tablespoons olive oil
3 red onions, finely sliced
6 garlic cloves, finely chopped
I teaspoon turmeric
½ teaspoon *ras el hanout* or garam masala
I teaspoon ground cinnamon
450 g (I lb) butternut squash, peeled, deseeded and cut into cubes
150 g (5 oz) dried apricots
Grated zest of 2 lemons and juice of I lemon
5 saffron threads mixed with 2 tablespoons boiling water or hot stock
6 fillets white fish (sea bream, sea bass, haddock or cod), small bones and skin removed
450 g (I lb) salad tomatoes, quartered
I teaspoon sugar
100 ml (4 fl oz) white wine

Salt and freshly ground black pepper
500 g (I lb 2 oz) couscous
I litre (1¾ pints) vegetable stock

To garnish:
I bunch fresh parsley, roughly chopped
110 g (4 oz) toasted whole almonds
2 lemons, cut into wedges

- Heat the oil in a large frying pan. Add the onions and garlic and sauté over a medium heat for 3 minutes until they are soft but not brown. Add the turmeric, *ras el hanout* or garam masala and cinnamon and fry for a further minute. Add the butternut squash, 150 ml (¼ pint) water, apricots, the zest of one lemon and the saffron. Bring to the boil, then reduce the heat and simmer, covered, for 15 minutes.

- Add the fish fillets, tomatoes, sugar, lemon juice and wine. Season well with salt and pepper and continue to cook, covered, for a final 10 minutes or until the butternut squash and fish are cooked.

- Place the couscous in a large bowl, pour over the stock, stir in the remaining lemon zest and season well. Cover with cling film and leave until the stock is absorbed. Fluff up with a fork just before serving.

- To serve, line individual warmed plates with generous helpings of couscous and spoon over the fish tagine. Sprinkle with the parsley and almonds and place the lemon wedges on the side of the plate.

Salmon Fish Cakes
with Tartare Sauce

FISH CAKES ARE a good example of a Jewish recipe that has travelled around the world, transforming itself as it goes. My Dutch friends use minced white fish – hake, cod or haddock – while I like to use fresh and smoked salmon.

I find that these delicious fish cakes, made with both fresh and smoked salmon, are ideal for a Shabbat or Yom Tov lunch, or a light supper when major cooking is just not on the agenda. For the best results, the secret is to add the salmon flakes gently so that large pieces are still visible.

Preparation: 25 minutes + 30 minutes chilling
Cooking: 20 minutes
Serves 4–6 (makes 15 fish cakes)

600 g (1 lb 5 oz) potatoes, cut into chunks
600 g (1 lb 5 oz) fresh salmon fillet
100 ml (4 fl oz) white wine or vegetable stock
100 g (3½ oz) smoked salmon, cut into small pieces
4 spring onions, finely chopped
Handful of fresh parsley, finely chopped
Salt and freshly ground black pepper
200 g (7 oz) plain flour
2 eggs, lightly beaten
300 g (11 oz) breadcrumbs
Vegetable oil, for frying
Lemon wedges, to garnish

For the tartare sauce:
200 g (7 oz) mayonnaise
Grated zest of 1 lemon
1 teaspoon horseradish sauce
2 tablespoons capers
2 tablespoons finely chopped fresh parsley
Salt and freshly ground black pepper

- Boil the potatoes for 15 minutes or until soft, then drain and mash with a potato ricer or fork.

- Place the fresh salmon in a pan. Pour in the wine or stock, bring to a gentle simmer, then cover and cook for 6–8 minutes or until the salmon is cooked through. Drain and set aside to cool.

- Flake the salmon into large pieces and add to the mashed potato, together with the smoked salmon, spring onions and parsley. Season well with salt and pepper and gently mix everything together.

- With wet hands shape the mixture into 15 cakes. Lightly dust each cake with some of the flour, dip it into the eggs and then coat with some of the breadcrumbs. Chill the fish cakes in the fridge for at least 30 minutes (important, or they will come apart in the frying pan).

- For the tartare sauce, combine all the ingredients. Keep in the fridge until ready to use.

- Heat 1 cm (½ in) oil in a large frying pan. Fry the fish cakes, in batches, over a high heat for 3–4 minutes on each side or until they are golden, crisp and heated through. Drain on kitchen paper.

- To serve, place the fish cakes on individual warmed plates, pour the sauce over them and garnish with lemon wedges.

NOTE: The sauce can be kept for up to four days, covered and refrigerated, provided all the ingredients are fresh.

Poultry

CHICKEN FALLS UNDER the *kashrut* laws for meat. Any part of the permitted bird can be eaten – chicken and turkey carcasses and giblets are traditionally used to make soups and stocks. Chicken is the main bird eaten by Sephardi and Ashkenazi Jews alike although, as my recipes show, it is treated in many different ways. Schnitzel is eaten in Israel – possibly the true Sephardi-Ashkenazi fusion dish – it is found there on every meaty menu in restaurants.

Roast Chicken with Apricots

FOR DECADES ASHKENAZI Jews have been eating chicken on Friday nights. There is no *halachic* (scriptural-based) reason for this; it is simply the age-old cuisine that European Jewry has adopted. It is for many families the only time everyone sits down together and the extended family is present. The three-course Friday night dinner is the best meal of the week, and more effort with the cooking is expected, and certainly appreciated, by the family.

My children take it in turns to choose the menu and this is one of their all-time favourite main courses. I tend to prepare the chicken in the morning, cover it and leave it in the fridge until just before I place it in the oven. This gives time for the flavours of the red wine and rosemary to permeate into its flesh. The dried apricots swell up and become melt-in-the-mouth fruits as they soak up the wine and chicken juices. Serve this with roast potatoes, *kugel* or rice and a selection of green vegetables.

Preparation: 10 minutes
Cooking: 2 hours + 10 minutes resting
Serves 6

1 x 2.3 kg (5 lb) roasting chicken, giblets removed (keep these for chicken soup)
6 sprigs of fresh rosemary
1 onion, roughly chopped
450 ml (¾ pint) red wine
250 g (9 oz) dried apricots
Salt and freshly ground black pepper

- Preheat the oven to 190°C/375°F/Gas Mark 5.

- Loosen the skin from the breast of the chicken and carefully insert the rosemary sprigs between the skin and the breast.

- Place the chicken, breast-side down, in a roasting tin. Sprinkle with the onion and pour over the wine and 200 ml (8 fl oz) water. Arrange the apricots around the bird and season well with salt and pepper. Cover with foil and roast in the oven for approximately 2 hours.

- Remove the chicken from the oven and leave it to rest for 10 minutes before carving.

Hameen: The Shabbat Classic

THIS IS THE classic Shabbat lunch eaten by Indian Jews of Sephardi and Far Eastern origin. A whole meal, not just a single dish, it is made on the Friday before Shabbat and is cooked very slowly in a low oven, then served for lunch the following day. Don't just make this for Shabbat – it is just as filling and delicious eaten during the week. Remember to start cooking it the night before.

The word *hameen*, or *hamin*, comes from the Hebrew *cham*, meaning hot – or the French *chaud*, as the stew resembles a Jewish French cassoulet. It is actually the Sephardi equivalent of the Ashkenazi *cholent*. There is one main difference – the Sephardi kitchen uses mostly wholewheat grain and rice while it is customary for the Ashkenazi to use pearl barley. As for the meats, the Ashkenazi use beef, duck, goose and *schmaltz* (fat), and the Sephardi use beef, mutton, chicken, mutton fat and oil. Because of the length and gentleness of cooking, the meat used is cheap, gelatinous and tough.

When the Sephardi Jews of Spain were expelled in 1492 they took with them to Morocco and North Africa the tradition of making *hameen* for the Sabbath. They cooked their overnight stew as they had before, using local ingredients and flavours. Mutton replaced beef, and rice – cooked in a cloth bag to prevent sogginess – was used instead of barley. The mixture was spiced with hot red peppers, saffron or turmeric, and ground coriander. Syrian Jews place the mixture inside a hollowed-out pumpkin or squash and Jews throughout the Mediterranean often add chick-peas or cracked wheat.

Aunt Nina's Hameen

THIS PARTICULAR RECIPE is from my husband's Aunt Nina, now in her eighties, who spent many years in Singapore and used to prepare it most Fridays. She was taught how to make *hameen* by a Chinese cook who was trained by an Orthodox family. 'It is wonderful to share with family and friends as it makes a large quantity,' she says. She also says that the secret of a good *hameen* is plenty of cinnamon, so thick sticks of the fresh spice should be used. The smell fills the kitchen with its unique aroma. Another secret is to resist the temptation to check the dish while it's cooking – once it is sealed it is best left well alone.

Preparation: 30 minutes
Cooking: Overnight or a minimum of 3 hours

2 tablespoons vegetable oil
2 onions, roughly chopped
3 garlic cloves, finely chopped
3 teaspoons turmeric
2.5 cm (1 in) piece of fresh root ginger, finely chopped
1 x 2.3 kg (5 lb) roasting chicken, cut into 8 portions
400 g (14 oz) basmati rice
450 g (1 lb) salad tomatoes, roughly chopped
2 tablespoons tomato purée
7 cardamoms
3 cinnamon sticks
2 litres (3½ pints) chicken stock
Salt and freshly ground black pepper

- Preheat the oven to 120°C/250°F/Gas Mark ½ or its lowest setting.

- Heat the oil in a very large frying pan. Add the onions, garlic, turmeric and ginger and sauté over a medium heat for 2 minutes until the onions and garlic start to colour. Add the chicken pieces and sauté for 5–7 minutes until they are brown all over. Add the rice, tomatoes, tomato purée, cardamoms and cinnamon. Cook for a further 2 minutes then pour in the stock. Make sure the stock completely covers the rice. Season with salt and pepper.

- Mix well so that the cinnamon flavours infuse into the chicken. Bring to the boil, then reduce the heat and simmer for 10 minutes. Transfer to a large ovenproof dish and cover with foil and then a lid.

- Place in the oven and cook overnight or for a minimum of 3 hours.

- Serve in warmed bowls.

Roast Turkey with Apple Dumplings and Apple Gravy

THIS IS THE recipe for anyone who wants a new and unique dish that is family friendly and captures all the flavours of the Jewish New Year. It is perfect for a large gathering and ideal served cold for the rest of Yom Tov.

Jews in America tend to celebrate Thanksgiving with a roast turkey and this recipe is also perfect for this occasion. The Jewish population in the United States is the second largest in the world after Israel. It is composed mostly of Ashkenazi Jews, but there are also Sephardi and Mizrachi

(Middle Eastern) Jews, along with members of other Jewish ethnic groups, so there is a wide range of cultural traditions. I have a lot of close family in America, including a twin sister and numerous cousins. Frequent trips have been great culinary adventures discovering 'what's new that is kosher', as most developments tend to stem from the United States.

When cooking turkey allow at least 300 g (11 oz) per person and approximately 20 minutes per 450 g (1 lb) for roasting. It is important to cover the bird with foil and baste regularly so that it remains moist and tender. Once the turkey is cooked allow 15 minutes resting time, so that the juices can seep back into the meat; this makes the bird easier to carve and more succulent to eat. The best way to carve turkey is to remove the legs, and then slice the breast, using long sawing movements.

Preparation: 25 minutes
Cooking: 4 hours + 15 minutes resting
Serves 8–10

1 litre (1¾ pints) cider
100 ml (4 fl oz) kosher calvados
1 teaspoon ground cinnamon
2 tablespoons clear honey
100 ml (4 fl oz) soy sauce
Salt and freshly ground black pepper
1 x 5 kg (11 lb) turkey, giblets and neck removed

For the apple dumplings:
2 apples, peeled, cored and quartered
3 spring onions, trimmed
3 slices of white bread
75 g (3 oz) ground almonds
Salt and freshly ground black pepper

For the apple gravy:
2 tablespoons cornflour
Cooking stock (see below)
4 apples – peeled, cored and quartered

- Preheat the oven to 180°C/350°F/Gas Mark 4.

- First make the dumplings. Whiz all the ingredients together in a food processor until combined. Roll into 25 small balls and set aside.

- Now make a cooking stock for the turkey. Mix the cider, calvados, cinnamon, honey and soy sauce with 150 ml (¼ pint) water and season with salt and pepper.

- Rinse the turkey inside and out and pat it dry. Sprinkle the main cavity with salt and pepper. Place the bird in a roasting tin, breast-side down, and pour in half the cooking stock. Cover with foil and roast for 1½ hours.

- Remove the turkey from the oven. Pour over the remaining cooking stock, re-cover the bird with foil and return it to the oven for a further 1½ hours.

- Check the turkey again, baste with the stock and turn the bird over so that it is breast-side up. Continue cooking it, covered with foil, for another 30 minutes.

- Line a baking sheet with baking parchment, place the apple dumplings on it and bake them for 25–30 minutes at 180°C/350°F/Gas Mark 4. When the dumplings are cooked, leave them in an oven at 150°C/300°F/Gas Mark 2 to keep warm, or microwave for 2–3 minutes.

- Remove the foil from the turkey and roast, uncovered, for a final 30 minutes. The turkey should be golden. Check that it is cooked by piercing a thigh with a sharp knife. The juices should run clear.

- Remove the turkey from the oven and transfer all the cooking stock in the roasting tin to a pan. Remove the scum and fat. Re-cover the turkey with foil and leave it to stand for 15 minutes.

- To make the gravy, mix the cornflour with 2 tablespoons of the cooking stock. Add this to the rest of the stock. Bring to the boil, then reduce the heat and simmer for 10 minutes to reduce by a third of the original liquid. While the gravy is simmering, cook the apple quarters in a clean pan with a little water over a low heat until softened. Mix the softened apples into the gravy and season to taste.

- To serve, carve the turkey into thin slices and place on individual warmed plates, with three dumplings, in a pool of apple gravy.

NOTE: The turkey can be stuffed one day in advance.

Jews in Hungary

THE JEWISH COMMUNITY in Hungary was virtually destroyed by the Holocaust. At the start of the Second World War there were about 800,000 Jews in the country, making up about five per cent of the total population. Initially there were small-scale pogroms and riots but these gradually worsened, with the first massacre of Hungarian Jews by SS troops in the autumn of 1941, followed by transports to the concentration camps – mainly to Auschwitz in Poland. Between 15 May and 8 July 1944, in the final weeks of the war and with Soviet troops advancing, the pace of death intensified and over 400,000 Hungarian Jews were exterminated.

Today there are 20 synagogues in Hungary and a community of approximately 100,000 Jews. Hungary exports *matzah*, kosher meat and kosher wine.

Chicken Paprikash

SOMETIMES REFERRED TO as chicken paprika, this is a Hungarian speciality for Yom Kippur. I like to use chicken pieces but whole breasts de-boned can be substituted if you prefer. The chicken is served with thick egg noodles or pappardelle; a dish made with family favourite ingredients that are suitable for fasting on.

Paprika is a major flavouring in Hungary. It is a fine powder ground from certain varieties of sweet pepper. Known as 'pimiento', these vary in size, shape and redness. The powder can range in colour from bright red to rusty brown, and in taste from sweet to smoky to spicy. When cooking paprika, remember it releases its colour and flavour only when heated.

Chicken paprikash is delightfully simple to make and is popular with everyone I've served it to.

Preparation: 20 minutes
Cooking: 1¾ hours
Serves 4–6

2 tablespoons olive oil, plus 2 tablespoons for the noodles (optional)
1 x 150 g (5 oz) chicken, cut into 8 pieces

3 tablespoons smoky or sweet (not hot) paprika
400 g (14 oz) mushrooms, sliced
1 onion, roughly chopped
1 green pepper, deseeded and cut into strips
475 ml (15 fl oz) chicken stock or water
225 g–350 g (8 oz–12 oz) large egg noodles (50 g/2 oz per person)
2 tablespoons margarine (optional)

- Preheat the oven to 160°C/325°F/Gas Mark 3.

- Heat the oil in a large frying pan. Add the chicken pieces and paprika, and sauté over a medium heat for 3 minutes until the chicken pieces are nicely brown. Then add the mushrooms, onion and green pepper. Cook for 5–8 minutes until the vegetables are soft.

- Transfer to an ovenproof dish. Add the stock or water, cover and place in the oven for 1½ hours.

- Cook the noodles according to the instructions on the packet. Drain and add the margarine or oil, whichever you prefer, to the noodles so that they do not stick together.

- To serve, place the egg noodles on a warmed serving platter and top with the chicken paprikash.

Persian Stuffed Chicken with Mushroom Gravy

STUFFING POULTRY WITH dried fruit is a popular style of Persian cooking, particularly for festivals. The original gravy for this dish was a thin, slightly spicy broth which I have made much more substantial and tasty.

There have been Jews in Iran (formerly Persia) for thousands of years. The Purim story of Esther is one of many with references to Jewish experiences in Persia, celebrating the rescue of the Jews from extermination at the hands of the chief minister to the king of Persia. Today, the Jewish community is officially recognised as a religious minority group by the Iranian government. During the Seder service many Persian Jews have mock fights, using spring onions as symbols of the Egyptian whips.

Over the centuries Iranian-Jewish cooking has adopted the character of the national cuisine. It makes great use of spices, herbs and nuts – particularly nutmeg, cinnamon and pistachios – but the overall effect is subtle rather than hot or sharp.

This luxurious dish is ideal for Seder night – prepare it in advance, cook it just before it's needed and serve it plated or buffet style. I like to serve it with individual potato *kugel* and a selection of green vegetables.

❄ Ⓟ (substitute cornflour for potato flour)
Preparation: 30 minutes
Cooking: 40 minutes
Serves 6

6 chicken breasts, skinned and boned
110 g (4 oz) raisins

110 g (4 oz) dried apricots
50 g (2 oz) pistachios
2 garlic cloves
3 tablespoons medium *matzah* meal
1 teaspoon ground cinnamon
Salt and freshly ground black pepper
2–3 tablespoons olive oil

For the mushroom gravy:
350 g (12 oz) mixed mushrooms, finely sliced
475 ml (¾ pint) chicken stock
200 ml (8 fl oz) red wine
2 tablespoons cornflour (potato flour for Pesach)
Salt and freshly ground black pepper

- Cover the chicken breasts with cling film and pound them with a rolling pin until they are 1 cm (½ in) thick.

- Place the raisins, apricots, pistachios, garlic, *matzah* meal and cinnamon in a food processor and whiz to form a paste. Season well with salt and pepper.

- Spread the flattened chicken breasts evenly with the paste. Roll up each breast like a Swiss roll and secure firmly with string or two or three cocktail sticks.

- Heat the oil in a large frying pan. Add the chicken rolls and sauté over a medium heat for 5 minutes until they are brown. Remove and set aside.

- For the gravy, place the mushrooms in the same pan. Cook over a high heat for about 5 minutes or until they start to wilt. Add the stock and wine and continue cooking for a further 5 minutes. Mix 2 tablespoons water with the cornflour to form a paste. Add the paste to the frying pan, stirring well to prevent lumps. Season with salt and pepper.

- Place the chicken rolls back in the frying pan, cover and cook over a medium heat for a final **30 minutes**.

- To serve, pour the mushroom gravy on to a warmed serving platter. Remove the string or cocktail sticks from the chicken rolls and place the rolls on top of the gravy.

NOTE: This dish can be prepared a day in advance and refrigerated.

Breast of Duck with the Flavours of France

EATING DUCK AND goose is a particular Ashkenazi tradition as they are the favourite meat ingredient in many Middle Eastern and Asian dishes, and some Persian ones. This is a French recipe that is similar to one I enjoyed while staying with a Parisian family in my teens. It was made for the grandparents' anniversary and was served as part of a buffet.

The current Jewish community in France numbers around 600,000 and is one of the largest in the world. It includes all types of Jews from the ultra-orthodox Haredi to the completely secular. The dominant tradition in France is Sephardi and many French Jews have their ancestry in Arab lands. Despite increasing anti-Semitism in France, particularly in Paris, the Jewish lifestyle is flourishing.

For the French, a Friday night meal would be a chicken dish with couscous, or possibly duck for a special occasion.

Duck is available all year round. When buying it, check that the flesh is plump and the cavity has a clean fresh smell. The meat is rich and has a stronger flavour than that of chicken. This recipe uses breasts but it's fine to use a whole bird, cut into portions. Some crusty bread is all that is needed to soak up the juices and complete the meal in the true French way.

Preparation: 15 minutes
Cooking: 55 minutes
Serves 4

1 tablespoon vegetable oil
4 duck breasts
250 g (9 oz) dried pitted prunes
2 aubergines, cut into large cubes
300 ml (½ pint) fruity red wine
300 ml (½ pint) chicken stock
1 large bunch fresh thyme (to be added as a bunch)
225 g (8 oz) Puy lentils, cooked
Salt and freshly ground black pepper
Sprigs of fresh thyme, to garnish
Crusty bread, to serve

- Preheat the oven to 180°C/350°F/Gas Mark 4.

- Heat the vegetable oil in a large frying pan. Add the duck breasts and brown them over a high heat for 5-6 minutes or until the skin is crispy. Remove and place in a large casserole dish.

- Add the prunes, aubergines, wine, stock, thyme and lentils and season with salt and pepper. Mix together and pour over the duck breasts. Remove the bunch of thyme, cover and place in the oven for 50 minutes.

- To serve, place a generous helping of the vegetables on individual warmed plates and sit a crispy breast of duck on top. Garnish with sprigs of thyme and serve at once with crusty bread.

Chicken, Date and Raisin Tagine with Couscous

THIS IS A dish that you will want to make time and time again – the combined flavours work well and produce a chicken meal that has a lemony spiced flavour without heat. I wrote this recipe with Rosh Hashanah in mind as its selection of sweet fruits captures the essence of the festival.

Sweet dates are served to symbolise the wish that the New Year will be equally sweet. While most Sephardi Jews eat them plain, some Moroccan Jews dip them in a mixture of ground sesame seeds, aniseeds and powdered sugar. (Apples are also dipped in this mixture.) Another tradition, between Rosh Hashanah and Simchat Torah, a joyous holiday celebrating the end and beginning of the annual cycle of weekly Torah readings, is to dip the Friday night *challah* in honey and not salt.

Dates have a special place in the Bible as they are one of the seven species listed as native to the land of Israel. They originally grew in the Jordan valley, but with modern irrigation techniques they have also taken root near the Dead Sea. In biblical times dates were made into honey, and many believe that the honey referred to in the 'land flowing with milk and honey' was actually date honey. Today, dates are a popular sweet snack before or after meals, and are exported all over the world.

This recipe does not need any additional vegetables, which makes serving it for a dinner party very straightforward.

Preparation: 20 minutes
Cooking: 1½ hours
Serves 6

3 tablespoons olive oil
6 chicken breasts, boneless and skinless
1 large red onion, roughly chopped
4 garlic cloves, roughly chopped
2 teaspoons ground cinnamon
2 teaspoons ground cumin
110 g (4 oz) dates, pitted
2 lemons, sliced
8 saffron threads
150 ml (¼ pint) chicken stock
300 ml (½ pint) red wine
150 g (5 oz) raisins
Salt and freshly ground black pepper

To garnish:
150 g (5 oz) blanched almonds, toasted
Sprigs of fresh parsley, preferably flatleaf

For the couscous:
570 ml (1 pint) hot vegetable or chicken stock
300 g (11 oz) couscous
Salt and freshly ground black pepper

- Heat the oil in a deep frying pan. Add the chicken breasts and sauté, in batches, over a medium heat for 5 minutes until brown. Remove from the pan and place in a deep ovenproof dish.

- Sauté the onion, garlic, cinnamon and cumin in the frying pan for 2 minutes, add to the chicken and mix well. Add the dates, lemons, saffron, stock, wine and raisins, and season well with salt and pepper. Stir, then cover and simmer for 1–1¼ hours.

- For the couscous, pour the stock over the couscous. Cover immediately with cling film and leave for 10 minutes. Remove the cling film and fluff up the couscous with a fork. Season with salt and pepper.

- To serve, place a generous helping of couscous on individual warmed plates and spoon over a portion of chicken tagine. Garnish with the toasted almonds and sprigs of parsley.

NOTES: The best way to reheat couscous is to cover the bowl with cling film and place it in a microwave. To toast almonds place them in an oven preheated to 200°C/400°F/Gas Mark 6 for 10 minutes or until golden.

Roast Duck with Orange Sauce

IF THERE WAS ever a recipe that I will always remember my mother making when I was little, it is this one. Duck is expensive and quite fatty, so it was only made on special occasions like birthdays or anniversaries.

The connection between Jews and oranges has to be Jaffa! The Jaffa orange, also known as the Shamouti orange, is very sweet and almost seedless, and is exported from Israel. Today the industry has declined somewhat due to competition from Spanish and other European markets. The name comes from the city of Jaffa.

The Jaffa orange serves as a symbol for Israelis and also for Palestinians, many of who see it as symbolising the bounty of their lost homeland – during the 1948 Arab-Israeli War some Palestinian farmers were separated from the orange groves their families had tended for generations. In Jewish Israeli culture, the oranges are associated with the pioneering age of Zionism.

Keep this recipe for Tu B'Shvat, the Jewish festival for the New Year for Trees. Oranges are a perfect example of Israeli produce.

Preparation: 20 minutes
Cooking: 2 hours
Serves 4

2.3 kg (5 lb) duck, giblets removed (keep for stock or soup)
2–3 tablespoons salt, plus extra for seasoning
Freshly ground black pepper
1 large cooking apple, peeled, cored and quartered
1 onion, sliced
2 oranges, cut into slices, to garnish

For the orange sauce:
125 g (4½ oz) caster sugar
300 ml (½ pint) white wine vinegar
Juice and grated zest of 2 oranges
4 tablespoons brandy
1 tablespoon cornflour
Salt and freshly ground black pepper

• Preheat the oven to 180°C/350°F/Gas Mark 4.

- Rinse the duck well and pat it dry. Pull out excess fat from the cavity and around the neck. Then prick the skin all over, and season the bird inside and out with salt and pepper. Put the apple and onion inside the cavity and rub the 2–3 tablespoons salt all over the bird – this helps to break down the fat.

- Place the duck, breast-side up, on a rack in a roasting tin and roast in the oven for approximately 2 hours until it is golden, draining off the fat from time to time. The duck is cooked when the juices run clear when a thigh is pierced.

- Meanwhile, make the sauce. Dissolve the sugar in the vinegar. Bring to the boil, then reduce the heat and simmer until the sugar starts to caramelise. Add the orange juice and zest, stir in the brandy and season.

- Blend the cornflour with 2 tablespoons water to make a paste. Stir this into the sauce to thicken it.

- When the duck is cooked, cut it into four portions. Pour over the sauce and garnish with orange slices.

Honey- and Sesame-glazed Chicken with Apple Rice

THIS RECIPE CAPTURES all the flavours for a sweet and happy New Year. You can never have enough main-course family dishes and this one is definitely a winner. When Rosh Hashanah falls during the week and Shabbat follows, food planning is essential and this is an ideal dish that can be prepared in advance.

On a health note, apples are an excellent choice, especially during festive times when eating is a continuous pleasure: 'An apple a day keeps the doctor away.' Research suggests that apples may reduce the risk of colon cancer, prostate cancer and lung cancer. Like many fruits, they contain vitamin C as well as a host of other antioxidant compounds that may reduce the risk of cancer by preventing DNA damage.

Preparation: 15 minutes
Cooking: 30 minutes
Serves 6

6 chicken breasts, skinned and boned
6 tablespoons sesame oil
4 tablespoons clear honey
300 ml (½ pint) hot chicken stock

To garnish:
3 tablespoons sesame seeds
6 sprigs fresh flatleaf parsley

For the apple rice:
2 tablespoons olive oil
50 g (2 oz) vegetable margarine
1 small onion, roughly chopped
6 spring onions, trimmed and roughly chopped
300 g (11 oz) long grain rice
900 ml (1½ pints) chicken stock
150 ml (¼ pint) fresh apple juice
75 g (3 oz) raisins or sultanas
1 green apple, cored and roughly chopped
1 red apple, cored and roughly chopped
Salt and freshly ground black pepper

- Preheat the oven to 200°C/400°F/Gas Mark 6.

- Score the chicken breasts – this helps them to absorb the cooking flavours and gives the meat a stylish look. Place in a shallow ovenproof dish. Pour the sesame oil, honey and hot chicken stock over the breasts, cover and place in the oven for 20 minutes.

- For the apple rice, heat the oil and margarine in a large pan. Add the onion and spring onions and sauté over a medium heat for 2 minutes or until softened. Add the rice, stock, apple juice and raisins or sultanas, cover and simmer for 15 minutes.

- Stir in the chopped apples, season well with salt and pepper, and continue cooking, covered, for a further 5 minutes.

- Toast the sesame seeds for the garnish in a dry frying pan over a high heat for 2 minutes until just golden. (If they burn they will taste bitter, so watch them carefully.)

- To serve, place a generous helping of apple rice on individual warmed plates, slice a chicken breast at an angle and fan it on top. Spoon a tablespoon of the sesame and honey cooking juices over it. Garnish with a sprinkling of sesame seeds and a sprig of parsley. Serve at once.

NOTE: This dish can be prepared a day in advance and refrigerated, and served cold if desired.

Crispy Lemon Schnitzels

THIS HAS TO be one of the most popular classic Ashkenazi dishes with my family and many others. The schnitzels are enjoyed by young and old alike and can be eaten hot or cold for picnics and packed lunches.

Turkey schnitzels are one of the most frequently eaten dishes in Israel – usually accompanied by chips and Israeli salad. Try them with *latkes*, fried onions, mash, rice and pickles.

You can either use ready-prepared turkey schnitzels, which are thin, or prepare your own chicken schnitzels from boneless, skinless breasts. If you decide on chicken breasts, cover them with baking parchment or cling film and bash them gently with a rolling pin, taking care not to break the fibres.

Ⓟ

Preparation: 20 minutes
Cooking: 25 minutes
Serves 6

6 chicken breasts, skinned and boned, and pounded until thin, or 6 turkey schnitzels
Salt and freshly ground black pepper
250 g (9 oz) medium *matzah* meal
Grated zest of 2 lemons
3 eggs
6 tablespoons vegetable oil
100 ml (4 fl oz) Kiddush wine

- Preheat the oven to 200°C/400°F/Gas Mark 6. Line a baking sheet with baking parchment.

- Season the chicken breasts or turkey schnitzels with salt and pepper.

- Combine the *matzah* meal and lemon zest on a plate and lightly beat the eggs in a shallow dish. Dip the breasts or schnitzels in the beaten eggs, then coat them with the lemon *matzah* meal. Repeat this process twice to ensure a really good coating.

- Heat the oil in a frying pan and fry the breasts or schnitzels over a high heat for 4–5 minutes on each side until brown. If the oil starts to burn clean the pan and use fresh oil.

- Place the breasts or schnitzels on the baking sheet, sprinkle with the wine and place them in the oven for 15–20 minutes or until they are no longer pink inside. (The wine prevents them from going dry.)

- Serve immediately.

NOTE: The coated breasts or schnitzels can be refrigerated for up to 4 hours until you are ready to cook them.

Golden Chicken Salad

THIS IS THE perfect light supper meal for making when the weather has been warm and you don't want to spend serious time near a hot stove. File the recipe away for summer, but you can also use it over Pesach as it has no *matzah* or nuts. Its golden colour comes from the delicious mix of orange and yellow peppers together with pineapple and sweet potatoes.

It can be made with freshly cooked chicken breasts or leftovers from Friday night's dinner. It can be served hot, cold or warm. I like to prepare it in stages, by roasting the vegetables and then combining them with the remaining ingredients at the last minute.

Preparation: 25 minutes
Cooking: 20 minutes
Serves 6

1 orange pepper, deseeded and roughly chopped
1 yellow pepper, deseeded and roughly chopped
450 g (1 lb) sweet potatoes, roughly chopped
4 garlic cloves, finely chopped
Salt and freshly ground black pepper
3 tablespoons olive oil
600 g (1 lb 5 oz) cooked chicken, cubed or sliced
1 medium-size pineapple, peeled, cored and roughly
   chopped
5 tablespoons mayonnaise
1 bunch fresh chives, snipped, to garnish

- Preheat the oven to 200°C/400°F/Gas Mark 6.

- Place the peppers and sweet potatoes on a baking sheet. Sprinkle with
  the garlic and season well with salt and pepper. Coat the vegetables
  with the oil and roast them for 20 minutes or until they are soft and
  slightly golden. Set aside to cool for 10 minutes.

- Put the chicken and pineapple in a large serving dish. Add the
  mayonnaise and vegetables, mix together and check the seasoning.

- To serve, garnish the salad with snipped chives.

NOTE: The salad can be made a day in advance and refrigerated – a
great Shabbat lunch.

Spanish Escalopes with Red Rice

THIS TASTY DISH is served with courgettes and red rice for added colour. Although the rice normally comes from Camargue in south-west France, rather than Spain, it works well with this recipe: its unique nutty consistency is similar to that of brown rice but the grains are firmer and less sticky. It takes 20–25 minutes to cook, a lot longer than regular long grain rice. Red rice can also be used for pilafs and salads.

If you prefer you can use chicken breasts instead of turkey schnitzels, but allow approximately 5 minutes more to cook them depending on the size and thickness of the portion.

Preparation: 20 minutes
Cooking: 35 minutes
Serves 6

450 g (1 lb) red rice rinsed
900 ml (1½ pints) chicken stock
4 tablespoons olive oil
6 turkey escalopes (thin schnitzels)
5 garlic cloves, crushed
4 tablespoons roughly chopped fresh flatleaf parsley
Juice and grated zest of 1 lemon
Freshly ground black pepper
600 g (1 lb 5 oz) cherry tomatoes on the vine, cut into small wedges
150 g (5 oz) pimiento-stuffed olives, sliced
4 courgettes, roughly chopped
6 sprigs of fresh parsley, to garnish

- Cook the rice in the stock according to the instructions on the packet – this will take around 20–25 minutes. Drain and set aside.

- Meanwhile, heat 2 tablespoons of the oil in a large frying pan. Add the turkey escalopes and fry them over a high heat for about 7 minutes until golden, turning them halfway through.

- Whisk together the garlic, parsley, lemon zest and juice, the remaining oil, pepper and 4 tablespoons water. Add the whisked ingredients to the escalopes along with the tomatoes, olives and courgettes. Stir, and continue to cook for a further 5 minutes or until the courgettes are tender.

- To keep the escalopes warm while the rice is cooking, place them in an oven preheated to 200°C/400°F/Gas Mark 6 for a maximum of 10 minutes.

- To serve, spoon some rice on to individual warmed plates. Place an escalope and vegetables on top and garnish with a sprig of parsley.

Citrus Turkey Roll

TURKEY MAKES AN impressive but economical main course, especially for those times when you are catering for a number of people. I love this tasty stuffing with herbs and cranberries that is revealed, Swiss roll style, as the roll is sliced. Cooked in a stock of lemon and orange juice with white wine, the turkey will not dry out even if it is cooked slightly longer than planned.

Preparation: 25 minutes
Cooking: 55 minutes + 10 minutes resting
Serves 6

750 g (1 lb 10 oz), skinless, boneless turkey breast
2 slices of white bread
3 garlic cloves
1 tablespoon clear honey
4 tablespoons finely chopped fresh flatleaf parsley
4 tablespoons finely chopped fresh basil
3 tablespoons dried cranberries
Grated zest of ½ orange
1 egg
Salt and freshly ground black pepper
1–2 tablespoons olive oil
300 ml (½ pint) white wine
750 ml (1¼ pints) chicken stock
2 lemons, cut into wedges
Roughly chopped fresh parsley, to garnish

- Preheat the oven to 200°C/400°F/Gas Mark 6.

- Using a sharp knife, make a sideways cut, from left to right, part of the way through the turkey breast; it must go far enough to allow you to open the two halves like a book. Open the two halves, place a piece of baking parchment over the turkey and use a mallet or rolling pin to pound the breast into a flatter piece of meat of even thickness.

- Place the bread, garlic, honey, parsley and basil in a food processor and pulse gently until the mixture is very roughly chopped. Transfer to a bowl and stir in the cranberries and orange zest. Add the egg, season with salt and pepper, and mix together.

- Spread the mixture over the meat, in one layer, leaving a small border all round.
- Roll the turkey up and tie the roll with string in several places.
- Heat the oil in a casserole dish on the hob; it must be slightly larger than the turkey roll. When the oil is hot, fry the turkey roll over a high heat on all sides for 7–10 minutes so that it is nicely browned. Remove from the heat. Add the wine and stock, and arrange the lemon wedges around the roll. Cover and place in the oven for 40–45 minutes.
- Remove from the oven and allow to stand for 10 minutes before slicing.
- To serve, place the turkey slices on a large serving platter and dust with chopped parsley.

NOTE: To make individual servings, you can replace the turkey breast with 6 turkey schnitzels and flatten and roll the meat as above. Cook the schnitzels for 15–20 minutes.

Turkey Goulash

CHOOSING THE MAIN course for Seder night always poses a dilemma and I know everyone is looking for a good new idea. Why not try this recipe at next year's Seder table? Turkey is economical and this goulash is easy to prepare and straightforward to serve. It will keep well on a hot plate, so if you spend more time than expected discussing the details of the Exodus story it will not spoil.

I like to serve this on a bed of curly kale or stir-fried shredded Savoy cabbage. All the vegetables are in the goulash and the cabbage just gives the dish some extra colour.

❄ Ⓟ

Preparation: 25 minutes
Cooking: 1¼ hours
Serves 10

3 tablespoons vegetable oil
4 large onions, roughly chopped
6 garlic cloves, crushed
1 kg (2¼ lb) boneless turkey, cut into small cubes
2 teaspoons ground cinnamon
2 tablespoons sweet paprika
Salt and freshly ground black pepper
3 tablespoons potato flour
1 kg (2¼ lb) potatoes, cubed
750 g (1 lb 10 oz) mushrooms, sliced
10 medium-size carrots, cut into chunks
6 sticks celery, sliced
4 tablespoons tomato ketchup
450 ml (¾ pint) chicken stock
200 ml (8 fl oz) red wine
Paprika, for dusting
Cooked cabbage, to serve
Sprigs of fresh parsley, to garnish

- Heat the oil in a large frying pan. Add the onions and garlic and sauté over a medium heat for about 4 minutes or until the onions are no longer transparent. Add the turkey, cinnamon and paprika, and season with salt and pepper. Cook the turkey gently on all sides for approximately 10 minutes.

- Stir in the flour and cook for 1 minute. Add the potatoes, mushrooms, carrots, celery and tomato ketchup, and pour in the stock and wine.

Bring to the boil, then cover and reduce the heat to a simmer for
1 hour. Taste and adjust the seasoning accordingly.

- To serve, dust individual warmed plates with paprika. Make a circle of
cooked cabbage, place a large helping of turkey goulash in the centre
and garnish with sprigs of parsley.

Meat

KOSHER MEAT HAS been a luxury at the Jewish table. In less affluent times it was saved for Shabbat and stretching it with other ingredients is still popular. For reasons of *kashrut*, only cuts from the front part of the animal are permitted in the United Kingdom. These tend to adapt well to long, slow cooking and make melt-in-the-mouth dishes. Separating milk from meat is a fundamental rule of *kashrut*. For most observant Jews, after eating meat it is essential to wait a prescribed time before consuming dairy. This varies quite considerably within communities and family groups and can be any time from three to six hours. The Dutch Jewish community observe a one hour time lapse for example.

If you are eating dairy produce there is no prescribed time as to when you can eat meat. Very often a glass of water, the cleaning of one's teeth or the saying of the *Birchat Hamazon* grace after meals will be sufficient.

Cholent: A Shabbat Staple

THIS BOOK IS all about Jewish flavours, and this recipe is essential for anyone exploring the roots of Jewish cooking. It is essentially a slow-cooked stew that is made on the Friday before Shabbat comes in and is ready to eat the following day. It is a meal in itself, traditionally made with meat, potatoes, vegetables, grains and pulses, and is therefore extremely filling. The ingredients differ considerably – there are recipes for vegetarian *cholents* that are not so heavy on the stomach – but what they all have in common is that they produce a unique and overwhelmingly distinctive aroma that fills the kitchen as it cooks on a Shabbat.

The Jewish religion forbids any form of work during the Sabbath and this includes cooking. Around the world, *cholent* is also known by names that vary from *adafina* to *hameen*. It is very popular and every home and country has its own special ingredient and flavour.

Some Orthodox sages say that on Shabbat a person is endowed with an extra soul (*neshama yeteirah* in Hebrew) which manifests itself in an increased capacity to consume food during the Shabbat meals. Therefore, there is an underlying spiritual reason why it is easier, quantitatively and qualitatively, to eat more foods such as *cholent*, *kishka* (a kosher beef intestine stuffed with *matzah* meal, rendered fat (*schmaltz*) and spice), *kugels*, chopped liver and other 'heavy' foods on Shabbat than on a regular weekday.

Cholent from Alsace

THIS PARTICULAR RECIPE is an old one that originated with the Ashkenazi Jews of the Alsace region of France/Germany. It is made with shoulder of lamb, dried fruits and fresh rosemary.

Preparation: 20 minutes + soaking haricot beans overnight
Cooking: 18–20 hours
Serves 8

200 g (7 oz) haricot beans
1.8 kg–2.3 kg (4 lb–5 lb) shoulder of lamb, bone removed
4 garlic cloves, sliced
2 tablespoons olive oil
2 onions, sliced
570 ml (1 pint) red wine
900 g (2 lb) potatoes, quartered
4 tablespoons fresh rosemary leaves
1 tablespoon sugar
50 g (2 oz) raisins
200 g (7 oz) mixed dried fruit (apricots, pears, peaches)
570 ml (1 pint) vegetable stock
Salt and freshly ground black pepper

- Soak the haricot beans overnight according to the instructions on the packet, then drain and rinse them.

- Using a sharp knife, make slits in the lamb. Insert the garlic slices into the meat.

- Heat the oil in a large casserole dish on the hob. Add the onions and lamb and sauté over a high heat for 5–10 minutes or until the meat is brown. Add the wine, potatoes, rosemary, beans, sugar, raisins and dried fruit, and pour in enough stock to cover all the ingredients. Season well with salt and pepper. Bring to the boil and simmer for 1½ hours. If preferred, simmer the *cholent* ahead of time, cook to this stage and chill until just before Shabbat starts.

- Preheat the oven to its lowest temperature. Cover the casserole dish with foil and then a lid; this helps to keep the heat in and prevents the flavours escaping. Place the dish in the oven and leave to cook overnight.

- Serve the *cholent* when you return from the Sabbath morning synagogue service.

NOTE: If you wish, the *cholent* can be cooked in a crock pot instead of a casserole dish; turn the light to its lowest setting and cover the crock pot with foil and a lid. Another alternative is to transfer the contents of the pan to a slow cooker once the *cholent* has simmered for 1½ hours.

Adafina

ADAFINA IS THE Sephardi version of the Ashkenazi *cholent*. Both are prepared on Friday, cooked overnight and eaten for Shabbat lunch. In North Africa the dish is called *dfina*, from the Arabic 'to hide away', as the dish hides in the oven being cooked for Shabbat. However, the mouth-watering distinctive aroma that fills the kitchen can't be hidden! The long slow cooking makes the meat beautifully succulent and full of flavour. A large slow cooker is perfect for this recipe.

The dish is four courses in one: soup/broth, meatballs, vegetables (chick-peas and potatoes) and finally rice and eggs. A light dessert of fresh fruit is all that is needed to complete this meal as it is extremely filling.

Variations include soaking whole grains, haricot beans and omitting the chick-peas and rice. Every family has its own preference and *adafina* is made to personal taste; very often what the cook's mother made!

Preparation: 30 minutes
Cooking: 2 hours 25 minutes + 18–20 hours slow cooking
Serves 10–12

1 large onion, roughly chopped
450 g (1 lb) brisket or shin of beef

2 x 400 g cans chick-peas, drained and rinsed
2 teaspoons turmeric
I teaspoon sweet paprika
6 dates, pitted
2 tablespoons clear honey
Salt and freshly ground black pepper
900 g (2 lb) small potatoes
300 g (11 oz) long grain rice
I tablespoon vegetable oil
I tablespoon ground cinnamon
Pinch of freshly grated nutmeg
10–12 eggs (1 per person), hard-boiled, unshelled

For the meatballs:
350 g (12 oz) minced beef
2 tablespoons ground almonds
50 g (2 oz) breadcrumbs
I teaspoon sugar
I egg
2 tablespoons finely chopped fresh parsley
Salt and freshly ground black pepper

- Bring 3 litres (5¼ pints) water to the boil in a large pan. Add the onion, beef, chick-peas, turmeric, paprika, dates and honey, and season with salt and pepper. Reduce the heat and simmer, covered, for 2 hours.

- For the meatballs, mix all the ingredients together and shape into 10–12 balls, one for each person.

- Preheat the oven to 120°C/250°F/Gas Mark ½.

- Add the meatballs and potatoes to the beef and chick-peas in the pan and simmer for a further 10 minutes. Set aside.

- Meanwhile, place the rice, oil, cinnamon and nutmeg in another pan with 570 ml (1 pint) water and season with salt and pepper. Bring to the boil and simmer until the rice is cooked, approximately 15 minutes.

- Wrap the rice in baking parchment, then wrap it in foil or put it in a roasting bag (make sure the bag is securely tied) and place it in the pan containing the beef, chick-peas, meatballs and potatoes. Add the hard-boiled eggs, cover and place in the oven until required for Shabbat lunch. Alternatively, transfer the *adafina* to a slow cooker.

- To serve, shell the eggs and slice the beef, and arrange them on a deep serving platter with the potatoes, meatballs, chick-peas and rice. Some people like to drink the broth/gravy separately while others prefer to pour it over the meat.

NOTE: After the initial 2-hour simmering period for the beef and chick-peas I like to transfer the contents of the pan to a bowl to cool, then chill them in the fridge so that I can remove the surface level of fat before placing everything in a slow cooker.

Beef and Prune Tagine with Coriander Mashed Potatoes

TAGINES ARE A key part of the Moroccan Jewish heritage, but I have adapted this recipe to suit modern Jewish fusion cooking. It is the ideal dish for Seder night as it can be left to cook slowly while the service is taking place or, alternatively, it can be frozen and reheated. The joy is that it does not need constant attention; in fact, the longer you cook the beef, the more tender it becomes. Add more wine if the meat starts to stick to the bottom of the pan.

Doubling the quantities works well, making the tagine suitable for large numbers, and serving is simple. As well as the coriander mashed potaoes in this recipe, I like to accompany it with sliced roast potatoes or plain mashed potatoes. Dried fruits are plentiful in kosher supermarkets during Pesach and this dish makes good use of them, and allows a small amount of beef to go a long way.

Preparation: 20 minutes
Cooking: 2½ hours
Serves 6

2 tablespoons vegetable or olive oil
900 g (2 lb) chuck steak, cut into cubes
4 onions, sliced
2 teaspoons ground cinnamon
2.5 cm (I in) piece of fresh ginger, peeled and grated
3 tablespoons fine *matzah* meal
300 ml (½ pint) red wine
450 ml (¾ pint) beef stock
250 g (9 oz) dried prunes, pitted
200 g (7 oz) sultanas
Salt and freshly ground black pepper

To garnish:
3 tablespoons whole almonds
Sprigs of fresh coriander
3 tablespoons pistachios

For the coriander mashed potatoes:
1.3 kg (3 lb) potatoes, cut into chunks
3 tablespoons margarine
1 tablespoon olive oil
3 tablespoons roughly chopped fresh coriander leaves
Pinch of freshly grated nutmeg
Salt and freshly ground black pepper

- Heat the oil in a large deep pan. Add the beef and fry over a medium heat for 5 minutes until browned. Add the onions, cinnamon, ginger and *matzah* meal to the pan and continue to fry for a further 5 minutes. Add the wine, stock, prunes, sultanas and season. Bring to the boil, then cover and reduce the heat to a simmer for 2 hours.

- Preheat the oven to 200°C/400°F/Gas Mark 6.

- Place the almonds for the garnish on a baking sheet in an even layer. Put them in the oven and toast for about 10 minutes until golden. Keep an eye on them or they will burn. Remove from the oven and set aside.

- For the mashed potatoes, boil the potatoes for 15 minutes or until soft. Drain and use a fork or potato ricer to mash them. Add the margarine, oil, coriander and nutmeg, stir, and season with salt and pepper.

- To serve, place generous helpings of potato mash on individual warmed plates and top with the beef tagine. Garnish with sprigs of coriander, the toasted almonds and the pistachios.

Italian Lamb Casserole with Lemon and Parsley

ITALIANS ARE PASSIONATE about their food, but Italian Jews take that passion to another level. Their ingredients ooze flavour and this recipe for a lamb casserole certainly reflects that.

The lamb needs to marinate overnight in lemon, breadcrumbs, chilli and garlic before it is cooked in a low oven for 3 hours (or in a slow cooker). But it is worth it – one of my friends calls this casserole a modern-day designer *cholent*. The lamb is cooked in red wine and vegetable stock, which have the power to make it exceptionally tender.

The special flavours of garlic, lemon, chilli, red wine and parsley work well together and can be tasted in every bite. Serve with mashed potatoes, polenta or rice.

Preparation: 15 minutes + overnight marinating
Cooking: 3 hours
Serves 6

110 g (4 oz) white bread (preferably 2–3 days old)
Grated zest of 2 lemons
4 tablespoons finely chopped fresh parsley
½ teaspoon chilli powder
3 garlic cloves, finely chopped
2 tablespoons lemon juice
5 tablespoons extra virgin olive oil
1½ teaspoons salt
Freshly ground black pepper
1.3 kg (3 lb) shoulder of lamb, bone removed, cubed
120 ml (4½ fl oz) red wine

2 x 400 g cans cannellini beans, drained and rinsed
300 ml (½ pint) vegetable stock

To garnish:
6 sprigs of fresh parsley
1 lemon, sliced

- Preheat the oven to 150°C/300°F/Gas Mark 2.

- Place the bread in a food processor and whiz to make fine crumbs. Spread the breadcrumbs on a baking sheet and place in the oven for 10–15 minutes or until dry.

- Combine the breadcrumbs, lemon zest, parsley, chilli powder, garlic, lemon juice and oil. Season with the salt and some pepper and stir well.

- Place the lamb in a bowl. Spoon the breadcrumb mixture over the meat and mix thoroughly until every bit of lamb is coated with shiny crumbs. Refrigerate overnight.

- The next day, put the lamb and all the bits into a casserole dish. Add the wine, beans and stock, cover and place in the oven. Now turn the oven on to 160°C/325°F/Gas Mark 3. (There is no need to preheat the oven as slow cooking is the secret of the casserole's success.)

- Cook for 3 hours. From time to time, check to see that there is enough liquid in the casserole – if it gets too dry add a few tablespoons of boiling water.

- Serve on individual warmed plates and garnish each helping with a sprig of parsley and a slice of lemon.

Chicken Liver, Fennel and Watercress Salad

KOSHER BUTCHERS NOW supply ready-koshered chicken livers. This means that recipes like this one can be made in no time at all. Quickly pan-fried in sesame oil and finely glazed with red wine, these chicken livers make a delicious starter or main-course salad for an impromptu dinner party. Chicken livers are a great source of protein, iron, vitamins A, B_6 and B_{12}, thiamin, zinc and copper.

Lower-cholesterol alternatives to the chicken livers include hot-smoked salmon and smoked mackerel. Both can be purchased vacuum-packed and ready to use.

Ⓟ (change sesame to olive oil)
Preparation: 10 minutes
Cooking: 5 minutes
Serves 6

110 g (4 oz) pine nuts
Juice of 1 orange
4 tablespoons sesame oil (change to olive oil for Pesach)
675 g (1½ lb) koshered chicken livers, sliced
3 tablespoons red wine
250 g (9 oz) watercress
2 bulbs fennel, trimmed and sliced
Salt and freshly ground black pepper

- Toast the pine nuts in a dry frying pan over a high heat. This will take about 2 minutes; watch them as they burn very quickly. Remove from the pan and set aside.

- Mix the orange juice with 2 tablespoons of the oil and set aside.

- Heat the remaining oil in a large frying pan. Add the chicken livers and sauté over a high heat for 2 minutes until the livers start to turn brown, then pour the wine over them. Cook for a further minute so that the wine infuses into the livers.

- Decorate individual plates with some of the watercress and fennel, and scatter with the chicken livers. Season with salt and pepper and drizzle with the orange juice and sesame oil mixture.

- Sprinkle with the toasted pine nuts and serve immediately.

Steak with Butter Bean and Chilli Tomato Salad

JEWISH MEN LOVE steak, and knowing that a way to a man's heart is through his stomach I could not write a book without a recipe for the ultimate red meat. The best kosher steak you can buy is rib steak; cooked to perfection it just melts in the mouth. Take your orders for cooking the steaks from anaemic to cremated and everyone will be happy. I have accompanied this recipe with a 'no cook' healthy salad that uses butter beans, also known as lima beans. Like most beans, they are rich in the best sort of fibre – soluble fibre – which helps to eliminate cholesterol from the body. They are a good source of potassium, iron and copper. As a high potassium, low sodium food they help to reduce blood pressure, which makes them a great companion with steak – a rich red meat.

To peel tomatoes easily, make a small cross in the base of each one and place them into a bowl. Pour boiling water over them and leave for 30 seconds. Remove the tomaties from the boiling water, then when they are cool enough to handle, slip off the skins. If you leave the tomatoes in the water for too long they will start to cook and go mushy.

Preparation: 15 minutes
Cooking: 20 minutes
Serves 4

4 x 170 g–225 g (6 oz–8 oz) rib steaks
Salt and freshly ground black pepper
2 tablespoons vegetable oil

For the butter bean and chilli tomato salad:
2 x 400 g cans large butter beans
600 g (1 lb 5 oz) tomatoes, peeled and cored
2 small red chillies, halved and deseeded
1 bunch fresh basil
3 garlic cloves, roughly chopped
4 tablespoons olive oil
1 tablespoon red wine vinegar
Salt and freshly ground black pepper

- First make the salad. Drain and rinse the beans and place in a mixing bowl. Chop the tomatoes and add them to the beans.

- Place the chillies, basil (reserve a few small leaves for the garnish), garlic, oil and vinegar in the small bowl of a food processor and whiz until smooth. Add to the tomatoes and beans, season well with salt and pepper and mix together.

- Season steaks with salt and pepper. Heat the oil in a large frying pan and sauté the steaks over a high heat in two batches. Allow 3 minutes per side for very rare steaks, 5–6 minutes for medium and 10 minutes for well done. This is just a guide, as the times will vary slightly depending on the thickness of the meat.

- To serve, put a large spoonful of salad on individual plates and place a steak alongside. Garnish with the reserved basil sprigs.

Hungarian Stuffed Peppers in Tomato Sauce

POPULAR JEWISH-HUNGARIAN food includes goulash and stuffed carp, and dishes that use peppers, paprika and chestnuts. 'Stuffed' food is something of a Jewish cooking style throughout the cuisine – from nut- and honey-stuffed baklava to apple- and raisin-stuffed Ashkenazi strudel. Savoury stuffed dishes such as *holishkes* (stuffed cabbage) feature especially at festival time.

This recipe will work well with courgettes, aubergines and onions as well as peppers. I like to dust the serving plates with paprika to continue the Hungarian theme. Should you have any tomato sauce left over, freeze it and use it with pasta or meatballs. It is traditional to serve the peppers with *mamaliga* – boiled, baked or fried polenta.

Preparation: 20 minutes
Cooking: 1½ hours
Serves 6

300 g (11 oz) long grain rice
450 g (1 lb) minced beef
1 onion, grated (use a food processor)
2 garlic cloves, finely chopped
4 tablespoons finely chopped fresh parsley
1 egg
Salt and freshly ground black pepper
3 large green peppers
3 large yellow peppers

For the tomato sauce:
2 tablespoons vegetable oil
1 onion, very finely chopped
1 teaspoon hot paprika
3 teaspoons sweet paprika
2 garlic cloves, finely chopped
750 ml (1¼ pints) passata
Juice of 1 lemon
1 teaspoon sugar
Salt and freshly ground black pepper

- Preheat the oven to 180°C/350°F/Gas Mark 4.

- Bring 475 ml (15 fl oz) water to the boil. Add the rice and cook for 8 minutes. Drain and set aside to cool.

- Mix the rice with the beef, onion, garlic, parsley and egg. Season well with salt and pepper.

- Slice the tops (stem end) off the peppers and set aside. Remove the cores, seeds and white membrane from the inside of each pepper; be careful not to break the skin. Stuff each pepper with some of the beef and rice mixture. Do not pack the peppers too tightly or fill them completely as the rice will expand during cooking. Cover each pepper with its reserved lid.

- For the sauce, heat the oil in a large pan with a lid. Add the onion and sauté over a medium heat for 5 minutes until translucent and soft. Add the hot and sweet paprikas and the garlic, reduce the heat to low (i.e. not simmering) and cook for a further 5 minutes. Add the passata, lemon juice and sugar, and season with salt and pepper.

- Pour the tomato sauce into an ovenproof dish with a lid. Place the stuffed peppers in an upright position in the sauce. Cover the dish tightly with foil and then the lid, and place in the oven for 1¼ hours. Just before serving, taste the sauce and adjust the seasoning if necessary.

Lamb Pilau with Apricots

THIS IS A delicious rice pie with a lamb filling sandwiched between two layers of rice. It is flavoured with my favourite Sephardi spices: cinnamon, saffron, nutmeg and coriander. I like to make it for a mid-week dinner as it can be prepared in advance and reheated, or for a Sunday supper when the family are all at home, hungry and ready for a tasty meal. The secret to the success of this recipe is to cook the lamb slowly in the spices, which blends the flavours together. Serve with steamed or boiled cabbage.

Preparation: 20 minutes
Cooking: 2 hours 20 minutes
Serves 8

1 kg (2¼ lb) cubed shoulder of lamb
1 tablespoon ground cinnamon
1 teaspoon ground coriander
1 teaspoon freshly grated nutmeg
Salt and freshly ground black pepper
3 tablespoons olive oil
2 onions, roughly chopped
300 ml (½ pint) boiling water
10 saffron threads
100 ml (4 fl oz) red wine
400 g (14 oz) dried apricots
110 g (4 oz) raisins
500 g (1 lb 2 oz) basmati rice

To garnish:
Sprigs of fresh coriander
6 radishes, sliced

- Season the cubed lamb with the cinnamon, coriander, nutmeg and salt and pepper.

- Heat 2 tablespoons of the oil in a large frying pan with a lid. Add the onions and sauté over a medium heat for 5 minutes until just golden. Add the lamb and cook for 5–6 minutes until the cubes are nicely brown all over.

- Add the boiling water to the saffron and pour into the frying pan. Add the wine, apricots and raisins, stir, then cover and cook over a very low heat for 1½ hours.

- Preheat the oven to 180°C/350°F/Gas Mark 4. Grease an ovenproof dish large enough to take all the ingredients with the remaining oil.

- In a separate pan, cook the rice according to the instructions on the packet and drain it 5 minutes before it is completely cooked.

- Put half the rice into the dish and spoon it evenly over the base. Spread the meat mixture over the rice and cover with the remaining rice. Cover the dish with foil and bake for 30 minutes.

- Garnish with coriander sprigs and the radish slices, and serve.

Greek Croquettes in Tomato Sauce

THE JEWISH COMMUNITY in Greece is now very small; however, its culinary influences are far from insignificant. The communities in Rhodes and Crete may go back 2000 years and their food reflects Roman, Byzantine, Persian, Arab, Spanish and Ottoman influences. A typical Shabbat evening meal invariably consists of *hameen* eggs, beef with bulghar wheat or casseroled poultry. These meat croquettes are very popular, especially on the meze menus.

Meatballs appear in just about every cuisine in the world. In Italy they are partnered with spaghetti, and in Syria they are served with rice and flavoured with cumin and coriander. They can be spicy, sweet, sour, large or small. Another Jewish tradition is to make very tiny meatballs and serve them with soup.

I like to serve these croquettes on a bed of broccoli and rice or a combination of white and wild rice. On Passover, I serve them with potato *kugel*.

(P) (substitute plain flour for potato flour)
Preparation: 15 minutes
Cooking: 35 minutes
Serves 6–8 people (makes 15 croquettes)

450 g (1 lb) minced beef
½ teaspoon ground cumin
2 tablespoons roughly chopped fresh mint
1 teaspoon ground coriander
4 tablespoons roughly chopped fresh oregano
1 egg
2 tablespoons fine *matzah* meal
1 teaspoon salt
¼ teaspoon freshly ground black pepper

For the tomato sauce:
2 tablespoons olive oil
1 onion, finely chopped
2 garlic cloves, finely chopped
1 tablespoon plain flour (change to potato flour for Pesach)
1 tablespoon clear honey
½ teaspoon ground cinnamon
120 ml (4½ fl oz) red wine
1 x 400 g can chopped tomatoes
Salt and freshly ground black pepper

- Put the beef, cumin, mint, coriander, 2 tablespoons of the oregano, egg, *matzah* meal, salt and pepper in a large bowl or food mixer and mix well.
- With wet hands, form the mixture into 15 small oval shapes.
- For the tomato sauce, heat the oil in a saucepan. Add the onion and garlic and sauté gently over a low heat for 5 minutes until the onion has

softened. Stir in the flour and cook, stirring, for 1 minute. Season with salt and pepper.

- Add the cinnamon, wine, tomatoes and honey and simmer slowly for 10 minutes, stirring occasionally. Transfer the sauce to a food processor and whiz until smooth.

- Return the sauce to the pan and add the croquettes. Simmer, covered, for 20 minutes.

- Sprinkle with the remaining oregano and serve.

Honey-glazed Lamb with Lemon Potatoes

COOKING FOR ROSH HASHANAH requires food that is easy to serve and will be enjoyed by the whole family. Nothing too spicy, time consuming or complicated is on the menu!

I thought long and hard about this recipe, and hope I have captured the essential flavours of the festival. The lamb is cooked in red wine and pomegranate juice, ensuring that it is both tasty and succulent. Lemon potatoes contrast well with its sweetness.

Preparation: 25 minutes
Cooking: 1½ hours + 10 minutes resting
Serves 6

2 kg (4½ lb) shoulder of lamb, bone removed
10 garlic cloves

Juice of 2 lemons
Salt and freshly ground black pepper
100 ml (4 fl oz) red wine
100 ml (4 fl oz) pomegranate juice
2 kg (4½ lb) floury potatoes (such as Maris Piper), unpeeled
    and scrubbed
4 tablespoons extra virgin olive oil
6 sprigs of fresh thyme
6 sprigs of fresh oregano
300 ml (½ pint) chicken stock

To garnish:
Sprigs of fresh thyme
Seeds of 3 pomegranates

- Preheat the oven to 180°C/350°F/Gas Mark 4.

- Using the point of a sharp knife, score the top of the lamb with diagonal criss-cross lines.

- Slice two of the garlic cloves. Make slits in the lamb along the scored lines and press the garlic slices into them.

- Place the lamb in a deep roasting tin. Sprinkle with a quarter of the lemon juice and season well with salt and pepper. Pour the wine and pomegranate juice over the lamb.

- Cover with foil and bake for 1½ hours.

- Meanwhile, roughly chop the potatoes. Bring a pan of water to the boil, add the potatoes and simmer for 5 minutes. Drain the potatoes and place them in a separate roasting tin. Drizzle with the oil and toss to coat.

- Scatter the thyme and oregano, and the remaining garlic cloves, over the potatoes and sprinkle with the remaining lemon juice. Season well and add the chicken stock.

- Place the potatoes in the oven with the lamb and roast them for approximately 40 minutes or until golden.

- When the lamb is cooked remove it from the oven and leave to rest for 10 minutes before serving. Carve into thick slices.

- To serve, place several slices of lamb on individual warmed plates with helpings of the lemon potatoes. Garnish with thyme sprigs and a spoonful of pomegranate seeds.

Noodles, Kugels and Pies

NOODLES, *KUGELS* AND PIES are on the Jewish table as weekday main dishes and Shabbat and Yom Tov accompaniments. They are filling, tasty and economical. *Kugels* are particularly associated with Jewish cuisine. *Kugel* is German for 'ball' and describes the round, puffy sweet or savoury casserole made from grated potatoes or noodles that has featured on the Jewish menu for nearly a thousand years. Modern versions include blueberry, sweet potato, pineapple and broccoli *kugels* – a far cry from the dish's humble beginnings as a bread-based pudding.

According to Hassidic tradition, *kugels* are imbued with mystical powers and have an important place as stars of the Friday night meal and Shabbat morning Kiddush.

Jews in Greece

IN 1939, there were over 70,000 Jews in Greece living in communities whose histories stretched back over 2000 years. In 1945, the total Jewish population of Greece was given as 10,000. Some 60,000 had died in Poland. In some towns a few Jews escaped deportation, and emerged from hiding at the end of the war – others even survived the camps – but returned to their homes to find emptiness. Of the Jews from Crete, none survived and Chania has only an empty synagogue, abandoned by Jews and Christians alike, and not even a monument to commemorate the tragedy. In Salonika, 15 train-loads over a period of 18 months emptied the city of its Jews.

It is said that the few remaining Jews in Greece are now vanishing, and it has been predicted that within 20 years there will be no Jewish communities, only individuals living isolated and secularised lives. This remains to be seen. Unlike the Jewries in other parts of Europe, with the exception of the Second World War there has never been a moment of unrelenting persecution during the two millennia of the Jewish presence in Greece.

Rabbi Simon Frances, of the Reform community in Harrow, London, is from Greece. He was born in Larissa and his family went into hiding in Athens during the war. Some recipes are still very popular in Greece and we discussed my variation of a delicious Greek dish: *spanakopita*.

Spanakopita
(Greek Spinach and Feta Pie)

THIS RECIPE IS a variation on the original, but captures extra flavour with the addition of peas seasoned with ground cumin and coriander. It is perfect to eat all year round.

I have used frozen spinach and frozen peas for convenience, but use the fresh vegetables when they are in season – I always like to promote 'fresh is best'. You will need 900 g (2 lb) fresh spinach and the same quantity of fresh peas as frozen ones. The sizes of filo pastry sheets vary according to the manufacturer, but essentially you will need 6 large sheets or 12 small ones; if you use small ones, lay them side by side on a lined baking sheet. The uncooked pie can be frozen.

I like to serve this with grilled sliced red peppers and black olives. Very simple and very Greek.

❄

Preparation: 25 minutes
Cooking: 35–40 minutes
Serves 8

6 sheets of filo pastry
110 g (4 oz) unsalted butter, melted
2 tablespoons sesame seeds

For the filling:
450 g (1 lb) frozen leaf spinach
200 g (7 oz) frozen peas
1 tablespoon olive oil
4 spring onions, finely sliced
450 g (1 lb) feta cheese
2 eggs
1 teaspoon ground cumin
2 teaspoons ground coriander
Salt and freshly ground black pepper

- Preheat the oven to 200°C/400°F/Gas Mark 6. Line a large baking sheet with baking parchment.

- First make the filling. Defrost the spinach and squeeze out the excess liquid. Set aside.

- Cook the peas in boiling water for 5 minutes, then drain and set aside.

- Heat the oil in a frying pan. Add the spring onions and sauté over a medium heat for 5 minutes until just soft.

- Place the feta, eggs, spring onions, spinach, peas, cumin, coriander and salt and pepper in a food processor. Whiz until well combined.

- For the pastry, place a sheet of filo on the lined baking sheet. Brush with some of the melted butter and cover with another sheet. Repeat this with the remaining sheets.

- Spoon the filling along the length of the pastry leaving a 5 cm (2 in) gap on the edge nearest to you. Fold the lower edge (the one furthest away from you) of the pastry to enclose the filling, then roll up the pastry like a Swiss roll. Brush with more melted butter and sprinkle the top with the sesame seeds.

- Bake in the oven for 35–40 minutes or until the pastry is golden.

- Cut into slices to serve.

NOTE: The pie can be made a day in advance and refrigerated.

Potato Kugel

POTATO *KUGEL* IS a classic example of Jewish comfort food. Its versatility knows no bounds. Serve it for Shabbat, Yom Tov and every day. Eat it hot, cold or warm. My recipe is traditional – you can ring the changes by adding a carrot or courgette, or make individual *kugels* in ramekins (reduce the baking time to 20 minutes). In my house, my son and husband fight over the crispy topping – to increase this precious element, score the top of the *kugel* with a fork before cooking.

The secret of a light *kugel* is the addition of baking powder, so don't forget this crucial ingredient.

Preparation: 15 minutes
Cooking: 40 minutes
Serves 6–8

I tablespoon vegetable oil, for greasing
1.3 kg (3 lb) potatoes, grated
4 eggs, lightly beaten
3 tablespoons fine *matzah* meal
2 teaspoons salt
2 teaspoons baking powder
I onion, grated
2 tablespoons finely chopped fresh parsley (optional)
Freshly ground black pepper

- Preheat the oven to 200°C/400°F/Gas Mark 6. Line the base of a shallow 22 x 22 cm (9 x 9 in) baking tin with baking parchment and grease the sides with the oil.

- Squeeze the grated potatoes with a clean cloth or kitchen paper so that they are dry. (Potatoes contain an enormous amount of water!) Mix in the eggs, *matzah* meal, salt, baking powder, onion, parsley, if using, and pepper to taste.

- Bake in the oven for 40 minutes or until firm.

- To serve, turn the baking tin upside down, remove the baking parchment and cut the *kugel* into squares.

Chicken and Mushroom Pie

ANOTHER EXAMPLE OF a Jewish recipe based on the 'waste not, want not' principle, this was often made with the boiling chicken left over from chicken soup. Boiling chicken alone can be quite dry and tasteless, but when it is made into a pie it seems to absorb more flavour and can make a tasty meal. Dried mushrooms are a great store cupboard ingredient. Adding them to the hot chicken stock/soup produces the most amazing mushroom aroma and enhances the flavour of the whole recipe. Serve with a selection of seasonal vegetables.

❅

Preparation: 30 minutes
Cooking: 40 minutes
Serves 6

2 tablespoons olive oil
2 onions, roughly chopped
4 garlic cloves, finely chopped
750 g (1 lb 10 oz) fresh mushrooms (brown cap or button),
    sliced
2 tablespoons plain flour, plus extra for dusting
250 ml (9 fl oz) hot chicken stock or strained chicken soup
20 g (¾ oz) dried mushrooms
4 tablespoons white wine
3 tablespoons roughly chopped fresh parsley
750 g (1 lb 10 oz) cooked chicken, roughly sliced
Salt and freshly ground black pepper
450 g (1 lb) puff pastry (ready-rolled if possible)
1 egg yolk

- Preheat the oven to 200°C/400°F/Gas Mark 6.

- Heat the oil in a large frying pan. Add the onions, garlic and fresh mushrooms and sauté over a medium heat for 5 minutes until all the juice has been extracted from the mushrooms. Add the flour and cook, stirring, for a further 2 minutes.

- Stir in the chicken stock or soup, dried mushrooms, wine and parsley. Simmer for 3 minutes to soften the dried mushrooms then add the chicken slices and season with salt and pepper. Transfer to a 30 x 22 cm (12 x 9 in) rectangular ovenproof dish.

- If the pastry isn't ready-rolled, roll it out on a lightly floured work surface. Trim the pastry to an oval about 5 cm (2 in) larger than the dish. Cut a 2.5 cm (1 in) strip from all round the oval and press this on to the rim of the pie dish.

- Lightly whisk the egg yolk with 1 teaspoon water and brush the pastry rim with a little of the mixture, then position the pastry oval on top to make a lid. Press the edges together to seal, then, using a sharp knife, knock up the edges. Decorate the top with leaves made from pastry trimmings, if desired. Brush the pastry all over with the remaining beaten egg.

- Bake for 30 minutes or until the pastry is well risen and golden brown. Serve immediately.

Sambusaks

THESE ARE FLAKY, sesame-seed-crusted pastries filled with a savoury beef or cheese mixture. They are popular throughout much of the

Middle East and northern and eastern Africa, and are traditional Chanukah and Shabbat pastries from the Egyptian, Syrian and Iranian-Jewish communities. The origin of the name is uncertain; but the 'ak' ending is characteristically Persian.

Sambusaks, also known as *simbusak* or *samboussa*, may be either half-moon shaped or triangular. A thin circular piece of dough is folded over the filling, either in the centre to form a semicircle or at three edges, like a pyramid, to form a triangular shape. The resulting pastry is shallow-fried on both sides or baked. Traditional fillings are: chick-peas, onions and peppers; minced meat and onions; and cheese (usually feta or halloumi).

Preparation: 25 minutes
Cooking: 30 minutes
Serves 4 (makes 50 sambusaks)

450 g (1 lb) plain flour, plus extra for dusting
2 teaspoons salt
225 g (8 oz) margarine
200 g (7 oz) sesame seeds, for the topping

For the cheese filling:
450 g (1 lb) feta or cream cheese
2 eggs, lightly beaten
1 teaspoon baking powder
1 teaspoon salt
3 tablespoons sesame seeds

For the meat filling:
2 tablespoons olive oil
2 onions, finely chopped

1 teaspoon allspice
1 teaspoon salt
½ teaspoon ground cinnamon
450 g (1 lb) minced beef
50 g (2 oz) pine nuts

- Place the flour, salt and margarine in a food mixer with 120 ml (4½ fl oz) water and mix using the metal blade until the dough leaves the sides of the bowl clean. Alternatively, work the dough with your hands for 5 minutes. Cover with cling film, flatten, place on a plate and leave in the refrigerator until ready to use.

- For the cheese filling, mix the cheese, eggs, baking powder, salt and sesame seeds together.

- For the meat filling, heat the oil in a frying pan. Add the onions and sauté over a low heat for 5 minutes until soft but not brown. Add the allspice, salt and cinnamon. Stir in the beef and cook over a medium heat for 5 minutes until brown. For a smooth mixture, transfer to a food processor and whiz briefly. Transfer to a bowl and mix in the pine nuts by hand.

- Preheat the oven to 200°C/400°F/Gas Mark 6. Line two to three baking sheets with baking parchment.

- Lightly dust a work surface with flour. Roll out the pastry dough to a thickness of 5 mm (¼ in). Using a 7 cm (3 in) cutter, stamp out approximately 50 circles.

- Place 1 teaspoon of filling in the centre of each circle and fold the dough in half. Tightly crimp the edges with a fork. Repeat until all the dough and fillings are used up.

- Put the sesame seeds for the topping on a plate and turn the pastries in them to coat.

- Transfer the *sambusaks* to the prepared baking sheets and bake in the oven for 15–20 minutes until golden brown.

Lokshen Kugel

LOKSHEN KUGEL MEANS 'noodle pudding' in Yiddish and it is a comforting dessert that is delicious hot or cold. It is simple to make and one of those recipes that has been passed down the generations and is still as popular as ever. You will find it on the menus of many kosher restaurants and it never fails to please.

It originated in Eastern Europe where Yiddish was the main language spoken in Jewish communities. *Lokshen* pudding is often served as dessert on a Friday night, although this particular cheese version is a favourite for Shavuot when dairy foods are favoured.

❄

Preparation: 10 minutes + 1 hour soaking
Cooking: 45 minutes
Serves 8

50 g (2 oz) raisins
3 tablespoons brandy or whisky
2 tablespoons melted butter
600 g (1 lb 5 oz) thick *lokshen* noodles
600 g (1 lb 5 oz) cream cheese
5 eggs, beaten
2 tablespoons ground cinnamon

200 g (7 oz) sugar
250 ml (9 fl oz) soured cream

- Soak the raisins in the brandy or whisky for 1 hour.

- Preheat the oven to 180°C/350°F/Gas Mark 4. Grease a large casserole dish (about 32 x 24 cm/13 x 9½ in) with some of the butter.

- Cook the noodles according to the instructions on the packet, then drain them. Stir in the cheese, raisins, eggs, cinnamon, sugar and soured cream. Add the remaining butter to the noodle mixture.

- Pour the noodle mixture into the prepared dish and bake in the oven for 45 minutes or until set.

Crunchy Leek and Potato Gratin with Orange and Fennel Salad

I LOVE THE look and taste of this delicious vegetarian dish – leeks, red onion and spinach with a sliced potato and walnut topping. It is also ideal for those on a gluten-free diet. Served with my orange and fennel salad it makes a complete meal. The use of fresh ginger may surprise readers who avoid strong flavours. However, once it is cooked and mixed with the other ingredients the small quantity of this spice is quite inoffensive, but gives the dish a delicate taste. On a health note, ginger is said to stimulate gastric juices, and has a warming and soothing effect when you have a cold or cough.

Leeks tend to be difficult to clean, but I find the easiest way is to slit them lengthways and rinse them under cold running water to remove any grit.

I use a food processor to slice the potatoes, which certainly speeds up the preparation of the gratin, but if time is of the essence you can cook the whole dish in advance and reheat it later.

❄

Preparation: 25 minutes
Cooking: 50 minutes
Serves 6

3 leeks, trimmed and sliced
900 g (2 lb) potatoes, finely sliced
I red onion, sliced
250 g (9 oz) leaf spinach, cooked and well drained
3 garlic cloves, finely chopped
2 cm (¾ in) piece of fresh root ginger, peeled and finely chopped
Salt and freshly ground black pepper
100 ml (4 fl oz) vegetable stock
3 tablespoons double cream
25 g (I oz) Parmesan cheese, grated
50 g (2 oz) walnuts, roughly chopped

For the orange and fennel salad:
4 tablespoons olive oil
I teaspoon clear honey
Salt and freshly ground black pepper
4 oranges, peeled and cut into segments
I orange pepper, deseeded and roughly chopped
2 bulbs fennel, roughly chopped

- Preheat the oven to 200°C/400°F/Gas Mark 6.

- Place a layer of half the leeks and then a layer of half the potatoes in a large casserole dish. Add the onion, spinach, garlic and ginger, and season with salt and pepper. Layer with the remaining leeks and then the remaining potatoes.

- Pour over the stock and cream. Season again and bake, uncovered, in the oven for 40 minutes. Remove the gratin from the oven and sprinkle with the Parmesan and walnuts.

- Return the dish to the oven for a final 10 minutes or until the potatoes are tender.

- Meanwhile, for the salad, mix the oil and honey together and season with salt and pepper. Place the orange segments, orange pepper and fennel in a salad bowl.

- Toss the salad with the oil and honey dressing. Put a slice of the gratin on individual warmed plates and serve portions of the salad as side dishes.

NOTE: The gratin can be cooked a day in advance and refrigerated.

Dainty Asparagus Tarts

THESE ARE GREAT starters or accompaniments to a fish meal over Succot. This recipe is for individual little tarts as puff pastry tends to crumble when cut. If you have time, make double the quantity as extra friends and family always seem to come to meals during this festive period. If you want a non-dairy starter, replace the cream cheese and herbs with 2 tablespoons sun-dried tomato purée or 2 tablespoons tapenade.

Make the tarts larger if you want to serve them as a main course, and vary the fillings with sliced tomatoes, caramelised onions or sliced courgettes.

P (use non-dairy cream cheese)
Preparation: 15 minutes
Cooking: 12 minutes
Serves 6

Plain flour, for dusting
375 g (13 oz) puff pastry (ready-rolled if possible)
300 g (11 oz) fine asparagus spears (5–7 spears per pastry rectangle)
1 egg, lightly beaten
3 tablespoons finely chopped mixed fresh herbs (basil, chives, coriander, mint)
150 g (5 oz) cream cheese (use non-dairy for a *parev* option)
Salt and freshly ground black pepper
Extra virgin olive oil, to serve

- Preheat the oven to 220°C/425°F/Gas Mark 7. Line a baking sheet with baking parchment.

- Lightly dust a work surface with flour. If the pastry isn't ready-rolled, roll it out to 30 cm (12 in). Cut the pastry in half and cut each half into three 10 cm (4 in) length rectangles.

- Trim the asparagus spears to about 10 cm (4 in) lengths. Cook the asparagus in boiling water for 2 minutes until al dente. Drain and set aside.

- Place the pastry rectangles on the prepared baking sheet and score a rectangular border in each one, about 2 cm (¾ in) from the edge. Brush the borders with the beaten egg.

- Mix the herbs with the cream cheese. Spread the mixture over the pastry rectangles, keeping within the border.

- Trim the cooked asparagus spears so that they are all the same size and fit within the border of the pastry. Lay 5–7 spears on top of the cream cheese mixture – tail to end, then end to tail. Season with salt and pepper.

- Bake in the oven for 12 minutes or until golden brown.

- Serve either hot or warm, with a drizzle of extra virgin olive oil and a dusting of pepper.

NOTE: The tarts can be made a day in advance and refrigerated.

Borekas

THESE ARE POPULAR little puff pastry parcels filled with potatoes and mushrooms or spinach and cheese. Nearly every street in Israel has a bakery that includes hot *borekas* among its delicacies. I like to decorate the pastry by sprinkling sesame seeds on top.

Sometimes known as pastilles, *borekas* come from the Turkish Sephardi tradition and are eaten as snacks with drinks at Kiddush or in the *succah* during Succot. They also make enticing appetisers and delicious side dishes, and can be stored in the freezer before baking. You can vary the size of the *borekas* to suit the occasion, but make them all the same size so that they all cook at the same time. This recipe gives you a choice of two fillings: potato and mushroom, and, for variety, the more colourful spinach and cheese. The sesame seeds on the potato and mushroom *borekas* will enable you to know which is which.

❄ Ⓟ (if using potato and mushroom filling)
Preparation: 30 minutes
Cooking: 25 minutes
Serves 6–8 (makes 36 borekas)

Plain flour, for dusting
900 g (2 lb) puff pastry (ready-rolled if possible)
2 egg yolks, lightly beaten

For the potato and mushroom filling:
450 g (1 lb) potatoes, cut into chunks
Salt and freshly ground black pepper
2 tablespoons vegetable oil
1 onion, finely chopped
225 g (8 oz) fresh mushrooms, finely chopped
1 egg
3 tablespoons sesame seeds

For the spinach and cheese filling:
225 g (8 oz) frozen spinach, thawed and well drained
110 g (4 oz) feta cheese, crumbled
200 g (7 oz) ricotta or cream cheese
1 tablespoon finely chopped fresh oregano
1 garlic clove, finely chopped
Salt and freshly ground black pepper
2 teaspoons *zaatar* (optional), for dusting

- Boil the potatoes for 15 minutes or until soft, then drain and mash with a potato ricer or fork. Season with salt and pepper.

- Heat the oil in a large frying pan. Add the onions and mushrooms and sauté over a medium heat for 5 minutes until they are soft and all the liquid has evaporated. Remove from the heat and stir in the mashed potatoes and egg. Check the seasoning and adjust accordingly.

- Combine the spinach, cheeses, oregano and garlic, and season with salt and pepper.

- Preheat the oven to 200°C/400°F/Gas Mark 6. Line a baking sheet with baking parchment.

- Lightly dust a work surface with flour. Cut the pastry in half and, if it is not ready-rolled, roll each half into a 23 x 23 cm (9 x 9 in) square. Do this twice. Cut the pastry into a total of 36 squares, each 8 x 8 cm (3 x 3 in) each.

- Transfer the squares to the lined baking sheet and place 1 tablespoon of your chosen filling in the centre of each square. Fold the pastry diagonally over the filling. Press or crimp the edges to seal and brush with the beaten egg. Sprinkle or dust with the relevant topping: sesame seeds for potato and mushroom *borekas* or a dusting of *zaatar*, if you wish, for the spinach and cheese ones.

- Bake in the oven for 25 minutes or until golden brown.

Carrot Kugel

FOR ME, *KUGELS* are for Yom Tov and Shabbat; to eat them on a regular day would just seem odd. However, this *kugel* is a bit different and is a brilliant recipe for families seeking ways for their children to eat more vegetables. It tastes delicious, can be served hot or cold, and, of course, can be prepared in advance.

The cinnamon adds a great flavour and the carrots have numerous health benefits. They are naturally high in beta-carotene, a substance that is converted to vitamin A in the body and has a powerful antioxidant effect in fighting against some forms of cancer, especially lung cancer. Current research suggests that it may also protect against stroke and heart disease. So let them eat carrots!

As this recipe freezes well, double the quantities and keep half for another occasion. The *kugel* is cut up into squares, which makes serving easy. Serve it cold with cold meats or hot for the Friday night or Yom Tov meal.

Preparation: 20 minutes
Cooking: 40 minutes

Serves 8–10 (makes 25 squares)

1 tablespoon vegetable oil, for greasing
1 kg (2¼ lb) carrots, grated
1 onion, grated
2 teaspoons ground cinnamon, plus extra for serving
1 teaspoon salt
Freshly ground black pepper

3 tablespoons brown sugar
1½ teaspoons baking powder
1 teaspoon bicarbonate of soda
6 eggs, beaten
110 g (4 oz) plain flour
110 g (4 oz) fine *matzah* meal
Sprigs of fresh parsley, to garnish

- Preheat the oven to 200°C/400°F/Gas Mark 6. Line the base of a 22 x 22 cm (9 x 9 in) tin with non-stick baking parchment and grease the sides with the vegetable oil.

- Place the carrots, onion, cinnamon, salt, pepper to taste, brown sugar, baking powder and bicarbonate of soda in a mixing bowl. Add the eggs, flour and *matzah* meal and mix well.

- Spoon the mixture into the prepared tin and level off the surface with a knife. Bake in the oven for 40 minutes or until the *kugel* is firm and crispy. Cool for 5 minutes then remove from the tin and cut into squares.

- To serve, dust a serving platter with ground cinnamon and garnish with sprigs of parsley.

NOTE: The *kugel* can be made one to two days in advance and refrigerated.

Apricot and Honey Lokshen Pudding

FRIDAY NIGHTS ARE special – for many they are the only time when the whole family sits down together for dinner. Every week one of my children decides which dessert we will have, and this apricot and honey *lokshen* pudding is a great favourite. Many *lokshen* pudding recipes are heavy but this is light, with a slight alcoholic twist.

This recipe is for individual portions, but one large dish will work just as well, although you will need to increase the cooking time to 45 minutes. The pudding is delicious served hot, cold or warm, so any leftovers can be eaten at Shabbat lunch. Serve with ice cream, sorbet or even cream.

Preparation: 20 minutes + 2 hours soaking
Cooking: 25 minutes
Serves 8

170 g (6 oz) dried apricots, roughly chopped
5 tablespoons Amaretto
20 g (¾ oz) margarine, melted, plus extra for greasing
225 g (8 oz) thin noodles or vermicelli
4 eggs
3 tablespoons clear honey
Icing sugar, for dusting, to serve

- Soak the apricots in Amaretto for a minimum of 2 hours or place, covered, in a microwave for 2 minutes. Drain and set aside, reserving the excess Amaretto.

- Preheat the oven to 180°C/350°F/Gas Mark 4. Line the bases of eight ramekins with baking parchment and grease the sides with margarine.

- Divide the apricots equally between the ramekins.

- Boil the noodles in a deep pan according to the instructions on the packet, until cooked. Drain and set aside.

- In a mixing bowl, whisk the eggs until fluffy, then add the honey and whisk again until you have a light mixture. Add the margarine, drained noodles and reserved Amaretto and mix well. Spoon the mixture carefully into the ramekins.

- Put the ramekins in a roasting tin and pour in enough boiling water to come about halfway up their sides. Bake in the oven for 25 minutes. The puddings are cooked when they are firm to the touch and set in the middle.

- To serve, invert the puddings on to individual warmed plates and dust with icing sugar.

NOTE: Can be made two days in advance and served cold if wished.

Moroccan Shepherd's Pie

SHEPHERD'S PIE IS a regular family dish in most households in the United Kingdom. I have included it in this book to demonstrate how English dishes can be transformed to become Moroccan with the addition of a few ingredients, all of which adhere to the rules of *kashrut*.

The recipe is also suitable for Pesach and does not contain *matzah*, ground almonds or eggs as too much *matzah* can upset the stomach.

As much as one loves these traditional ingredients, it is comforting to find something that is not only very tasty but healthy too. The addition of dried apricots sweetens the meat, which makes it more child friendly. If you are allergic to nuts, omit the pine nuts and replace them with 200 g/7 oz chopped spinach.

To serve this more stylishly, make it in individual ramekins and cook for 20 minutes. This may also be easier for serving and freezing. Serve the shepherd's pie with a selection of green vegetables or a green salad.

Preparation: 35 minutes
Cooking: I hour
Serves 6

2 tablespoons olive oil
I onion, roughly chopped
675 g (1½ lb) minced lamb
2 garlic cloves, finely chopped
2 tablespoons tomato purée
150 ml (¼ pint) chicken stock or strained chicken soup
2 teaspoons ground cinnamon
150 g (5 oz) dried apricots, roughly chopped
3 tablespoons pine nuts
Salt and freshly ground black pepper

For the topping:
1.5 kg (3½ lb) potatoes, cut into chunks
3 tablespoons non-dairy margarine
2 tablespoons olive oil
Salt and freshly ground black pepper

- First make the topping. Boil the potatoes for 15 minutes or until very soft, then drain. Mash them using a potato ricer or fork. Add the margarine and oil, and season with salt and pepper. Set aside.

- Preheat the oven to 200°C/400°F/Gas Mark 6.

- For the meat mixture, heat the oil in a large frying pan. Add the onion and sauté over a medium heat for 5 minutes until just soft. Add the lamb, garlic, tomato purée, stock or soup and cinnamon. Cook, stirring, over a medium heat until the lamb is completely brown. This will take about 10 minutes. Add the apricots and pine nuts, and season well.

- Place the lamb mixture in a large ovenproof dish. Spoon over the mashed potatoes, level them with a knife and make lines on the top with a fork.

- Bake for 35 minutes or until the topping is golden brown.

NOTE: The shepherd's pie can be made a day in advance and refrigerated.

Three Bean Mash Pie

WITH SO MUCH information about healthy eating I feel that home-fresh cooking is one of the easiest ways to achieve a balanced diet. Pre-packed foods often include above average levels of salt and sugar, and not enough fibre.

This vegetarian main course fulfils all the requirements of a balanced dish and would also suit a vegan diet. It is a delicious, warming winter dish that will also satisfy diehard hearty meat-eaters. It makes a pleasant change to cottage or shepherd's pie and works well if quantities are doubled for a large gathering. Serve with a green salad or a selection of green vegetables.

❄ Ⓟ

Preparation: 30 minutes
Cooking: 1 hour
Serves 10

2 tablespoons olive oil
1 red onion, roughly chopped
4 garlic cloves, finely chopped
1 red chilli, deseeded and finely chopped (optional)
2 teaspoons ground cumin
½ teaspoon mild paprika
1 x 400 g can red kidney beans, drained and rinsed
1 x 400 g can cannellini beans, drained and rinsed
1 x 175 g can borlotti beans, drained and rinsed
450 g (1 lb) carrots, roughly chopped
450 g (1 lb) swede, roughly chopped
2 x 400 g can chopped tomatoes
Handful of fresh coriander leaves, roughly chopped
Salt and freshly ground black pepper

For the topping:
900 g (2 lb) potatoes, cut into chunks
50 g (2 oz) unsalted butter or margarine (*parev*)
    or olive oil
Salt and freshly ground black pepper

- Heat the oil in a large pan. Add the onion, garlic, chilli, if using, cumin and paprika and sauté over a medium heat for 2 minutes until the onions start to soften. Stir in the beans, carrots, swede and tomatoes and pour in 150 ml (¼ pint) water or enough to just cover the vegetables. Season with salt and pepper. Bring to the boil, then reduce the heat and simmer for 30 minutes or until the vegetables are soft. Add a little extra water if necessary. Add the coriander and transfer the vegetables to a deep ovenproof dish.

- Meanwhile, preheat the oven to 200°C/400°F/Gas Mark 6.

- While the vegetables are simmering, boil the potatoes for 15 minutes or until soft. Drain and add the butter or margarine, or the oil. Mash with a potato ricer or fork and season well. Spoon the mashed potatoes over the vegetables, level them with a knife and make lines on top with a fork.

- Place in the oven for 30 minutes or until golden brown.

NOTE: The pie can be made a day in advance and refrigerated.

Potato, Olive and Pesto Tarts

THIS IS A new recipe that I have written especially for breaking the fast at Yom Kippur. After years of trial and error, I have decided that a buffet with light tasty dishes is the best way to end the fast – with lots of cups of tea! And this tart is an excellent addition to the normal festive foods. Although the recipe uses simple store-cupboard ingredients it is incredibly versatile. By varying the size of the tarts you can produce a dinner party starter, a light supper, a vegetarian main course or even canapés. Slice the potatoes as thinly as possible with a food processor or mandolin. Try varying the flavour by using marinated peppers, sun-dried tomatoes or capers instead of olives.

❄ Ⓟ (substitute pesto for non-dairy pesto or tomato paste)
Preparation: 25 minutes
Cooking: 25 minutes
Serves 6

Plain flour, for dusting
250 g (9 oz) puff pastry (ready-rolled if possible)
2 egg yolks, lightly beaten, to glaze
2 tablespoons pesto sauce (substitute for non-dairy pesto
 or tomato paste for a *parev* option)
2 medium-size potatoes, finely sliced
2 tablespoons olive oil
1 courgette, cut into thin rounds
2 tablespoons black olives, stoned
Salt and freshly ground black pepper

To garnish:
6 sprigs of fresh rosemary
100 g (3½ oz) mixed salad leaves

- Preheat the oven to 200°C/400°F/Gas Mark 6. Line a baking sheet with baking parchment.

- Lightly dust a work surface with flour. If the pastry isn't ready-rolled, roll it out to a 30 cm (12 in) rectangle. Using a 10 cm (4 in) round cutter, cut out six circles of pastry. Brush each circle with the beaten egg and spread with the pesto, leaving a 2 cm (¾ in) border round the edge.

- Cook the potatoes in a pan of simmering water for 5 minutes until they are just soft. Drain and leave to cool for 5 minutes.

- Heat the oil in a medium-size frying pan. Add the courgette and sauté over a medium heat for 3 minutes until just cooked. Remove and set aside.

- Place alternate slices of potato and courgette in a spiral; the slices must overlap so that the pesto base is covered. Scatter with the olives and season with salt and pepper.

- Transfer the tarts to the prepared baking sheet and bake in the oven for 25 minutes or until the potatoes are tender and the pastry is brown and crisp.

- Garnish each tart with a sprig of rosemary and mixed salad leaves, and serve.

Spaghetti with Wild Mushrooms

IN ITALIAN COOKING fewer ingredients very often provide more flavour, and this is certainly the case here where the dried wild mushrooms (which should be available in most good supermarkets) need few additions.

Dried mushrooms have a long shelf-life, so don't worry about buying a large quantity. They do not lose their flavour provided they are kept away from sunlight and stored in a dry place in an airtight container.

P (omit grated Parmesan)

Preparation: 15 minutes
Cooking: 15 minutes
Serves 4
75 g (3 oz) dried wild mushrooms
2 tablespoons olive oil
2 garlic cloves, crushed
1 large bunch fresh parsley, roughly chopped
300 g (11 oz) spaghetti
1 large bunch fresh basil, finely torn
Salt and freshly ground black pepper

To serve:
Freshly grated Parmesan cheese (omit for *parev* option)
Truffle oil (if available) or extra virgin olive oil

- Reconstitute the dried mushrooms by covering them with a minimum of cold water for 10 minutes. (Using cold water, and as little as possible, ensures that not too much flavour is extracted from the mushrooms.)

- Heat the oil in a large pan. Add the drained mushrooms and cook over a medium heat for 5 minutes until the mushrooms soften and start to cook. Add the garlic and parsley and cook gently for a few more minutes.

- Cook the spaghetti according to the instructions on the packet or until it is al dente.

- Drain the spaghetti thoroughly and pile into individual warmed bowls. Pour the mushrooms over the spaghetti, mix well, add the basil, season and mix together.

- Serve each portion with a generous helping of grated Parmesan and a drizzle of truffle oil or extra virgin olive oil.

Grains and Potatoes

A WIDE RANGE of grain- and potato-based dishes take their place on the Jewish table. Bulghar wheat and *kasha* (buckwheat) join the humble potato to make substantial starchy Ashkenazi recipes. Sephardi ones favour rice and couscous – often mixed with fruit and nuts. Unusual Jewish cuisines from both traditions think nothing of using grains and potatoes of different kinds in one dish to create wholesome and unique combinations such as *kasha varnishkes* (*kasha* cooked with pasta bows).

Hot Potato Salad

THIS IS A Dutch-Jewish recipe that is traditionally eaten on Shabbat with fish cakes, and is a perfect accompaniment for that other Jewish staple: coleslaw. It is called 'hot' potato salad because it is prepared while the potatoes are still hot, which allows the flavours of the dressing to be absorbed to great effect.

Dutch Jews suffered badly during the Second World War with their community of 139,000 being reduced to just 35,000 by 1945. One of the most famous Holocaust victims in the Netherlands was Anne Frank. The house (now a museum) where she and her family hid for over two years is a remarkable testament to her bravery and inner strength. Today there are both Sephardi and Ashkenazi communities in Holland, focused around Amsterdam, Rotterdam, The Hague and Utrecht. Recent immigration from Russia and Israel has given an international flavour to modern Dutch-Jewish cuisine.

Preparation: 10 minutes
Cooking: 15 minutes
Serves 6–8

**I kg (2¼ lb) new potatoes, unpeeled, cut into I cm
(½ in) cubes**
3 eggs, hard-boiled and shelled
I tablespoon French mustard
3 tablespoons roughly chopped fresh curly parsley
3 tablespoons vegetable oil
I tablespoon white wine vinegar
2 teaspoons salt
Freshly ground black pepper
2–3 tablespoons mayonnaise

- Cook the potatoes for 15 minutes or until soft. Drain, place in a bowl and set aside.

- Meanwhile, make the dressing. Mash the eggs with a fork. Add the mustard, parsley, oil, vinegar and salt and pepper to taste. Mix together; the dressing should be quite moist.

- While the potatoes are still hot, add the dressing. Combine well, taste and adjust the seasoning. Add the mayonnaise and mix gently to coat the potatoes.

- Transfer the salad to a serving dish.

Moroccan Sweet Potato Stew

THIS RECIPE IS perfect for Rosh Hashanah and Succot when you may have to cook for larger numbers. It is almost a meal in itself – just add some warm pitta bread with *zhug*, harissa or hummus. My kind of meal!

Don't be tempted to stir the stew too often as the sweet potatoes will break.

Preparation: 20 minutes
Cooking: 35 minutes
Serves 6–8

3 tablespoons vegetable or sunflower oil
1 large onion, roughly chopped
3 garlic cloves, finely chopped
2 teaspoons turmeric
1 teaspoon ground cinnamon
1 teaspoon medium curry powder
1 teaspoon ground cumin
¼ teaspoon freshly grated nutmeg
3 teaspoons salt
1 teaspoon freshly ground black pepper
1 red pepper, deseeded and cut into large squares
1.3 kg (3 lb) sweet potatoes, cut into cubes
1 aubergine, cut into cubes
2 x 400 g cans chick-peas, drained and rinsed
2 x 400 g cans chopped tomatoes
475 ml (15 fl oz) vegetable stock
Sprigs of fresh coriander, to garnish

- Heat the oil in a large deep pan. Add the onion, garlic, turmeric, cinnamon, curry powder, cumin, nutmeg, salt and pepper and sauté over a medium heat for about 3 minutes to bring out the flavour of the spices. Add the red pepper, sweet potatoes, aubergine, chick-peas and tomatoes. Add the stock.
- Bring to the boil, then reduce the heat and simmer for 35 minutes.
- Serve on a large warmed serving platter, garnished with sprigs of coriander.

NOTE: The stew improves with time, so make it a day ahead and refrigerate it to achieve the best flavour.

Sautéed Potatoes with Onions

THIS IS AN Eastern European dish that is often served with salt beef, tongue, roast chicken or lamb cutlets. It is simple but very tasty – so make plenty as seconds will need to be catered for.

The secret of this recipe is to sauté the onions over a low heat so that they cook without burning. Burnt onions are bitter and will not enhance the flavour!

Preparation: 10 minutes
Cooking: 50 minutes
Serves 6

5 tablespoons vegetable oil
3 medium-size onions, roughly chopped

1.2 kg (2½ lb) potatoes, thinly sliced
Salt and freshly ground black pepper

- Heat 2 tablespoons of the oil in a large frying pan with a lid. Add the onions and sauté over a low heat for 5–8 minutes or until golden. Remove the onions from the pan and set aside.

- Add the remaining oil to the pan. Add the potatoes, cover and fry over a low heat for 35 minutes or until tender. Stir in the onions, season well with salt and pepper and cook for a further 10 minutes. Serve immediately.

NOTE: For an extra kick, add a teaspoon of your favourite mustard to the pan when you fry the onions.

Persian Rice Cake

THIS IS A popular layered rice and potato dish that follows the Persian-Jewish tradition. The combination of textures – crispy potatoes and nutty rice – is delicious and the saffron adds a tasty aromatic flavour, and a colour that infuses the white rice and turns it pale yellow.

It has become particularly popular in my household on a Friday night, and looks suitably impressive when the 'cake' is inverted on to a serving platter to reveal the neatly fanned, crispy potato layer.

Whether or not you soak your rice depends on time and tradition. Soaking can shorten its cooking time and allows for the maximum expansion of long grain rice, particularly basmati. It also makes the grains less brittle so they're less likely to break during cooking. Rinsing rice before use washes off any dirt and excess starch and makes it less sticky. Why not ask your mother if she soaked her rice before cooking? And if she did, why not carry on the family tradition? Serve the rice cake with tagines and stews.

P (use *parev* chicken stock)

Preparation: 10 minutes + 2 hours soaking
Cooking: 30 minutes + 10 minutes steaming
Serves 6–8

375 g (13 oz) basmati rice
2 teaspoons salt, plus extra to taste
1 tablespoon chicken stock powder or 1 chicken stock
    cube (vegetable stock for a *parev* option)
10 saffron threads
2 tablespoons vegetable oil
300 g (11 oz) potatoes, thinly sliced
2 eggs, lightly beaten
Freshly ground black pepper

- Rinse the rice well – about five times – until the water runs clear. Place in a bowl, pour in water to cover and add the salt. Soak for 2 hours, then drain.

- Add the rice in 750 ml (1¼ pints) water to a saucepan with a lid. Add the stock powder or stock cube and saffron. Cook in the flavoured water for 8–10 minutes over a medium heat.

- Heat the oil in a medium-size frying pan. Carefully place the potatoes in two layers on the base. Fry them over a low heat for 15 minutes, but be careful not to burn them.

- Drain the rice and put in a bowl. Add the eggs and season well with salt and pepper. Place the rice on top of the potatoes in the frying pan.

Even it out with a fork and press down gently to seal it with the potatoes. Continue to cook, covered, for a further 10 minutes.

- Take the frying pan from the heat, cover with a clean tea towel or a lid, and leave to steam for 30 minutes.

- Remove the tea towel or lid, and invert the cake on to a warmed serving platter so that the potato base is on the top.

Kasha Varnishkes
(Buckwheat with Pasta Bows)

KASHA VARNISHKES IS buckwheat cooked with bow-shaped pasta. It originated in Eastern Europe, probably in Russia and the Ukraine, where it was once ceremonial food served at weddings and banquets. As recipes developed, other ingredients were added and the dish became an indispensable part of life for Jewish peasants – perhaps because the buckwheat plant grew well in poor soil and difficult weather, and was an excellent source of fibre and cheap protein.

It is still very popular in America but few Jews in Britain have heard of it! However, we can change this. Try this classic dish as an accompaniment to a pot roast or brisket on a Friday night or for a filling meal on a winter's day. Add chopped nuts for a bit of crunch.

P (use *parev* chicken stock)
Preparation: 20 minutes
Cooking: 30 minutes
Serves 6–8

4 tablespoons corn or vegetable oil, plus extra for greasing
250 g (9 oz) coarse ground *kasha*
1 egg, beaten
1 teaspoon salt, plus extra to taste
570 ml (1 pint) vegetable or chicken stock
225 g (8 oz) pasta bows
1 large onion, finely chopped
Freshly ground black pepper
2 tablespoons walnuts, roughly chopped

- Preheat the oven to 180°C/350°F/Gas Mark 4. Grease an ovenproof dish with oil.

- In a dry, heavy-based frying pan with a lid, toast the *kasha* for 2–3 minutes over a medium heat until it begins to turn golden and gives off an aroma. Immediately stir in the egg, using a wooden spoon. Add the teaspoon of salt and stock and cover the frying pan. Reduce the heat to a simmer and cook for about 15 minutes until the *kasha* has absorbed all the stock.

- Meanwhile, cook the pasta according to the instructions on the packet until al dente. Drain and set aside.

- Heat 3 tablespoons of the oil in a pan. Add the onion and sauté over a medium heat for 5 minutes until soft. Add the pasta and cooked *kasha* mixture. Transfer the contents to the prepared dish, and check and adjust the seasoning. Drizzle the remaining oil over the top and stir in the walnuts.

- Bake in the oven for 15 minutes until the top is slightly brown and crunchy.

Mejadera (Lentil and Rice Salad)

RECIPES THAT COMBINE two grains are classically found in Sephardi cooking. This dish is a delicious combination of lentils, rice and onions, and is a typical Sephardi Middle Eastern accompaniment for fish, chicken and lamb. I love the blend of spices: cinnamon, cumin, turmeric and coriander. Traditionally, *mejadera* was served on a Thursday night, when cheaper foods were eaten in anticipation of a lavish meal on Friday night. This dish is completed with a layer of fried onions, and for many this is their favourite part!

Brown lentils combine well with the basmati rice, but be careful not to overcook them as they may become soft and mushy. They are mild in flavour but will consequently absorb the spices I have included in the recipe.

Preparation: 15 minutes + 30 minutes soaking
Cooking: 1 hour 10 minutes
Serves 8

175 g (6 oz) brown lentils
200 g (7 oz) basmati rice
4 tablespoons vegetable oil
5 onions, finely chopped
2 garlic cloves, finely chopped
1 teaspoon turmeric
2 teaspoons ground coriander
2 teaspoons ground cinnamon
1 teaspoon ground cumin
1 tablespoon tomato purée

1 litre (1¾ pints) vegetable stock or *parev* chicken stock
Salt and freshly ground black pepper
2 tablespoons roughly chopped fresh coriander, to garnish

- Place the lentils in a pan with 750 ml (1¼ pints) water. Bring to the boil, then reduce the heat and simmer for 30 minutes. Drain and rinse. Set aside.

- Rinse the rice and leave it to soak in cold water for 30 minutes.

- Heat 2 tablespoons of the oil in a large deep pan with a lid. Add two of the onions and the garlic and cook over a medium heat for 10 minutes or until soft. Stir in the turmeric, ground coriander, cinnamon and cumin and cook for a further minute.

- Drain the rice thoroughly and add it to the onions.

- In a bowl, mix the tomato purée with the stock then pour the liquid into the rice mixture. Season with salt and pepper. Bring to the boil, and simmer for 20 minutes or until cooked. Stir in the lentils, cover and set aside.

- Heat the remaining oil in a separate pan. Add the remaining onions and sauté over a medium heat for 5 minutes until golden. Taste and adjust the seasoning.

- Transfer the rice and lentils to a warmed serving dish and layer the fried onions on top. Garnish with sprigs of coriander and serve immediately.

Crispy Saffron and Thyme Potatoes

IF YOU ARE looking for an impressive side dish for chicken, beef, lamb or even fish, this roasted potato recipe is the perfect solution. It presents potatoes in an unusual way and as the saffron cooks it provides an orange-red colour and a beautiful aromatic flavour that penetrates the potatoes. The potatoes are presented like a fan – this is called hasselback potatoes.

Saffron threads are the dried stigmas of the saffron crocus and it takes about 80,000 hand-picked crocuses to produce 450 g (1 lb) of them, so it is hardly surprising that it is the world's most expensive spice! I recommend buying it fresh and in small quantities as the aroma does weaken with time.

When cooking with saffron do not add it directly to a dish – always infuse it in hot water for at least 5 minutes before blending, as this promotes its pungent flavour and vivid colouring. Add the soaking water together with the threads. Never fry saffron in hot oil or butter as this will ruin the flavour.

 (use vegetable or *parev* chicken stock)

Preparation: 20 minutes
Cooking: 1–1¼ hours
Serves 6

4 tablespoons olive oil
4 saffron threads
570 ml (1 pint) hot vegetable or chicken stock
   (use vegetable stock for a *parev* option)
12 medium-size roasting potatoes
2 garlic cloves, finely chopped

15 g (½ oz) fresh thyme leaves
Salt and freshly ground black pepper
Sea salt, for sprinkling
Sprigs of fresh thyme, to garnish

- Preheat the oven to 190°C/375°F/Gas Mark 5. Lightly grease a large ovenproof dish with some of the oil.

- Soak the saffron threads in 2 tablespoons of the stock for 10 minutes, then stir in the remaining stock.

- Slice each potato vertically at 5 mm (¼ in) intervals, cutting to within 5 mm (¼ in) of its base. Place the potatoes in the prepared dish in a single layer, cut sides up.

- Spoon the remaining oil over the potatoes, sprinkle with the garlic and thyme, and season with salt and pepper. Pour the hot saffron stock over the potatoes.

- Bake in the oven, uncovered, for 1–1¼ hours, basting two or three times until the liquid is completely absorbed and the potatoes are crisp, golden brown and fanned open.

- Sprinkle with sea salt and serve garnished with sprigs of thyme.

Rice with Broad Beans and Dill

THIS DISH IS popular in many Sephardi households as an accompaniment for a wide range of dishes. For a dairy meal you can serve it with a sauce of yoghurt and herbs. The fresh dill flavours fuse well in the layers of rice and the herb produces flecks of vibrant green throughout the dish.

Broad beans are in many ways a neglected vegetable and are not often seen on the menu. I feel this is a shame because they are delicious when used fresh in salads, risottos, soups and stews. In addition, they are highly nutritious – full of phosphorus and vitamins A and C, and notably rich in protein.

However, be aware that broad beans are seasonal and the best time to buy them is in summer. De-pod them, simmer them in water for about 3 minutes, then remove their tough skins and use as required. The frozen broad beans that I have used in this recipe are a viable alternative and are, of course, available all year round.

Preparation: 10 minutes + 2 hours soaking
Cooking: 15 minutes
Serves 6

450 g (1 lb) basmati rice
400 g (14 oz) frozen broad beans
2 teaspoons salt
4 tablespoons finely chopped fresh dill
2 tablespoons sunflower or vegetable oil, for drizzling

- Rinse the rice several times. Place in a bowl, pour in enough water to cover and leave to soak for 2 hours, then drain.

- Defrost the beans and remove the outer skins.

- Place the rice in a pan and add enough water to cover it by the length of your thumbnail. Add the salt and begin to heat the rice very gently. Once it starts to swell and comes to the surface, add the beans. Bring to the boil, then reduce the heat and simmer for 8 minutes or until the beans and rice are soft.

- Cover the pan, turn the heat off and leave for 8 minutes.

- Stir in the dill, transfer the rice to a serving platter and drizzle with a little oil.

Bulghar Wheat and Vermicelli Pilau

BULGHAR WHEAT IS kernels of wheat that have been boiled, allowed to dry and then crushed. It is also known as cracked wheat and sold in three grades: fine, medium and coarse. Bulghar wheat is the staple ingredient of one of my favourite salads – tabbouleh, made with cracked wheat and parsley. The delight of using bulghar wheat is that, like all grains, it takes on the flavours of the ingredients it is cooked with. In this recipe, I have added turmeric, garlic and onions, all powerful ingredients that in turn produce a delicious pilau.

℗ (use vegetable rather than chicken stock)
Preparation: 20 minutes
Cooking: 15 minutes
Serves 8–10

2 tablespoons olive oil
2 onions, sliced
1 yellow pepper, deseeded and sliced
1 aubergine, cut into cubes
2 garlic cloves, finely chopped
1 teaspoon turmeric
110 g (4 oz) fine vermicelli

225 g (8 oz) coarse bulghar wheat
1 litre (1¾ pints) chicken or vegetable stock (use vegetable
stock for a *parev* option)
Salt and freshly ground black pepper
3 tomatoes, roughly chopped
2 tablespoons roughly chopped fresh parsley, to garnish

- Heat the oil in a large frying pan. Add the onions, pepper, aubergine and garlic and sauté over a medium heat for 5 minutes until they start to soften. Add the turmeric and fry for a further minute.

- Cook the vermicelli according to the instructions on the packet until al dente. Drain and set aside.

- Rinse the bulghar wheat in cold water, then add it to the vegetables in the frying pan. Pour in the stock and bring to the boil, then reduce the heat and simmer, covered, for 15 minutes. Season well with salt and pepper.

- Add the tomatoes, vermicelli and more stock if required. Check that the bulghar wheat is cooked, then garnish with the parsley and serve.

Risotto Salad with Summer Vegetables

VERY FEW SALADS will keep once dressed, but this one can be fully prepared up to 4 hours in advance, making it useful for Shabbat, Yom Tov, picnics and the organised hostess!

Italian Jewish food is simple, relying not on exotic ingredients or complicated procedures but on the right proportions of foods of the highest quality. I have included this recipe because Italian cuisine is not only the most popular internationally, but it is also able to trace its origins back to Roman times.

Remember to plan ahead as making a risotto involves that special ingredient: risotto rice. This is short grain and requires nearly three times more water than regular long grain rice. However, once you have mastered the art of making a risotto, you will make it again and again.

Preparation: 35 minutes
Cooking: 20 minutes
Serves 4 as a main course, 8 as a side dish

250 g (9 oz) Arborio risotto rice
1 litre (1¾ pints) vegetable stock
110 g (4 oz) fresh shelled peas or fresh or frozen broad beans
110 g (4 oz) fine green beans, trimmed
110 g (4 oz) thin asparagus spears, cut into 2.5 cm (1 in) lengths, tough ends discarded
4 spring onions, trimmed and finely sliced
1 red pepper, deseeded and finely chopped
2 tablespoons pitted black olives
1 tablespoon finely chopped fresh dill
1 tablespoon finely chopped fresh flatleaf parsley
1 tablespoon finely chopped fresh mint leaves
Salt and freshly ground black pepper
3–4 tablespoons lemon-infused olive oil or extra virgin olive oil, for drizzling

- Rinse the rice in a sieve until the water runs clear.

- Bring the stock to the boil in a pan.

- Place the rice in another pan and cook over a medium heat, adding ladles of boiling stock one at a time and stirring continuously until each ladleful is absorbed and until the rice is tender. This will take about 20 minutes.

- When the rice is cooked, rinse it in cold water and drain again. Transfer to a large serving dish.

- Cook the peas or broad beans, fine green beans and asparagus in boiling salted water until al dente. Drain and submerge in iced water (this keeps the vegetables bright green and prevents further cooking). Dry with kitchen paper or a clean tea towel.

- Add the vegetables to the rice, then stir in the spring onions, red pepper, olives, dill, parsley and mint. Season with salt and pepper.

- Drizzle with lemon-infused olive oil or extra virgin olive oil and serve.

NOTE: Lemon-infused olive oil (olive oil flavoured with slices of lemon) is available from supermarkets or you can make your own.

Pilau Chicken Rice

THIS IS TYPICALLY served by Iranian Jews at celebratory buffets and banquets (on a much larger scale, of course). Rice and chicken are favourite Jewish ingredients and you will find them on the menu for Ashkenazi and Sephardi dishes.

I suggest you use a boiling chicken minus the breasts. In Iran, boilers are used far more often in main dishes than they are in the UK, where we tend to use them only for soup. The flavour of the curry merges well with the chicken stock, so the boiling chicken ends up tasty.

Preparation: 40 minutes
Cooking: 30 minutes
Serves 6

450 g (I lb) boiling chicken (dark meat – bottom quarters, legs, wings)
2 tablespoons chicken stock or 2 chicken stock cubes
450 g (I lb) basmati rice
I tablespoon curry powder
I tablespoon tomato purée
Salt and freshly ground black pepper

For the topping:
2 tablespoons vegetable oil
2 onions, sliced
110 g (4 oz) blanched almonds
110 g (4 oz) raisins

- Place the chicken in a large pan, cover with water and add I tablespoon of the stock or one of the stock cubes. Bring to the boil, then reduce the heat and simmer for 30 minutes

- Meanwhile, rinse the basmati rice well – about five times – until the water runs clear. Place the rice in another pan and add 1.2 litres (2 pints) water, the remaining stock or stock cube, curry powder, tomato purée and seasoning. Bring to the boil, then reduce the heat and simmer for 8 minutes. Cover and leave for 5 minutes with the heat turned off.

- For the topping, heat the oil in a frying pan. Add the onions and almonds and sauté over a medium heat for 5 minutes or until golden. Stir in the raisins and cook for a further 2 minutes.

- Drain any excess liquid from the rice and place it on a serving platter in a mound. Top with the almonds, onions and raisins. Arrange the chicken portions around the sides and serve immediately.

Vegetables and Salads

VEGETABLES AND SALADS – hot and cold, cooked and uncooked – enhance the Jewish table at most meals. While all fruits, vegetables and salads are kosher, their preparation according to the *kashrut* laws is often complex. This is because of the prohibition against eating insects. Very thorough cleaning to prevent accidental insect ingestion is the order of the day, and this is clearly prescribed by rabbis. Some ingredients, such as apples, carrots, cucumber, tomatoes, peppers, courgettes and aubergines, are simple to wash and use. However, it is much more difficult to ensure that salad leaves, strawberries, asparagus, raspberries and parsley are not hiding unwanted bugs.

Stuffed Aubergines

WHILE STUFFED VEGETABLES feature in both Ashkenazi and Sephardi cuisines, aubergines, couscous and aromatic herbs and spices are firmly in the Sephardi camp. Serve one of these great creations per person as a whole meal, or half as a starter or light lunch. The cumin seeds and herbs give them a truly authentic Middle Eastern flavour and they are ideal for vegetarians. Serve with a plain green salad as they are quite filling.

During the eight days of Succot it is traditional to eat stuffed vegetables – tomatoes, onions, peppers, courgettes and aubergines – perhaps because it is harvest time and these vegetables are at their best and most plentiful.

Preparation: 30 minutes
Cooking: 50 minutes
Serves 6

3 large aubergines, halved lengthways
3 tablespoons olive oil
2 large red peppers, halved and deseeded
570 ml (I pint) hot vegetable stock
225 g (8 oz) couscous
I tablespoon vegetable oil
2 tablespoons cumin seeds
6 garlic cloves, finely chopped
I x 400 g can chick-peas, drained and rinsed
50 g (2 oz) raisins
3 tablespoons finely chopped fresh basil
3 tablespoons finely chopped fresh mint
3 tablespoons finely chopped fresh coriander
Salt and freshly ground black pepper
I tablespoon smoked paprika, for dusting

• Preheat the oven to 200°C/400°F/Gas Mark 6. Line a baking sheet with baking parchment.

- Score the flesh of the aubergines and place the halves, cut-sides up, on the baking sheet. Drizzle with 2 tablespoons of the olive oil and bake in the oven for 25 minutes.

- Meanwhile, preheat the grill to its highest setting. Place the peppers on another baking sheet and brush with the remaining olive oil. Grill them for 10 minutes or until blackened. Remove immediately, put into a dish and cover with cling film. Leave to cool.

- Remove the aubergines from the oven (keep the oven turned on) and scoop the flesh out of each half, leaving a 1 cm (½ in) thick shell. Set the shells aside. Chop the removed flesh and set aside.

- Pour the hot stock over the couscous. Cover with cling film and set aside.

- Heat the vegetable oil in a medium-size frying pan. Add the cumin seeds and sauté over a medium heat for 1 minute, then add the garlic and the chopped aubergine flesh. Cook for 10 minutes or until soft.

- Peel the skins off the peppers and roughly chop the flesh. Add to the aubergine mixture. Stir the aubergine and pepper mixture into the couscous. Add the chick-peas, raisins, basil, mint and half the coriander. Season well with salt and pepper.

- Divide the mixture between the six aubergine shells and bake in the oven for 15 minutes.

- Dust with the paprika, garnish with the remaining coriander and serve.

Tzimmes in Orange Juice

TZIMMES IS TRADITIONALLY eaten as a side dish at Rosh Hashanah for at least two reasons. Firstly, it is very sweet – and reflects our thoughts for a sweet year ahead. Secondly, the carrot rounds in the dish look like coins – we also hope for a prosperous year to come.

There are numerous *tzimmes* recipes – my new version cooks the carrots in orange juice and chicken stock for a different flavour. If you are short of cooking space – as is often the case at Yom Tov – it can be cooked on the hob as here or in a medium oven for 1 hour or in a slow cooker; one of the benefits is that the prunes plump up with the delicious stock and the dish is melt-in-the-mouth soft and delicious. *Tzimmes* can also be cooked overnight in the lowest possible oven setting; you will need to add an extra tablespoon of chicken stock and 500 ml (18 fl oz) water to prevent it drying out.

 (use *parev* chicken stock)

Preparation: 15 minutes
Cooking: 1 hour
Serves 6–8

1 kg (2¼ lb) carrots, cut into rounds
250 g (9 oz) dried prunes, pitted, or apricots, roughly
   chopped
570 ml (1 pint) orange juice
2 tablespoons chicken stock or *parev* chicken stock or
   1 chicken stock cube
Grated zest of 1 lemon
Grated zest of 1 orange
½ teaspoon grated fresh ginger

1 teaspoon ground cinnamon
3 tablespoons clear honey
Salt and freshly ground black pepper

- Put the carrots, prunes or apricots and orange juice in a large pan. Add the chicken stock or stock cube, lemon and orange zest, ginger, cinnamon and honey. Season well with salt and black pepper.
- Bring to the boil, then reduce the heat and simmer, covered, for 1 hour.

North African Pitta Bread Salad

THIS FUSION RECIPE combines the traditional Israeli TCP (tomato, cucumber and pepper) salad, Italian *panzanella* (tomato and bread) salad and Sephardi bread flavours. Add the dressing at the last minute to keep the bread crunchy.

I like to grind my own spices – it's quick to do and they taste fresher. However, for a short cut, you can use them ready-ground.

Preparation: 15 minutes
Cooking: 10 minutes
Serves 6

4 pitta breads
2 teaspoons coriander seeds
1 teaspoon cumin seeds
3 tablespoons extra virgin olive oil
3 large salad tomatoes, deseeded and roughly chopped

I green pepper, deseeded and roughly chopped
I red pepper, deseeded and roughly chopped
4 tablespoons roughly chopped fresh mint
4 spring onions, trimmed and chopped
I garlic clove, crushed
I cucumber, halved, deseeded and chopped
4 tablespoons olive oil
Juice of I lemon
Salt and freshly ground black pepper

- Preheat the oven to 200°C/400°F/Gas Mark 6.

- Cut the bread into 2.5 cm (I in) squares. Grind the coriander seeds and cumin seeds with a pestle and mortar and mix with the 3 tablespoons extra virgin olive oil. Place the pitta squares on a baking sheet, drizzle with the spiced oil mixture and toast in the oven for 10 minutes or until crisp and light brown. Set aside.

- In a large bowl, combine the tomatoes, peppers, mint, spring onions, garlic and cucumber.

- In a separate bowl, mix the 4 tablespoons olive oil and lemon juice, and season with salt and pepper. Pour the dressing over the salad ingredients and stir in the toasted pitta squares.

- Mix well and serve immediately.

Caraway Cabbage Stir-fry

THIS IS A delightful mixture of different cabbages stir-fried in olive oil and seasoned with caraway seeds. Quick and easy to prepare and cook, it makes a delicious nutritious accompaniment to chicken and meat dishes, adding colour and texture. You can easily vary the recipe by using different varieties of cabbage.

Cabbage is one of the oldest vegetables known to man and continues to be a staple of the modern diet, as it is inexpensive and rich in vitamin C (an antioxidant) and fibre. To store cabbage, place the whole head in a plastic bag and keep in the refrigerator. This will help to retain its vitamin C. Wash cabbage as and when required as it tends to wilt and lose the vitamin content. Also avoid slicing or shredding in advance of cooking.

Preparation: 10 minutes
Cooking: 10 minutes
Serves 6

½ Savoy cabbage
½ green spring pointed cabbage
3 tablespoons olive oil
200 g (7 oz) curly kale, stalks removed
Sea salt and freshly ground black pepper
3 tablespoons caraway seeds
Extra virgin olive oil, for drizzling

- Wash and shred the Savoy and green cabbages.

- Heat the oil in a large frying pan or wok. Add the cabbages and kale and stir-fry over a medium heat for 10 minutes until just tender. Season with salt and pepper and stir in the caraway seeds.

- To serve, drizzle with a little extra virgin olive oil and spoon on to a warmed serving platter.

Roasted Autumn Vegetables

THIS IS A colourful combination of roasted vegetables that can be prepared in advance and cooked when required. Unlike some fruits and vegetables, they do not oxidise or wilt if peeled and chopped ahead of time. Another great benefit is that they don't require careful attention and will not spoil if slightly overcooked – ideal for Shabbat and Yom Tov cooking. They are also delicious served at room temperature for Shabbat lunch.

The carrots and squash (also known as a gourd) are both significant symbolic foods mentioned at the festive meal on the first night of Rosh Hashanah.

The symbolism linked to carrots is somewhat more direct. When sliced, they look like coins and reflect our desire for a prosperous year. In addition, the Yiddish word for carrots is *mehren*, which can also mean to increase. So we are wishing that our lives will increase in good fortune, in every aspect.

Preparation: 15 minutes
Cooking: 30 minutes
Serves 6

2 orange peppers, deseeded and quartered
2 yellow peppers, deseeded and quartered
675 g (1½ lb) butternut squash, peeled, deseeded and cut into cubes
4 carrots, cut into rounds

2 red onions, quartered
4 garlic cloves, finely chopped
Salt and freshly ground black pepper
4 tablespoons olive oil or sesame oil

- Preheat the oven to 200°C/400°F/Gas Mark 6. Line a baking sheet with baking parchment.

- Roughly chop the peppers and place on the baking sheet with the squash, carrots and onions. Sprinkle with the garlic, season with salt and pepper and drizzle with the oil.

- Bake in the oven for 30 minutes or until the vegetables are soft and golden.

NOTE: The vegetables can be prepared 2–3 hours in advance and refrigerated.

Tomato and Courgette Frittata

I THINK ONE of the most difficult meals during Pesach is breakfast/ brunch. *Matzah* does not really fill you up and I find myself constantly munching on yet another piece of the 'crumbly stuff' to satisfy the hunger pangs. This dish sets you up for the day and is extremely tasty and filling. It can also be served at lunch, either hot or cold, with a salad. It keeps well, so should there be any leftovers, cut it up into slices and use as part of a packed lunch.

(P)

Preparation: 25 minutes
Cooking: 50 minutes
Serves 6–8

3 tablespoons olive oil, plus extra for greasing
600 g (1 lb 5 oz) potatoes, sliced
2 onions, roughly chopped
2 garlic cloves, finely chopped
3 courgettes, cut into rounds
5 eggs, lightly beaten
150 ml (¼ pint) double cream
6 salad tomatoes, sliced
Salt and freshly ground black pepper
3 tablespoons finely chopped fresh coriander (or any
**   chosen herb)**
Fresh coriander leaves, to garnish

- Preheat the oven to 200°C/400°F/Gas Mark 6. Grease a loose-based 22 cm (9 in) baking tin and line the base with baking parchment.

- Boil the potatoes for 10 minutes or until they are just soft. Drain and set aside.

- Heat the oil in a large frying pan. Add the onions, garlic and courgettes and sauté over a medium heat for 5 minutes until they are just cooked.

- Mix the eggs and cream together.

- In a bowl, combine the potatoes, tomatoes and courgette mixture. Season well with salt and pepper and add the coriander (or your choice of herb). Spoon into the prepared tin and pour over the egg and cream mixture. Bake in the oven for 40 minutes or until set.

- Invert the frittata on to a plate and remove the parchment.
- Cut into thick wedges and place on a warmed serving platter. Dust with pepper, garnish with coriander leaves and serve immediately.

NOTE: The frittata will keep for up to three days in the fridge.

Pumpkin and Cauliflower Bake

I AM ALWAYS looking for new ways of enticing my children to eat different vegetables so that they get a balanced diet. This pumpkin and cauliflower bake is a great combination and makes a pleasant accompaniment to most roast dinners and fish dishes, and can be served as part of a hot buffet meal. It puffs up in the oven and falls on cooling yet still retains its moist soufflé texture. It freezes well, either raw or cooked, so if time permits make double the quantity and freeze one to keep for another time. Vegetables like carrots, butternut squash, broccoli and swede make delicious alternatives to either the pumpkin or the cauliflower – or both.

Pumpkin, an autumn vegetable, is traditionally eaten by Sephardi Jews at Rosh Hashanah. The Hebrew word for pumpkin is *qara*, which also means 'to call out'. This reflects the prayer asking that our good deeds be 'called out' before God at this time of judgement.

Preparation: 15 minutes
Cooking: 50 minutes
Serves 8

1 kg (2¼ lb) pumpkin, peeled and sliced
1 kg (2¼ lb) cauliflower (2 medium-size cauliflowers),
  divided into florets
4 eggs
2 egg whites
2 teaspoons ground cinnamon, plus extra for dusting
1 teaspoon baking powder
Salt and freshly ground black pepper

- In separate pans, cook the pumpkin 8–10 minutes and cauliflower for 10–12 minutes or until they are soft. Drain and set aside.

- Preheat the oven to 180°C/350°F/Gas Mark 4.

- Whisk the eggs and egg whites until thickened, then add the cinnamon and baking powder.

- Place the pumpkin and cauliflower in a food processor and whiz until smooth. Season well with salt and pepper.

- Combine the pumpkin and cauliflower mixture with the whisked eggs. Pour into a large ovenproof dish. Place in the oven for about 40 minutes. The bake is cooked when the top is golden and firm to touch.

- Dust with ground cinnamon just before serving.

Creamy Spinach Mash

MY FAMILY ENJOYS mashed potatoes at any time, and combining them with spinach gives them colour and texture, and also improves their nutritional value. This dish is quick and easy to make – especially if you use a potato masher or ricer – and will easily reheat in the microwave should you wish to make it in advance. You can replace the spinach with other vegetables such as spring onions, shredded cooked cabbage or shredded cooked celeriac. Adding margarine, cream and milk or olive oil, and seasoning well with salt and pepper or a pinch of nutmeg helps to maximise the flavour and enjoyment.

This particular recipe is ideal for Pesach and any Yom Tov meal when you have many guests. It can be prepared and cooked in advance and is perfect for buffet-style serving.

P (substitute double cream for soya cream) **P**

Preparation: 20 minutes
Cooking: 10 minutes
Serves 6

900 g (2 lb) potatoes, cut into chunks
225 g (8 oz) fresh baby spinach, stalks removed, roughly chopped
110 g (4 oz) margarine or unsalted butter
100 ml (4 fl oz) double cream (soya cream for a *parev* option)
2 tablespoons olive oil
2 tablespoons finely chopped fresh mint
Pinch of freshly grated nutmeg
Salt and freshly ground black pepper

• Boil the potatoes for 10 minutes or until soft, then drain.

- Wash the spinach well.

- Return the potatoes to the pan and mash, using a masher, ricer or fork. While they are still hot, stir in the margarine or butter, spinach, cream, oil and mint. Season well with the nutmeg and salt and pepper.

NOTE: Reheat in a microwave or place in the oven on non-stick baking paper at 180°C/350°F/Gas Mark 4 for 30 minutes.

Fennel, Red Cabbage and Avocado Salad

IT IS ALWAYS useful to have a quick salad that can be made in advance, especially during Pesach when it seems that you are constantly cooking for the next meal. I love this colourful combination of vegetables, which is completed with a delicious honey dressing. It can be part of a healthy lunch or served with grilled fish or chicken at a mid-week supper.

Preparation: 15 minutes
Cooking: 8 minutes
Serves 6

50 g (2 oz) pecan nuts
600 g (1 lb 5 oz) red cabbage, cored and thinly sliced
1 bulb fennel, cored and thinly sliced

2 cooked beetroot, sliced
2 tablespoons dried cranberries
2 large avocados, peeled and sliced

For the dressing (makes 150 ml/¼ pint):
9 tablespoons olive oil
3 tablespoons clear honey
3 teaspoons lemon juice
Salt and freshly ground black pepper

- Preheat the oven to 200°C/400°F/Gas Mark 6.

- Place the pecans on a baking sheet and toast in the oven for
  5–8 minutes or until golden. Set aside.

- Combine the cabbage, fennel, beetroot and cranberries. Gently mix in
  the avocados.

- For the dressing, combine the oil, honey and lemon juice in a bowl and
  season with salt and pepper. Pour over the salad.

- Place the salad in a large serving dish, sprinkle with the pecans and
  serve immediately.

NOTES: The salad can be prepared 2 hours in advance and refrigerated.
Mix with the dressing immediately before serving. The dressing can be
made up to three days in advance and refrigerated.

Oriental Salad

DURING THE HIGH holy days salads come as a welcome relief from the more traditional and heavy Jewish meals. This recipe is a perfect example of kosher fusion, where I blend contemporary ingredients with traditional food. It is a little different from regular coleslaw, and in my opinion even more delicious – and certainly just as popular. With kosher supermarkets now stocking supervised soy sauce and sesame oil, making dishes like this is much easier.

Serve the salad as part of a buffet table, or make it for barbecues or picnics as it transports well. I like to keep the dressing separate until I am ready to serve so that the vegetables stay fresh and crunchy.

Preparation: 15 minutes
Cooking: None
Serves 6–8

110 g (4 oz) cashew nuts
300 g (11 oz) fresh bean sprouts
110 g (4 oz) radishes, finely sliced
5 spring onions, trimmed and sliced
5 carrots, grated
1 bunch fresh coriander, leaves only

For the dressing:
Juice of 1 lime
2 tablespoons soy sauce
1 chilli, deseeded and finely chopped
3 tablespoons sesame oil
1 teaspoon clear honey

- Preheat the oven to 200°C/400°F/Gas Mark 6.

- Place the cashews on a baking sheet and toast in the oven for 10 minutes or until golden. Set aside.

- Combine the bean sprouts, radishes, spring onions and carrots. Mix in the coriander leaves. Roughly chop the cashews.

- Combine all the dressing ingredients and refrigerate until ready to use.

- To serve, pour the dressing over the salad, toss and sprinkle with the cashews.

NOTES: The salad can be made an hour in advance and refrigerated. The dressing can be made a day in advance and refrigerated.

Spinach, Avocado and Asparagus Salad with Pesto Dressing

HEALTHY EATING IS always in the news – and for many people Jewish food is associated with heavy, highly calorific foods. Throughout this book I have tried to ensure that the recipes are 'lite' in every respect. This particular salad is a perfect example of eating for health.

Spinach originated in the Middle East and arrived in Europe via Spain in the eighth century. It became very popular – and was known as the 'Spanish vegetable' by the English. Its leaves contain high amounts of iron, vitamins B and C and beta-carotene.

Avocados are a valuable source of protein, fibre, calcium, iron, potassium and vitamins. Their high levels of vitamin E are particularly beneficial – this antioxidant helps to prevent ageing (so no more wrinkles!) and plays a significant role in preventing infections, cancers, heart attacks and strokes. Avocados are high in calories and fat, but the fat is monounsaturated and helps to lower bad cholesterol levels.

Asparagus is an excellent source of folic acid as well as potassium, fibre, vitamins B_6, A and C, and iron and thiamine. It is high in protein, low in sodium and calories and has no fat or cholesterol. Eat five or six spears daily as one of your 'five portions of fruit and vegetables a day' healthy eating plan.

P

Preparation: 15 minutes
Cooking: 2–3 minutes
Serves 4

200 g (7 oz) fresh asparagus tips
2 avocados, peeled
Juice of 1 lemon
225 g (8 oz) baby spinach leaves
8 slices of Parmesan cheese

For the pesto dressing:
50 g (2 oz) pine nuts
50 g (2 oz) Parmesan cheese, grated
3 tablespoons fresh basil leaves
100 ml (4 fl oz) olive oil
Salt and freshly ground black pepper

• Cook the asparagus in boiling water for 2–3 minutes until just soft. Drain and refresh under cold water. This helps to prevent further cooking and preserves the beautiful green colour of the asparagus. Set aside.

- For the dressing, fry the pine nuts in a dry frying pan for approximately 2 minutes until golden. Remove from the pan and set aside.

- Place the grated Parmesan, basil, and pine nuts in a food processor and whiz to form a paste. Gradually add the oil and whiz for a further 5 minutes. Season with salt and pepper.

- Cut the avocados into lengthways slices and sprinkle with the lemon juice to prevent them going brown.

- To serve, arrange the spinach, asparagus, Parmesan slices and avocado slices on individual plates. Pour some of the dressing over each portion and serve immediately.

Winter Coleslaw

JEWISH PEOPLE LOVE coleslaw whatever the occasion or time of the year. They enjoy it with a jacket potato, as part of a buffet, as a sandwich filling or just as an accompaniment to most main courses. It is also a great salad to serve for Shabbat or Yom Tov as it does not wilt overnight like most salads. For this recipe I have used a colourful selection of vegetables with pecan nuts, in order to produce a tasty coleslaw; you can try it with walnuts, cashews or almonds. If you are preparing it in advance, stir in the dressing just before serving in order to keep the vegetables crispy and the nuts crunchy.

Although there is some evidence that coleslaw was probably eaten by the ancient Romans, it only emerged in its modern form in the eighteenth century with the invention of mayonnaise. 'Cole slaw' is a partial translation of the Dutch *koolsla*, a shortening of *kool salade*, which means 'cabbage salad'. It was commonly called 'cold slaw' in England until the 1860s, when 'cole' meaning cabbage was revived, based on the Latin word for cabbage: *colis*.

Preparation: 20 minutes
Cooking: 8–10 minutes
Serves 8

110 g (4 oz) pecan nuts
½ Savoy or green cabbage
½ red cabbage
2 red apples, quartered
110 g (4 oz) cranberries
Salt and freshly ground black pepper
3 bunches endive, leaves separated, to serve

For the dressing:
6 tablespoons mayonnaise
2 tablespoons crème fraîche or Toffuti non-dairy cream
    cheese
2 tablespoons Dijon mustard
Juice of ½ lemon
Salt and freshly ground black pepper

- Preheat the oven to 200°C/400°F/Gas Mark 6.

- Place the pecans on a baking sheet and toast in the oven for 10 minutes or until golden. Set aside.

- Remove the tough outer leaves from the cabbages, and finely shred the remaining leaves. (Use a food processor for a quick option.)

- Core the apples and cut them into slices. Mix with the cabbage, cranberries and pecans.

- For the dressing, combine the mayonnaise, crème fraîche, mustard and lemon juice and season with salt and pepper.

- Stir the dressing into the coleslaw. Taste and adjust the seasoning.

- To serve, place the coleslaw on a serving platter, arrange the endive leaves around the edge and dust with pepper.

NOTE: The coleslaw can be prepared the day before it is required and refrigerated.

Roasted Beetroot and Potato Salad with Garlic Mayonnaise

THIS IS A tasty variation on a popular favourite – a different potato salad on the menu is always welcome. It can be served with most main course meals, especially barbecues and buffets. Potatoes and beetroot are popular Jewish foods and a salad that combines the two is a great creation. Try it – I am sure your guests will not be disappointed.

Baby new potatoes are perfect as they provide a delicious creamy texture, and the fresh roasted beetroot adds a wonderful vibrant colour as well as nutritional value. I have combined the salad with a *parev* garlic mayonnaise which is also delicious with crunchy vegetables or with poached fish or grilled meats.

Preparation: 10 minutes
Cooking: 55 minutes
Serves 6

4 uncooked beetroots, peeled
2 tablespoons extra virgin olive oil
Salt and freshly ground black pepper
I kg (2¼ lb) new potatoes, unpeeled and halved
3 tablespoons snipped chives
3 tablespoons fresh basil leaves, torn
3 tablespoons roughly chopped fresh parsley
2 tablespoons roughly chopped fresh oregano

For the garlic mayonnaise:
I large garlic clove, finely chopped
I teaspoon English mustard
2 egg yolks
Squeeze of lemon juice
300 ml (½ pint) olive oil or sunflower oil
Salt and freshly ground black pepper

- Preheat the oven to 200°C/400°F/Gas Mark 6. Line a baking sheet with baking parchment.

- Cut the beetroot into thin slices and place them on the baking sheet, in a single layer. Drizzle with the extra virgin olive oil and season with salt and pepper. Roast in the oven for 40 minutes or until softened. Set aside to cool.

- Cook the potatoes for 15 minutes or until tender. Drain and set aside to cool.

- For the garlic mayonnaise, place the garlic, mustard, egg yolks and lemon juice in a food processor and blend to form a paste. When the paste has formed, and while the motor is still running, slowly add the oil. When all the oil has been absorbed, taste and season with salt and pepper.

- In a bowl, mix the potatoes with the herbs; reserve 2 tablespoons of mixed herbs for the garnish. Then stir in the mayonnaise and beetroot.

- Transfer to a large serving dish, dust with pepper and garnish with the reserved herbs.

NOTE: The garlic mayonnaise will keep in the fridge in a sealed jar for up to two days.

Moroccan Carrot Salad

THE EXOTIC FLAVOUR of this filling salad comes from the unique combination of rose water and cinnamon. Serve it as an accompaniment for chicken, lamb or beef, or as part of a buffet table.

Ⓟ Ⓟ (omit rose water)
Preparation: 15 minutes
Cooking: 10 minutes + 1 hour infusing
Serves 4

75 g (3 oz) flaked almonds
450 g (1 lb) carrots
2 teaspoons clear honey
3 tablespoons olive oil
Juice of ½ lemon
1 tablespoon rose water
50 g (2 oz) raisins

1 teaspoon ground cinnamon
Salt and freshly ground black pepper

- Preheat the oven to 200°C/400°F/Gas Mark 6.

- Place the almonds on a baking sheet and toast in the oven for 10 minutes or until golden. Set aside.

- Grate the carrots in a food processor or by hand and place in a large mixing bowl. Stir in the honey, oil, lemon juice, rose water, raisins and cinnamon. Season well with salt and pepper and mix well. Leave at room temperature for 1 hour for the flavours to infuse.

- Stir in the toasted almonds just before serving.

Desserts

VERSATILITY IS THE KEY to the range of desserts that grace the Jewish table. The Jewish cook's repertoire should include light and also more filling finales, adapted to follow the main dishes appropriately. More challenging, perhaps, is the need for a choice of good desserts to serve after a meat-based meal. *Kashrut* laws prohibit eating dairy and meat at the same time, and many of the desserts enjoyed in the wider world are more often than not dairy-based. Fortunately, the recent arrival of non-dairy substitutes such as soy-, rice- and oat-derived milks and creams in supermarkets has made many more recipes available to the Jewish table.

Almond Pear Bake

PEARS ARE A naturally versatile food. Eaten simply as fresh fruit or in a salad they are flavoursome, textured and healthy. And their perfumed flavour blends so well when they are cooked with other ingredients, such as coconut, wine and – in my bake – almonds. All the other ingredients are standard Pesach ones, but this dessert is a treat at any time.

The bake can be presented in individual ramekins for a more stylish look and cooked for 15 minutes. Line the base of each one with baking parchment circles so that the dessert comes out easily when the ramekin is inverted. Apples or plums can be substituted for pears if preferred. Serve with non-dairy ice cream or sorbet.

❄ Ⓟ

Preparation: 20 minutes
Cooking: 45 minutes
Serves 6

1 tablespoon margarine, for greasing
6 firm pears, peeled, cored and cut into 2 cm (¾ in) slices
2 tablespoons dark brown sugar
1 tablespoon ground cinnamon
6 tablespoons split almonds

For the almond mixture:
150 g (5 oz) margarine
150 g (5 oz) caster sugar
150 g (5 oz) ground almonds
2 tablespoons vanilla sugar
6 eggs
3 tablespoons plain flour (potato flour for Passover)

- Preheat the oven to 190°C/375°F/Gas Mark 5. Grease a 34 x 24 x 4 cm (13½ x 9½ x 1½ in) pie or casserole dish with margarine.

- Combine the pears with the sugar and cinnamon and put in the dish.

- Place all the almond mixture ingredients in a food processor and whiz until creamy. Spread over the pears and level with a spoon, then sprinkle with the split almonds.

- Bake in the oven for 45 minutes or until golden brown.

NOTE: The bake can be made 4 hours in advance and refrigerated.

Crunchy Biscuit Ice Cream

MY LATE FATHER loved to have ice cream as a dessert – in fact, he was quite passionate about this. This crunchy biscuit recipe kept him and the whole family happy on Friday nights and Yom Tov – and as it is *parev* it can be served at any time. It is a great dessert to make in advance and keep in the freezer as a versatile standby. I have used plain biscuits, such as digestive; be careful to check that they are *parev* if you are making a non-dairy meal. Ginger nuts, digestives, and chocolate chip cookies are good alternatives. The quantities in this recipe fill two loaf tins, which is an added bonus when you want to draw on your freezer stocks at a time of need!

Serve the ice cream on its own, or with fresh fruit, apple pie or your favourite pudding. It only takes 5–10 minutes to slightly defrost as *parev* whipping cream melts more quickly than its dairy equivalent.

Preparation: 25 minutes + 4 hours freezing
Cooking: 8–10 minutes
Serves 14–16 (makes 2 loaf tins)

Oil for greasing
150 g (5 oz) brown breadcrumbs
150 g (5 oz) demerara sugar
300 ml (½ pint) non-dairy whipping cream
2 teaspoons vanilla essence
3 eggs, separated
150 g (5 oz) plain biscuits, crushed
2 tablespoons caster sugar
Sliced strawberries, to serve

- Grease two 900 g (2 lb) loaf tins with oil and line them with baking parchment.

- Put the breadcrumbs and demerara sugar in a large, shallow frying pan and dry fry them over a medium heat until the mixture clusters together and turns medium brown, stirring all the time. Remove from the pan and cool slightly.

- Whisk the cream until thick. Add the vanilla essence and egg yolks and whisk again. Stir in the crushed biscuits and cooled crumbs.

- In a clean, grease-free bowl, whisk the egg whites into soft peaks. Gradually add the caster sugar, continuing to whisk until the egg whites are very stiff. Add 1 tablespoon of the egg whites to the biscuit mixture, then fold in the remaining egg whites. Combine well and pour into the prepared loaf tins.

- Freeze until firm. This will take about 4 hours.

- To serve, invert the ice cream on to a serving plate and surround with sliced strawberries.

Chocolate Apple Dessert

WHEN I PLAN my family menus for Rosh Hashanah I try to use apples (and honey) in as many ways as possible – I cook old favourites and develop new recipes that will become old favourites! The New Year deserves a luxurious delicious apple cake for tea or dessert. This new favourite will delight guests and freezes beautifully.

The chocolate topping takes 2 hours to set, so remember to allow time for this. I once made this cake without the chocolate and it was not so exciting, so do make the effort. The variety of apple is not critical, but if there is a choice I prefer Granny Smiths as they are firm in texture with a good flavour.

❊ Ⓟ

Preparation: 20 minutes + 30 minutes cooling and 2 hours setting
Cooking: 1 hour
Serves 8

1 tablespoon margarine or oil, for greasing
5 eggs
340 g (12 oz) icing sugar
3 teaspoons vanilla sugar
750 g (1 lb 10 oz) eating apples, peeled, cored and grated
110 g (4 oz) raisins
300 g (11 oz) plain flour
2 teaspoons baking powder
110 g (4 oz) walnuts, chopped

For the chocolate topping:
150 g (5 oz) plain chocolate
75 g (3 oz) margarine
2 tablespoons apricot or raspberry jam

- Preheat the oven to 180°C/350°F/Gas Mark 4. Grease a 22 cm (9 in) loose-base cake tin with the margarine and line the base with baking parchment.
- Whisk the eggs, icing sugar and vanilla sugar in a mixing bowl until the

mixture is pale and thick. Stir in the apple, raisins, flour, baking powder and nuts.

- Bake in the oven for 1 hour or until the cake is firm to the touch in the centre and golden brown.

- Remove from the cake tin and transfer on to a plate for 30 minutes before adding the topping.

- For the topping, place the chocolate and margarine in a double-boiler and heat gently, stirring, until both have melted. Spread the jam over the top of the cake, then pour over the chocolate topping.

- Chill in the refrigerator for 2 hours until the topping has set, or overnight.

Roasted Almond and Nectarine Pie with Chocolate Sauce

ALTHOUGH NECTARINES IN season are delicious eaten fresh, they also make the most delicious desserts. Here they are fanned in a spiral on top of an almond filling encased in a chocolate pastry. A shiny glaze gives the pie a final elegant touch.

This dessert can be made in stages. Prepare the pastry first – you can even freeze it and bake it from frozen – then the almond filling, and complete the pie with the nectarine slices. Apples, apricots and raspberries make ideal alternatives to nectarines should you prefer. And the chocolate sauce in the recipe can be replaced with a ready-made one. Serve with ice cream or thick yoghurt.

❄ (pastry) ◈P

Preparation: 35 minutes + 30 minutes chilling
Cooking: 1 hour
Serves 8

For the pastry:
110 g (4 oz) plain chocolate, broken into pieces
300 g (11 oz) plain flour, plus extra for dusting
150 g (5 oz) unsalted butter or non-dairy margarine
4 tablespoons ground almonds
2 drops of almond essence
1 egg

For the filling:
350 g (12 oz) blanched almonds
110 g (4 oz) caster sugar
150 g (5 oz) unsalted butter or margarine
3 eggs
1 egg white
2 drops of almond essence
5–6 ripe nectarines, stoned and sliced
4 tablespoons apricot jam

For the chocolate sauce:
110 g (4 oz) plain chocolate
2 tablespoons margarine

- To make the pastry, place the chocolate in a food processor and whiz until it resembles crumbs. Add the flour, butter or margarine, ground almonds, almond essence, egg and 1–2 tablespoons water. Continue to pulse until a dough has formed. Remove the dough from the bowl, slightly flatten it and place it in the fridge for 30 minutes.

- Lightly dust a work surface with flour. Roll out the pastry and line a 25 cm (10 in) loose-based flan tin. Chill in the fridge until ready to use.

- Preheat the oven to 190°C/375°F/Gas Mark 5.

- For the filling, place the almonds on a baking sheet and toast in the oven for 10 minutes or until nicely golden.

- Place the almonds and sugar in a food processor and pulse until finely ground. Add the butter or margarine, eggs, egg white and almond essence and pulse briefly until combined.

- Spoon the filling into the chocolate pastry case and top with the nectarines, positioning the slices in a spiral shape. Bake in the oven for 50 minutes or until set and golden.

- Put the jam into a small glass dish with 1 tablespoon water. Cover with cling film and melt in a microwave for 1 minute. (This is very hot so be careful.) Alternatively, place the jam and water in a small pan and stir over a low heat until the jam has melted. Brush the glaze over the nectarines.

- For the sauce, melt the chocolate in a dish set over a pan of simmering water. Add the margarine and stir from time to time. Drizzle the chocolate sauce over the flan and serve warm.

Boozy Pears

WHEN YOU THINK of pears, your mind conjures up an image of grace, sophistication and the ultimate in good taste. A teardrop shape and tender, golden skin surround fine-grained, buttery-textured flesh that has a juicy, sweet flavour and pleasant aroma. There are several varieties in the shops, the most common of which are Conference, Comice, Packham's, William's and Bartlett's.

Pears are great tossed in salads, made into jellies, jams or preserves, used in desserts and other baked creations, blended into fruit drinks, and used in a creatively fresh approach to salsas or chutney.

They are also highly nutritious – one medium-size pear provides 16 per cent of the daily requirement of dietary fibre (4 g) and 10 per cent of the daily requirement of vitamin C. Pears are also a source of potassium. They contain no cholesterol or sodium, and are virtually fat free.

This recipe is a great alternative to fruit salad. It uses predominantly store-cupboard ingredients and can be prepared in 10 minutes. Leave the pears to cook for 2 hours and they are transformed into a delicious, slightly alcoholic dessert. Serve with ice cream or thick yoghurt.

Preparation: 10 minutes
Cooking: 2 hours
Serves 6

6 large, ripe but firm pears
150 g (5 oz) golden caster sugar or soft brown sugar
275 ml (9 fl oz) Madeira, sweet sherry or Kiddush wine
Juice and thinly pared zest of 2 oranges
1 cinnamon stick
1 vanilla pod, split in half
Ground cinnamon, to serve

- Preheat the oven to 150°C/300°F/Gas Mark 2.
- Cut each pear in half from top to bottom, leaving the stem in place.

Remove the core with a teaspoon or melon-baller. Lay the halves, cut-sides up, in an ovenproof dish with a diameter of approximately 25 cm (10 in).

- Put the sugar, Madeira, sherry or wine, orange juice and zest, cinnamon stick and vanilla pod in a pan and add 200 ml (8 fl oz) water. Bring to the boil, stirring, and continue to stir until the sugar has dissolved. Pour over the pears (don't worry if the liquid does not cover them completely).

- Bake for 2 hours or until soft (the cooking time will vary according to the size and variety of the pears). Baste every 30 minutes, and pierce a pear with a skewer from time to time to test for tenderness.

- Dust individual plates with ground cinnamon and serve the pears either warm or cold.

Honey-spiced Apple Flan

BY SUCCOT THERE should be a wide range of apples in season including Braeburns, Pink Lady, Cox, Empire, Golden Delicious and Granny Smiths. Each has its own flavour and texture – the choice is yours. In most recipes, if cooking apples aren't specified any dessert apple may be used. However, in my experience Granny Smiths slice and cook well and don't make the dish too watery.

Apples are very healthy. They have no cholesterol or sodium, are low in calories, contain no more than 1 per cent fat, and are rich in many essential vitamins and minerals. They can even help to reduce stress and fight tooth decay. So the old wives' advice that 'an apple a day keeps the doctor away' is very true.

The flan is filled with a grated apple and honey mixture flavoured with mixed spice and cinnamon. It can be eaten hot or cold and will satisfy all apple pie addicts. For a short cut, buy ready-made pastry.

Preparation: 25 minutes + 30 minutes chilling
Cooking: 40–45 minutes
Serves 8

300 g (11 oz) plain flour, plus extra for dusting
150 g (5 oz) unsalted butter or margarine
3 tablespoons icing sugar, plus extra to serve
1 teaspoon mixed spice, plus extra to serve
1 egg
4 tablespoons apricot jam

For the filling:
3 eggs
3 tablespoons clear honey
1 teaspoon mixed spice
2 teaspoons ground cinnamon
1 teaspoon lemon juice
2 tablespoons breadcrumbs
4 eating apples, peeled and grated
2 eating apples, peeled and sliced

- Place the flour, butter or margarine, icing sugar, mixed spice and egg in a food processor and process until a dough has formed. Add a little water if the mixture is slightly dry. Wrap the pastry in cling film, flatten and place in the fridge for a minimum of 30 minutes to relax.

- Preheat the oven to 200°C/400°F/Gas Mark 6.

- To make the filling, whisk the eggs and honey until thick. Add the mixed spice, cinnamon, lemon juice, breadcrumbs and grated apple. Set aside.

- Lightly dust a work surface with flour. Roll out the pastry so that it fits a 22 cm (9 in) loose-based flan tin. Line the pastry case with foil, scatter with baking beans and blind bake for 20 minutes.

- Remove the baking beans and foil from the pastry case and pour in the apple mixture. Arrange the sliced apples on top in a circular pattern and bake in the oven for 40–45 minutes or until cooked and golden.

- Put the jam into a small glass dish with 2 teaspoons water. Cover with cling film and melt in a microwave for 1 minute. (This is very hot so be careful.) Alternatively, place the jam and water in a small pan and stir over a low heat until the jam has melted. Brush the flan with the glaze.

- Dust with icing sugar and mixed spice, and serve.

Halva

HALVA IS A confection or sweetmeat that originated in the Balkans and the eastern Mediterranean regions. It is made from ground sesame seeds and honey or sugar syrup, sometimes with the addition of other ingredients such as dried fruit, pistachios, chocolate and almonds. Cinnamon and cardamom are also added. The ingredients are blended together, then heated and poured into bars or long loaves. The name literally means 'sweetmeat' and various forms of the word may be found in Turkish, Greek, Yiddish, Arabic, etc. (*helva, halva, halvah, halwa, halawi*).

Marbled Halva Ice Cream

FOR THIS RECIPE I have added cocoa powder to enhance the slightly chocolatey flavour from the marbled chocolate *halva*, which is readily available from kosher delicatessens and supermarkets. Other flavours like vanilla, natural and pistachio are on supermarket shelves should you wish to change the recipe slightly. This ice cream has a beautiful silky texture and is delicious with most pies, crumbles and fruit desserts.

I prefer to use non-dairy cream for a less rich, *parev* option.

Preparation: 10 minutes + overnight freezing
Cooking: None
Serves 8–10

6 eggs, separated
2 tablespoons cocoa powder
75 g (3 oz) caster sugar
570 ml (1 pint) non-dairy cream
Pinch of salt
250 g (9 oz) flaked chocolate marbled *halva*
Cocoa powder and sliced strawberries, to serve

- Line a 900 g (2 lb) loaf tin with cling film.
- In a large mixing bowl, beat the egg yolks with the cocoa powder and sugar until very light and creamy.
- Lightly whip the cream in another bowl.
- In a clean, grease-free bowl, whisk the egg whites with the salt until stiff.
- Fold the cream carefully into the egg yolk and cocoa mixture, then add

the egg whites and, lastly, the *halva*. Pour into the prepared tin and freeze for at least 24 hours.

- Turn the ice cream out of tin and remove the cling film.
- To serve, dust individual plates with cocoa powder and place a slice of ice cream on top, along with some sliced strawberries.

Hazelnut Meringue Roulade with Raspberry Cream

ONCE YOU HAVE mastered the art of making roulades you will never consider them a challenge again. I feel that by following these three guidelines you will produce the perfect hazelnut roulade: use the right size tin; whip the meringue to the correct consistency, which is glossy and very stiff; and fold in the nuts carefully. Roulades always have a rustic appearance, which is part of their charm; so don't worry that yours cracks after rolling.

I love this crunchy meringue combination with a raspberry filling. If you want to make the roulade *parev*, use non-dairy plain 'cream cheese' instead of the double cream. Put it in a food processor with 2 tablespoons icing sugar, and perhaps a little cocoa powder or vanilla essence, and it will produce a spreadable mixture that does not crack the meringue.

Ⓟ Ⓟ (use potato flour for Pesach)
Preparation: 30 minutes
Cooking: 35 minutes
Serves 8

For the meringue:
75 g (3 oz) shelled hazelnuts, skinned
I teaspoon cornflour (potato flour for Pesach)
I teaspoon vanilla essence
I teaspoon ground cinnamon
6 egg whites
150 g (5 oz) caster sugar

For the raspberry cream:
150 g (5 oz) raspberries
2 tablespoons caster sugar
200 ml (8 fl oz) double cream (use non-dairy cream for a
** *parev* option)**

For the raspberry sauce:
200 g (7 oz) raspberries
2 tablespoons caster sugar

- Preheat the oven to 200°C/400°F/Gas Mark 6.

- Line a 26.5 x 38 cm (10½ x 15 in) shallow oblong tin with baking parchment; snip the corners so that it fits neatly.

- To make the meringue place the hazelnuts on a baking sheet and toast in the oven for 10 minutes or until golden. Then place in a food processor or coffee grinder and whiz to a powder.

- In a small bowl, blend together the cornflour, vanilla essence, cinnamon and 1–2 teaspoons water to form a paste.

- In a clean, grease-free bowl, whisk the egg whites until stiff then gradually add the sugar, a little at a time, along with the cornflour paste. The meringue should be very white and thick. Reserve 2 tablespoons of the powdered hazelnuts and tip the remainder into the meringue. Fold in lightly with a metal spoon.

- Spoon the meringue into the prepared tin and spread it evenly over the base with the back of a spoon. Sprinkle with the reserved hazelnut powder, reduce the oven temperature to 160°C/325°F/Gas Mark 3 and bake for 25 minutes or until the meringue is pale golden.

- Lay a sheet of baking parchment on a work surface, remove the meringue from the oven and carefully invert it on to the paper. Peel off the lining paper and leave the meringue to cool.

- For the raspberry cream, mix the raspberries with the sugar and cream. Spread the filling over the cooled meringue to within 1 cm (½ in) of its edges. Use the paper to roll the meringue up from one short edge. (It will crack slightly.)

- For the sauce, place the raspberries and sugar in a food processor and whiz until smooth. Push the sauce through a sieve to remove the seeds.

- Pour a pool of sauce on to the centre of each individual plate. Cut a thick slice of roulade, place it on top of the sauce and serve immediately.

NOTE: The meringue can be made a day in advance and stored in an airtight container; spread the filling over it a few hours before serving.

Roasted Winter Fruits

STEWED FRUIT, fruit compote, baked apples – warming winter desserts that involve concentrating the flavour of the chosen fruit are a strong Jewish tradition, as is the chosen spice, cinnamon, which goes so well with most fruits.

Cinnamon is the inner bark of an evergreen tree. I saw it growing recently at the Eden Project in Cornwall where there were numerous varieties. However, the best ground cinnamon I have ever bought came from a spice souk in Marrakech. It produced the most amazing aromatic flavour, quite different from that of the cinnamon in supermarket sachets. If you get the chance to buy authentic spices store them in a dry place away from sunlight to maximise their shelf life.

Cinnamon is mentioned in the Torah on several occasions. In Exodus it is described as one of the ingredients of the holy oil used in the Tabernacle to anoint priests and sacred vessels, and it features as a precious spice in the 'Song of Songs'. It was also used as a medicine to cure coughs. Cinnamon has a long history as a Jewish flavour and I love to use it in both savoury and sweet dishes.

This hot fruit salad is absolutely delicious – it is quick and simple to make and would work using Sharon fruit, pears and mangos. It is also a tasty, low-fat dessert and can be made in advance. Serve with vanilla ice cream, mascarpone cheese, thick Greek yoghurt or single cream.

P **P** (replace Amaretto with sweet Kiddush wine)
Preparation: 10 minutes
Cooking: 20 minutes
Serves 6

1 small pineapple, peeled, cored and cut into semicircles
4 plums, stoned and halved
6 fresh figs, quartered
4 star fruit, sliced and seeds removed
2 tablespoons clear honey
2 tablespoons soft brown sugar
Juice and grated zest of 1 lemon
1 teaspoon ground cinnamon
6 star anise

100 ml (4 fl oz) dessert wine or Amaretto
Seeds of 3 pomegranates

- Preheat the oven to 200°C/400°F/Gas Mark 6.

- Place the pineapple, plums, figs and star fruit in a deep oven-to-table dish.

- Combine the honey, sugar, lemon juice and zest, cinnamon, star anise and wine and pour over the fruit.

- Roast in the oven for 20 minutes or until the fruits are tender. Remove from the oven and add the pomegranate seeds, stirring so that they are evenly distributed.

NOTE: The fruits can be roasted 2 hours in advance and reheated gently in an oven heated to 180°C/350°F/Gas Mark 4.

Challah Bread and Butter Pudding

THIS IS A chocoholic's dream! The layers of crispy *challah* are wedged between a beautiful chocolate custard. The pudding is a Friday night treat and in most cases, because we have chicken as our main course, I tend to make it using soy cream. The flavours of soy products are an acquired taste but when they are mixed with alcohol, vanilla essence and chocolate you will have no idea that they are non-dairy. In addition, using them means the dessert is lower in calories and fat content.

The secret of success it to let the pudding stand overnight. The *challah* absorbs the custard mixture and in turn produces a very light dessert. Should you have some mixture left in the bowl that you can't quite pour into your dessert dish – wait. In time the *challah* absorbs the liquid and makes room for more. The final layer of apricot jam makes the topping crispy as well as shiny. If you don't have any *challah*, use bridge rolls or other sliced bread.

Preparation: 15 minutes + 2 hours soaking
Cooking: 50 minutes
Serves 8–10

75 g (3 oz) raisins
3 tablespoons brandy or Amaretto
2 tablespoons cocoa powder
2 tablespoons hot water
1 litre (1¾) pint milk or soy cream or soy milk
150 g (5 oz) plain chocolate, broken into chunks
2 teaspoons vanilla essence
6 eggs
110 g (4 oz) sugar
2 tablespoons unsalted butter or non-dairy margarine
8 medium-thick slices of *challah*
3 tablespoons apricot jam
1 tablespoon icing sugar

- Soak the raisins in the brandy or Amaretto for an hour. Mix 1 tablespoon of the cocoa powder with the hot water to make a paste.

- Put the milk, chocolate, vanilla essence and cocoa paste in a pan. Heat gently until the mixture is smooth, stirring from time to time. Whisk the eggs with the sugar until the mixture becomes thick and creamy and stir them into the chocolate mixture.

- Spread the butter or margarine on one side of the slices of *challah* and cut each slice into two triangles. Place half the triangles in overlapping rows, butter-sides down, in an ovenproof dish.

- Add the raisins and their soaking liquor to the chocolate mixture and pour over the *challah* triangles as evenly as possible. Arrange the remaining triangles over the mixture. Leave for about 2 hours, or overnight, for the mixture to soak into the *challah*.

- Preheat the oven to 180°C/350°F/Gas Mark 4.

- Put the ovenproof dish into a slighter larger roasting tin. Pour enough boiling water to come about halfway up the sides of the dish into the tin; be careful not to let any water splash on to the pudding.

- Bake in the oven for 45 minutes or until set.

- Put the jam into a small glass dish with 1 teaspoon water. Cover with cling film and melt in a microwave for 1 minute. (This is very hot so be careful.) Alternatively, place the jam and water in a small pan and stir over a low heat until the jam has melted. Mix the icing sugar with the remaining cocoa powder.

- Remove the pudding from the oven and brush the top with the glaze. Return the pudding to the oven for a final 5 minutes, for a crispy topping. Sprinkle with the cocoa powder and icing sugar mixture, and serve.

NOTE: The pudding can be made 2 hours in advance and refrigerated; reheat in a warm oven (180°C/350°F/Gas Mark 4) for 20 minutes.

Honey Syllabub

THIS IS A straightforward dessert that is ideal for Yom Tov as it captures the flavours of Rosh Hashanah. To embellish it a little, add some crumbled honey cake between layers of the syllabub. It has a very light and fluffy consistency and is a perfect ending to a rich meal. Pomegranate seeds can be used instead of strawberries.

The recipe uses kosher gelatine, which you can find at your local kosher delicatessen. It is a *parev* powder that comes in individual sachets. Kosher gelatine is made from fish bones, with no added colour or preservatives.

When using gelatine always weigh it accurately. Use too much and the food will be rubbery; too little and the food may fail to set. Pour the water on to the gelatine to soak in a measured amount of liquid so that it can start to 'sponge' or dissolve. Then warm it gently in a pan, but don't allow it to boil as it will become stringy and be unusable.

Preparation: 25 minutes + 3 hours setting
Cooking: 5 minutes
Serves 6

1 x 7 g sachet kosher gelatine
3 eggs, separated
75 g (3 oz) clear honey
150 ml (¼ pint) whipping cream (soy cream for *parev* option)

To decorate:
Sprigs of fresh mint
225 g (8 oz) strawberries or pomegranates, hulled and roughly chopped

- Place 2 tablespoons water in a small pan and sprinkle in the gelatine. Leave to soften.

- Whisk the egg yolks and honey together until pale and creamy.

- Once the gelatine has softened, warm it gently for 5 minutes or until it is clear. (Do not boil.) Pour the gelatine into the egg and honey mixture.

- Whisk the cream until it forms soft peaks. Add to the honey and egg mixture.

- Whisk the egg whites in a clean, grease-free bowl until they stand in peaks. Add 1 tablespoon to the honey and egg mixture, followed by the rest.

- Pour the honey syllabub into one large glass dish or six individual ones. Cover and refrigerate for at least 3 hours, or overnight, until set.

- Decorate with sprigs of mint and the strawberries, and serve.

Baked Apples with Muscat and Fig Filling

ALTHOUGH BAKED APPLES are perhaps considered a nursery food, by combining them with dessert wine, figs and roasted hazelnuts I have transformed them into a more adult pudding. The choice and availability of kosher sweet wines have increased quite substantially and there are numerous muscats, Sauternes, late harvest Rieslings, chenins blanc and Alfasi, and many many more. Your local wine merchant will advise you on the best wine available.

Despite its alcohol content, this is a great recipe for family gatherings. The flavour of the wine softens and mellows into the other ingredients. The apples are easy to prepare and straightforward to serve.

Choose eating apples that are perfect in shape and do not have any blemishes. (You could use cooking apples but they tend to be too sour.) If they don't stand up for baking, slice a very thin layer off the base of each apple.

Preparation: 25 minutes
Cooking: 55 minutes
Serves 8

50 g (2 oz) whole hazelnuts, skinned
150 g (5 oz) dried figs, stalks removed, thinly sliced
125 ml (5 fl oz) muscat (or other sweet wine)
1 tablespoon margarine
Juice and grated zest of 1 orange
25 g (1 oz) brown breadcrumbs
½ teaspoon freshly grated nutmeg
1 teaspoon ground cinnamon
Pinch of ground cardamom
8 large eating apples (such as Granny Smiths)

To serve:
450 ml (¾ pint) thick yoghurt (soy yoghurt for a *parev* meal)
2 tablespoons clear honey
1 tablespoon ground cinnamon

• Preheat the oven to 200°C/400°F/Gas Mark 6.

- Place the hazelnuts on a baking sheet and toast in the oven for 10 minutes or until golden. Remove and set aside to cool.

- Combine the figs, muscat, margarine, orange zest and juice in a pan. Stir over a medium heat until the mixture boils.

- Roughly chop the hazelnuts and stir them into the fig mixture. Add the breadcrumbs, nutmeg, cinnamon and cardamom.

- Reduce the oven temperature to 180°C/350°F/Gas Mark 4.

- Remove the core from each apple, leaving a wide opening at the top for the filling, and prick the skin with a fork to ensure the apple doesn't split when it is baked. Fill the apples with the fig mixture and stand them in a shallow ovenproof dish. Add 5 tablespoons water, cover with foil and bake in the oven for 30 minutes.

- Remove the foil and continue cooking for about 15 minutes or until the apples are tender.

- Meanwhile, combine the yoghurt and honey.

- To serve, dust individual plates with the cinnamon. Place an apple on each plate and serve hot, topped with a spoonful of the yoghurt and honey mixture.

Iced Pistachio and Poppy Seed Strudel

APPLE STRUDELS ARE especially popular in Ashkenazi households, and Viennese strudel pastry has its own special recipe. When I visited

Vienna I was keen to eat the city's well-known specialities – veal schnitzel and apple strudel – so I found a rather pleasant kosher restaurant. Portions were generous – Jewish style – but the food was so good that leaving any was not an option. Making your own strudel pastry requires skill, but once the process is mastered it is well worth the effort. In this recipe I have used bought filo pastry as it is an excellent alternative.

It is customary to have food containing poppy seeds, fruits and nuts at Purim. Tradition tells us that this is what Esther, the Jewish wife of the king of Persia, ate – they were some of the few ingredients she could obtain that were kosher. Not only do poppy seeds add flavour, they also enhance the appearance of breads, biscuits and cakes, dips and spreads, salads and dressings.

Preparation: 30 minutes
Cooking: 30 minutes
Serves 10–12

800 g (1¾ lb) cooking apples, peeled, sliced and chopped
150 g (5 oz) chopped dates (fresh or dried)
25 g (1 oz) breadcrumbs
110 g (4 oz) soft brown sugar
2 teaspoons ground cinnamon
200 g (7 oz) unsalted butter or margarine
6 sheets of filo pastry
Icing sugar, for dusting

For the icing:
150 g (5 oz) icing sugar
2 tablespoons lemon juice

3 tablespoons poppy seeds
2 tablespoons chopped pistachio nuts

- Preheat the oven to 180°C/350°F/Gas Mark 4. Line a large baking sheet with baking parchment.

- Mix the apples with the dates, breadcrumbs, brown sugar and cinnamon.

- Melt the butter or margarine in a small pan or in a microwave.

- Lay three sheets of the filo pastry side by side on a clean tea towel, overlapping the longest edges by 5 cm (2 in). Brush with a little of the melted butter or margarine. Cover with the remaining sheets of filo, overlapping them as before, and brush with butter or margarine.

- Place the apple mixture on the filo. Using the tea towel, roll the filo from the longest edge to form a thick parcel. Roll it on to the prepared baking sheet and form it into a horseshoe shape. Brush with a little more butter or margarine and dust with icing sugar.

- Bake in the oven for 20 minutes or until golden brown. Leave to cool for 10 minutes.

- For the icing, mix the icing sugar and lemon juice together. The consistency must be quite thick so that the icing sets on top of the strudel. After the strudel has been left to cool for 10 minutes, drizzle the mixture over the strudel and sprinkle with the poppy seeds and pistachios.

- Cut into slices and serve.

Figgy Almond Tart

EATING ON KOL NIDRE is always a rush regardless of when the Yom Kippur fast begins, so it is essential to have a dessert that is quick and easy to prepare. This recipe also works well with plums, apricots and nectarines if preferred – figs can be quite expensive and are seasonal. If any tart is left over, it is delicious with a cup of tea or coffee as part of the buffet meal to break the fast.

The tart is made up like a giant Danish pastry and can be served on its own or with whipped cream or a scoop of ice cream.

❄ ◆

Preparation: 15 minutes
Cooking: 30 minutes
Serves 6

110 g (4 oz) whole almonds
200 g (7 oz) marzipan
1 egg white or 3 tablespoons soy cream
375 g (13 oz) ready-rolled puff pastry (single sheet, thawed if frozen)
1 egg yolk, lightly beaten
50 g (2 oz) ground almonds
6–8 figs, cut into wedges
3 tablespoons flaked almonds
Icing sugar, to serve

- Preheat the oven to 200°C/400°F/Gas Mark 6.

- Place the whole almonds on a baking sheet and toast in the oven for 10 minutes or until golden. Remove and set aside. (Don't turn the oven off.)

- Put the marzipan, egg white or cream and toasted almonds in a food processor and whiz to form a thick paste.
- Line a baking sheet with baking parchment.
- Unroll the pastry and lay it on the baking sheet. Using the tip of a sharp knife, make a border by scoring a line all the way round the pastry about 2.5 cm (1 in) in from the edge. Brush the border with the egg yolk.
- With wet fingers, spread the marzipan paste over the centre of the pastry up to the border. Sprinkle evenly with the ground almonds and arrange the sliced figs so that they cover the marzipan paste. Top with the flaked almonds.
- Bake in the oven for 15–20 minutes or until golden and crispy.
- Dust with icing sugar just before serving.

Chocolate and Date Mousse

CHOCOLATE MOUSSE AND all its variations are always popular on the dessert menu. This particular recipe uses a brandy and date purée whisked into a chocolate and egg mixture. As the chocolate cools it sets the mixture. I like to present the mousse in individual wine glasses – it is impressive and makes serving straightforward. If you wish, you can replace the dates with the same quantity of chopped dried apricots (stones removed).

◈ Ⓟ

Preparation: 20 minutes + soaking
Cooking: 5 minutes + 3 hours chilling
Serves 6

110 g (4 oz) chopped dates
2 tablespoons brandy (kosher for Pesach)
125 g (4½ oz) plain chocolate
2 eggs, separated
50 g (2 oz) caster sugar
100 ml (4 fl oz) whipping cream or Rich's non-dairy cream
50 g (2 oz) grated chocolate, to serve

- Put the dates in a small bowl and cover with the brandy. Leave to soak for a minimum of 2 hours or cover and place in a microwave for 2 minutes.

- Place the dates and brandy in a food processor and whiz to form a paste.

- Melt the chocolate in a double-boiler for about 5 minutes or in a microwave. Remove from the heat and set aside.

- Beat together the egg yolks and sugar. Stir in the melted chocolate and the date and brandy paste. Whip the cream until it holds its shape and add to the chocolate mixture.

- In a clean, grease-free bowl, whisk the egg whites until firm peaks form. Carefully fold them into the chocolate mixture.

- Spoon the mousse into individual glasses or one large bowl and chill in the fridge for a minimum of 3 hours, or overnight.

- Dust with the grated chocolate and serve.

Cakes and Biscuits

NO JEWISH TABLE would be complete without something sweet, and throughout the centuries Jewish bakers have been renowned for their baking skills. Entertaining, especially at home, is a most enjoyable part of Jewish culture; no excuse is needed to put the kettle on and bring out the biscuit tin or cake stand. Kiddush on Shabbat and Yom Tov, *seudah* at Purim or just morning coffee and afternoon tea – there are so many occasions for coffee and cake.

Many of my recipes trace their origins back to local patisseries in countries where Jews settled – the dominant legacy is surely that of the great Austrian and Hungarian bakers of the late nineteenth and early twentieth centuries, with their apple strudels, *mandelbrot* (almond bread) and gateaux. Passover baking is an art – the use of ground nuts and eggs, and *matzah* meal instead of flour, can create the most delicious, unique cakes and biscuits.

Rugelach

THESE SMALL, sweet, crescent-shaped pastries are Ashkenazi in origin and increasingly popular. They are great eaten warm as part of Sunday brunch and noshed on Shabbat for Kiddush or *seudah* (the third meal on Shabbat).

This recipe is slightly unusual as the pastry of the *rugelach* is traditionally made with cream cheese and rolled up like French croissants. Some are made using non-dairy ingredients to keep them *parev*. I also like to make miniature versions as petits four to end a stylish dairy meal. Different fillings can include hazelnuts, chocolate or marzipan.

The pastry dough contains soft cream cheese that blends into the other ingredients, and also cold butter to form the little butter pockets that make the pastry flaky. This rich dough is sticky when mixed, but firms up during chilling and rolls out easily. Be sure to work on just one circle at a time, and keep others refrigerated. Don't overdo the filling as it tends to overflow and will burn on your baking sheet.

Remember to make *rugelach* for Shavuot when dairy is traditionally eaten.

❄

Preparation: 40 minutes + 3 hours chilling
Cooking: 20–25 minutes
Makes 24 rugelach

225 g (8 oz) unsalted butter
225 g (8 oz) cream cheese
400 g (14 oz) plain flour, plus extra for dusting
¼ teaspoon salt
1 teaspoon vanilla essence

I egg yolk, lightly beaten
2 tablespoons ground cinnamon
2 tablespoons caster sugar

For the filling:
50 g (2 oz) light brown sugar
2 tablespoons grated lemon zest
110 g (4 oz) walnuts or pecans
110 g (4 oz) raisins
I tablespoon ground cinnamon
6 tablespoons apricot jam

- Place the butter, cheese, flour, salt and vanilla essence in a food processor and combine to form a dough. Add extra flour if it seems too wet.

- Remove the dough from the food processor, cover with cling film and chill in the refrigerator for 3 hours.

- Preheat the oven to 180°C/350°F/Gas Mark 4. Line a baking sheet with baking parchment.

- For the filling, mix the sugar, lemon zest, walnuts or pecans, raisins and cinnamon together.

- Divide the pastry dough into four balls. On a lightly floured work surface, roll each ball out into a circle about 18 cm (7 in) in diameter and 5 mm (¼ in) thick. Using a knife, cut the circle into six triangular wedges.

- Spread a thin layer of the jam over each triangle, then add about I teaspoon of the filling over the jam. Roll up the triangles, starting with the wider curved end. Curve the crescents slightly, and place them on the prepared baking sheet and brush with the egg yolk. Bake for 20–25 minutes until golden brown.

- Mix the cinnamon and sugar together and sprinkle them over the warm *rugelach*.

Kiddush Jam Biscuits

DESPITE THEIR NAME, these biscuits are a sweet treat to be enjoyed by everyone at any time. They do look pretty on the Kiddush table, but fit equally well into a lunch box. They taste better after a couple of days as the jam softens them slightly.

These biscuits are great fun to make with children as little fingers enjoy rolling, stamping and spreading. I have used differently shaped cutters for their tops simply for variety and appearance.

Preparation: 20 minutes + 2 hours chilling
Cooking: 15 minutes
Makes 20 biscuits

300 g (11 oz) plain flour, plus extra for dusting
200 g (7 oz) margarine or butter
110 g (4 oz) caster sugar
1 egg
2 teaspoons vanilla essence
110 g (4 oz) blackcurrant or raspberry jam
2 tablespoons icing sugar, for dusting

- Place the flour, margarine or butter, caster sugar, egg and vanilla essence in a food processor and whiz to form a dough. Add 2 teaspoons water if the mixture is dry. The dough should leave the bowl clean.

- Remove the dough from the bowl, wrap with cling film and flatten. Chill in the fridge for 2 hours.

- Preheat the oven to 180°C/350°F/Gas Mark 4. Line two baking sheets with baking parchment.

- Lightly dust a work surface with flour. Cut the dough in half. Roll out one of the halves to a thickness of 3 mm (⅛ in). Use a 5 cm (2 in) cutter to stamp out circles and place them on one of the baking sheets.

- Roll out the remaining half to the same thickness and use the 5 cm (2 in) cutter to stamp out circles. Now use a 2 cm (¾ in) fancy cutter to stamp inner circles out of these circles. Put them on the second baking sheet.

- Transfer both baking sheets to the oven and bake for 15 minutes until golden.

- Leave to cool for 15 minutes. Spread the jam on the 5 cm (2 in) biscuits. Sit the 2 cm (¾ in) biscuits on top like a sandwich. Dust with the icing sugar.

Orange and Almond Cake
with Orange Cream

IT IS ALWAYS difficult to find suitable low-fat desserts other than fruit. This recipe contains no fat and transforms everyday ingredients into something delicious. The secret of its divine flavour is simmering two whole oranges for 1¼ hours and then incorporating them with the other ingredients.

This recipe also ticks all the boxes for a versatile cake: it can be made in advance, it is *parev* – and it is ideal for Pesach, when I omit the orange cream and it also makes a good dessert. It is the perfect finish to a Seder or Yom Tov meal – to turn it into 'afters', serve it with a ready-made sorbet (orange or lemon) or a *parev* ice cream (chocolate goes well with the orange and almond flavours.) During the rest of the year, I like to serve it topped with thick yoghurt mixed with icing sugar and a teaspoon of orange juice or an orange liqueur like Cointreau.

There are three basic varieties of orange. The sweet ones – Valencia and blood oranges are popular – are large and juicy but it is more difficult to remove their skins. Sour oranges, known as bitter oranges, are mainly used in cooking or for orange liqueurs where their essential oils and peel are often important ingredients. Loose-skinned oranges are sweet, and peel and segment easily. Always choose oranges that are heavy, firm and evenly shaped with smooth skins. As with lemons and limes, thicker skinned oranges give less juice. To maximise the amount juice from any citrus fruit, place it in a microwave on high for 1 minute before juicing.

Valued for their rich vitamin C content, oranges originated in Southeast Asia and are grown in warm-climate areas across the world, including Israel, North America, Africa, Spain and Portugal. The United States is the world's largest producer of oranges.

Preparation: 20 minutes + cooling
Cooking: 2 hours 15 minutes
Serves 8–10

2 large oranges
200 g (7 oz) caster sugar
6 eggs
200 g (7 oz) ground almonds
1 teaspoon almond essence
1 teaspoon baking powder
3 tablespoons split almonds

For the orange cream:
250 g (9 oz) thick plain yoghurt
2 tablespoons icing sugar, plus extra for dusting
Grated zest and juice of ½ orange
1 teaspoon Cointreau (more if desired)

- Put the oranges in a pan and cover with cold water. Bring to the boil, then reduce the heat and simmer, covered, for 1¼ hours. Top up with more water if necessary.

- Preheat the oven to 150°C/300°F/Gas Mark 2. Line a loose-based 20 cm (8 in) cake tin with baking parchment.

- Remove the oranges from the water and leave to cool a little. Using a sharp knife, carefully remove and discard the skin and pith. Cut each orange in half removing any pips. Place in a food processor with the sugar, eggs, ground almonds, almond essence and baking powder and whiz until smooth.

- Transfer the mixture to the prepared cake tin, sprinkle with the split almonds and bake for 1½ hours. Cover with foil if the top of the cake starts to burn.

- Leave to cool, then cut into slices.

- For the orange cream, combine the yoghurt with the sugar, orange juice and zest and Cointreau.

- Dust individual plates with icing sugar and serve slices of the cake with a generous spoonful of the orange cream.

NOTE: The cake can be made a day in advance and refrigerated.

Date and Nut Mandelbrot

FANCY COFFEE (latte, cappuccino, etc.) with a nutty crunchy biscuit is a modern morning or afternoon treat. When you munch on your *'biscotti'* you are eating something very close to the double-baked classic Jewish *mandelbrot* (almond bread) made for hundreds of years.

Sephardi Jews transported *mandelbrot* from their home countries to Spain and created a version that used anise, almonds and sesame seeds. The variations are endless: chocolate, hazelnut, walnut, raisin, cranberry, blueberry or even coconut. If you wish, you can choose your favourite ingredient and substitute it for the dates, walnuts or almonds.

Preparation: 15 minutes + 10 minutes cooling
Cooking: 40 minutes
Makes 72 slices approx.

450 g (1 lb) plain flour, plus extra for dusting
3 eggs
225 g (8 oz) sugar
Grated zest of 1 orange
1 teaspoon vanilla essence

1 teaspoon baking powder
110 g (4 oz) chopped dates
110 g (4 oz) chopped walnuts
110 g (4 oz) roughly chopped almonds

- Preheat the oven to 180°C/350°F/Gas Mark 4. Line a baking sheet with baking parchment.

- Place the flour, eggs, sugar, orange zest, vanilla essence and baking powder in a food processor and combine. Add the dates, walnuts and almonds and process until a dough has formed. Add extra flour if the dough is too wet.

- Divide the dough into three equal portions. On a floured work surface roll each portion into a 30 x 5 cm (12 x 2 in) log. Place the portions 5 cm (2 in) apart on the prepared baking sheet and bake for 25 minutes until golden.

- Cool the logs for 10 minutes then transfer them to a chopping board. Using a serrated knife, cut each log diagonally into 24 equal slices. Place the slices, cut sides down so it is flat facing upwards on the baking sheet.

- Reduce the oven temperature to 150°C/300°F/Gas Mark 2 and bake for a final 15 minutes or until the slices are lightly crusty on top.

- Cool on a wire rack before serving.

Pistachio, Almond and Hazelnut Cigars

MOROCCAN AND TUNISIAN Jews make these sweet filo pastries for festivals and family celebrations. The aromatic blend of roasted nuts and orange flower water or rose water is delightful – you will find both waters in the baking section of large supermarkets or in specialist grocery shops.

On a health note, pistachios, like all nuts, are an excellent source of protein. Unsalted ones have a high-potassium, low-sodium content, which helps to normalise blood pressure, maintain water balance in the body and strengthen muscles. Pistachios are also a good source of vitamin E, which boosts the immune system and alleviates fatigue. However, the salted variety should be eaten in moderation as too much sodium is not so good for you.

Preparation: 40 minutes
Cooking: 15 minutes
Makes 40 pastries

50 g (2 oz) hazelnuts, toasted
75 g (3 oz) split almonds, toasted
50 g (2 oz) pistachio nuts
1 egg, separated
25 g (1 oz) sugar
1 teaspoon orange flower water or rose water
5 sheets of filo pastry (50 x 24 cm/20 x 9½ in)
75 g (3 oz) unsalted butter or margarine, melted
Icing sugar, for dusting

- Preheat the oven to 200°C/400°F/Gas Mark 6. Line two baking sheets with baking parchment.

- Place the hazelnuts, almonds, pistachios, egg yolk, sugar and orange flower or rose water in a food processor and whiz to a thick paste.

- Cut each sheet of filo into eight rectangles, approximately 9 x 7.5 cm (3½ x 3 in), and cover with a clean damp cloth or cling film.

- Brush one of the rectangles with some of the egg white and spread 1 teaspoon of the nut paste along the short end. Fold the long sides slightly in over the paste and roll up the rectangle from the filled end. Place on one of the prepared baking sheets with the seam underneath and brush with some of the melted butter.

- Repeat with the remaining pastry rectangles and paste; keep the spare filo covered as you go, as it does dry out quickly.

- Bake for 15 minutes or until the pastries are crisp and golden. Transfer to a wire rack to cool.

- Dust with icing sugar just before serving.

Florentines

THE JEWISH COMMUNITY in Florence decreased greatly during the Second World War and today the community of 1000 has two synagogues. Although small, they are extremely active. These famous nutty biscuits are said to be a gift from Florence. The thin layer of chocolate over their undersides makes them taste positively decadent. I have made them with almonds and candied peel but other nuts like walnuts and hazelnuts can be substituted.

Keep this recipe for Purim when it is customary to send sweet gifts to friends, family and the less fortunate members of the community. This tradition, known as *mishloach manot* (sending portions), is still practiced today, when gifts of two different foods are wrapped and presented in little baskets.

❄ Ⓟ (omit chocolate)

Preparation: 15 minutes
Cooking: 10–12 minutes
Makes 25

75 g (3 oz) unsalted butter or margarine
85 g (3½ oz) golden syrup
150 g (5 oz) almonds, roughly chopped
110 g (4 oz) sultanas
50 g (2 oz) glacé cherries, chopped
50 g (2 oz) candied peel
25 g (1 oz) plain flour
110 g (4 oz) chocolate (plain, milk or white, or a combination)

- Preheat the oven to 180°C/350°F/Gas Mark 4. Line two baking sheets with baking parchment.

- In a medium-size pan, melt 50 g (2 oz) of the butter or margarine with the golden syrup over a low heat, stirring, until the syrup has dissolved in the butter. Add the almonds, sultanas, cherries and candied peel. Stir in the flour – add more if the mixture is too runny.

- Drop tablespoons of the mixture on to the prepared baking sheet, about 5 cm (2 in) apart, and flatten them slightly. Bake for 10–12 minutes or until golden and crisp.

- Remove the baking sheets from the oven and leave the florentines to cool until they are firm enough to be taken off the sheets without breaking, then transfer them to a wire rack to cool further.

- Place the chocolate in a bowl with the remaining butter or margarine and heat over a pan of simmering water, stirring, until melted and combined.

- When the florentines are completely cool, spread the flat side of each one with 1 teaspoon of the melted chocolate. Use a fork to draw wavy lines on the chocolate.

- Leave, chocolate sides up, until the chocolate has cooled, then store in the refrigerator.

Almond and Cream Cheese Sponge Cake

HISTORICALLY, EATING A slice of cake or a bun between meals filled you up when times were hard and main meals were low in nutritional value. When times were good Jewish baking could resemble an art form, especially in Austria where patisserie was amazing in its appearance, taste and form.

Nowadays, we need something traditional to have with coffee. This cake uses almonds, cream cheese and typical Jewish store-cupboard ingredients, and can be made in no time at all.

Almond (*sheked* in Hebrew) means 'the awakening one' or, literally, 'to be wakeful' because the almond tree was the first tree to awake from the sleep of winter and blossom. Almonds are mentioned six times in the Old Testament. The first reference is in Genesis 43 where Jacob, in an apparent attempt to gain favour with Egypt's ruler, orders his sons to take the pharaoh some of the 'best products of the land' including almonds.

This sponge cake can also be served as a dessert, with ice cream or custard.

❄

Preparation: 20 minutes
Cooking: 45 minutes

150 g (5 oz) unsalted butter or margarine, plus
1 tablespoon for greasing
175 g (6 oz) caster sugar
3 eggs
200 g (7 oz) self-raising flour
250 g (9 oz) light cream cheese, plain yoghurt or non-dairy
cream cheese
125 g (4½ oz) ground almonds
½ teaspoon almond essence

For the syrup:
250 g (9 oz) caster sugar
Juice of ½ lemon

- Preheat the oven to 180°C/350°F/Gas Mark 4. Grease a rectangular tin, approximately 30 x 25 cm (12 x 10 in), with margarine and line it with baking parchment.
- Cream the butter or margarine with the sugar until light and fluffy.

Add the eggs, one at a time, adding 1 tablespoon of the flour with the second egg and with the third egg. Mix in the cream cheese or yoghurt. Fold in the remaining flour, and the ground almonds and almond essence.

- Turn the mixture into the prepared tin and bake for 40 minutes or until the centre springs back when lightly pressed.

- To make the syrup, heat the sugar with 150 ml (¼ pint) water over a low heat, stirring, until the sugar has dissolved. Bring to the boil and simmer for 2 minutes, then add the lemon juice.

- Remove the cake from the oven and pour the syrup over it. Leave in the tin until cool. If there is more syrup than you need, keep it and pour it over the sliced cake.

Poppy Seed Roll

THIS IS ONE of those cakes that features in most Eastern European Jewish patisseries, particularly during Purim when nuts and seeds are favoured. This recipe makes the best sweet bread! It's tender, fluffy and tastes wonderful. It is made like any other bread, but has a higher yeast content to compensate for the quantities of sugar and milk. My recipe makes four rolled cakes or bread loaves, and although this sounds a lot they do freeze beautifully.

Alternative fillings like 250 g (9 oz) mixed chopped nuts (pistachios, walnuts and almonds, for example) combined with 125 g (4 ½ oz) icing sugar, or 125 g (4 ½ oz) cocoa powder with 125 g (4 ½ oz) icing sugar are delicious.

❄️ Ⓟ (use soya milk and non-dairy margarine)

Preparation: 25 minutes + 2 hours rising
Cooking: 20 minutes
Makes 4 rolls (each roll serves 8–10 people)

2 x 7 g (2 tablespoons) sachets dried yeast
570 ml (1 pint) warm milk (or soya milk for a *parev* option)
1 kg (2¼ lb) strong flour, plus extra for dusting
3 eggs
75 g (3 oz) sugar
1 teaspoon salt
200 ml (8 fl oz) vegetable oil
110 g (4 oz) margarine, melted (non-dairy for a *parev* option)
Icing sugar, for dusting

For the poppy seed filling:
400 g (14 oz) poppy seeds
200 g (7 oz) icing sugar
2 tablespoons milk (soya milk for a *parev* option)

- Dissolve the yeast in 2 tablespoons of the warm milk and leave for 5 minutes until frothy.

- In a large mixing bowl, combine the flour, eggs, sugar, salt, 100 ml (4 fl oz) of the oil, and the margarine, yeast mixture and remaining milk in a bowl. Using a dough hook, if available, knead the dough for 8 minutes until it is smooth and shiny. Alternatively, work the dough with your hands for 8–10 minutes.

- Remove the dough from the bowl and knead it by hand for 2 minutes, then shape it into a ball. Grease a bowl with 1 tablespoon of the oil.

Place the dough in the bowl, cover with cling film and leave to rise in a warm place for 2 hours.

- Knock back the dough and divide it into four pieces.

- Preheat the oven to 200°C/400°F/Gas Mark 6. Line two baking sheets with baking parchment.

- On a lightly floured work surface, roll each piece out to make a rectangle roughly 35 cm (14 in) long, 22 cm (9 in) wide and 5 mm (¼ in) thick.

- For the poppy seed filling, mix the poppy seeds with the icing sugar and milk.

- Brush the surface of each rectangle with 1 tablespoon of the oil. Spread with a quarter of the filling and roll the dough up like a Swiss roll.

- Put two rolls on each baking sheet, brush with some of the remaining oil and bake for 20 minutes.

- Once the rolls are cooked, brush the tops with more oil and dust with icing sugar.

- Cut the rolls into slices and serve warm or cold.

NOTE: I like to make two rolls with the poppy seed filling and two with a chocolate or nut filling (see age 295).

Honey Apple Cake

ONE OF THE many traditions at Rosh Hashanah is to dip sliced apples into honey in the hope that the forthcoming year will be filled with sweetness. I decided I would combine these two favourite ingredients in a delicious cake that is ideal both for tea and as a dessert. The result is subtly spiced, and mouth-wateringly sweet. I bake this in a round pan, symbolic of the hoped-for fullness in the New Year. This cake can be served not only on Rosh Hashanah but throughout the year.

I have used my favourite orange blossom honey; an all-round honey, it has an exceptional taste and is great in tea, or spread on breads or biscuits – however you choose to use it. It is often from a combination of sources, and is usually light in colour and mild in flavour, with a fresh scent and light citrus taste. Orange blossom honey is produced in Florida, southern California and parts of Texas.

Preparation: 25 minutes
Cooking: 1¼ hours
Serves 8–10

340 g (12 oz) orange blossom honey
4 tablespoons apple juice
Juice and grated zest of 1 large orange
4 tablespoons vegetable oil, plus extra for greasing
120 ml (4½ fl oz) strong coffee
3 eggs
300 g (11 oz) plain flour
1 teaspoon bicarbonate of soda
2 teaspoons baking powder
2 teaspoons ground cinnamon
2 apples, peeled and roughly chopped
110 g (4 oz) raisins
Icing sugar, for dusting

- Preheat the oven to 180°C/350°F/Gas Mark 4. Grease a 25 cm (10 in) cake tin and line it with baking parchment.
- Whisk together the honey, apple juice, orange juice and zest, oil, coffee and eggs until well combined.
- Mix the flour, bicarbonate of soda, baking powder and cinnamon in a separate bowl then gradually add the dry mixture to the wet ingredients. Stir in the apples and raisins.
- Bake for 1¼ hours or until the centre is firm to the touch.
- Invert the cake on to a serving plate and dust with icing sugar.

Passover Apple Squares

OVER PASSOVER I am always looking for something different to cook that is quick and easy to make. I find that apple recipes are always popular, especially if they are *parev* and can be made in advance. This recipe is similar to one for apple clafoutis, a cake mixture cooked in an egg and *matzah* meal batter. Pears and fresh apricots can be used instead of apples.

Note that the squares have the advantage of being nut-free. At Pesach I feel especially sorry for anyone who has an allergy to nuts, because so many recipes, whether for sweet or savoury dishes, use them. The squares are delicious for tea or as a dessert.

Preparation: 20 minutes
Cooking: 45 minutes
Makes 16 squares

1 tablespoon margarine, for greasing
225 g (8 oz) sugar
2 teaspoons ground cinnamon
½ teaspoon salt
200 g (7 oz) fine *matzah* meal or cake meal
5 eggs, separated
100 ml (4 fl oz) vegetable oil
Juice and grated zest of 1 lemon
2 large dessert apples, peeled, cored and thinly sliced
Icing sugar, for dusting

- Preheat the oven to 190°C/375°F/Gas Mark 5. Line the base of a 20 cm (8 in) square tin with baking parchment and grease the sides with the margarine.

- In a bowl, combine the sugar, cinnamon, salt and *matzah* or cake meal. Add the egg yolks, oil and lemon zest and juice and whisk until the mixture is thick.

- In a clean, grease-free bowl, whisk the egg whites until stiff, then fold them into the egg yolk mixture.

- Pour half the batter into the prepared tin and cover batter with the apples. Cover the apples with the remaining batter and bake for 45 minutes until the mixture is firm and set in the middle.

- Leave to cool, then cut into 16 squares.

- To serve, stack the squares up high and dust them with icing sugar.

Banana and Walnut Muffins

THESE MUFFINS ARE delicious at any time: straight out of the oven, as a dessert with custard or ice cream, in packed lunches or as a treat for the children when they come home from school. They also make an excellent energy-packed quick breakfast – good for late risers and reluctant early morning eaters. I like to make double the quantity and freeze one batch for another time.

For the best results, mix the dry and wet ingredients together only until no dry lumps remain. The mixture should not be light or smooth. When cooking with bananas, remember that ripeness equals sweetness and depth of flavour; a cake or muffin made with under-ripe fruit will lack true banana character. This is a perfect recipe if the bananas in the fruit bowl are beginning to turn. It is also a great one for young children to make, with help, as it is so quick and easy.

Preparation: 15 minutes
Cooking: 30 minutes
Makes 15

350 g (12 oz) plain flour
2 teaspoons baking powder
1 teaspoon bicarbonate of soda
Pinch of salt
200 g (7 oz) chopped walnuts
110 g (4 oz) caster sugar
3 eggs, lightly beaten
120 ml (4½ fl oz) vegetable oil
110 g (4 oz) clear honey
5 large bananas, mashed

- Preheat the oven to 190°C/375°F/Gas Mark 5. Line a muffin tin with 15 paper muffin cases.

- In a large bowl, combine the flour, baking powder, bicarbonate of soda, salt, walnuts and sugar. In a separate bowl, combine the eggs, oil, honey and bananas. Mix the wet ingredients into the dry mixture and stir until combined. Do not overwork the mixture as it is better for it to have some texture.

- Spoon the mixture into the paper cases, filling each one three-quarters full, and bake for 30 minutes or until the muffins are well-risen, golden brown and not sticky in the centre.

- Remove the muffins from the cases and cool on a wire rack.

Almond Brownies

THESE FUDGE-LIKE brownies are really delicious as part of an afternoon tea during Chanukah, the festival when the popular story of Judith is told. She was a brave Jewess who slew Holofernes, an Assyrian general who threatened to destroy the Israelites. She allegedly seduced him and fed him salty cheese. This made him thirsty so he drank too much wine – and once he was in a drunken sleep Judith cut off his head and ended his tyranny. So cheese-based food is eaten at Chanukah to recall this event.

These almond brownies are also great as part of a lunch-box meal, a snack on the run or a treat with a cup of coffee. They are different from the classic recipe as they are made with low-fat cream cheese, which gives them a wonderful fudge-like texture. They are extremely moreish, so making a double quantity and freezing the second batch might prove useful. Serve them with single cream.

Preparation: 15 minutes
Cooking: 20 minutes
Makes 20

400 g (14 oz) light low-fat cream cheese
200 g (7 oz) light muscovado or soft brown sugar
50 g (2 oz) cocoa powder
2 eggs
2 teaspoons almond essence
2 tablespoons ground almonds
110 g (4 oz) plain flour, sifted
2 tablespoons flaked almonds
2 tablespoons icing sugar

- Preheat the oven to 180°C/350°F/Gas Mark 4. Line a 22 cm (9 in) square tin with baking parchment.

- In a large bowl, combine the cheese with the sugar. Add the cocoa powder, eggs, almond essence, ground almonds and flour and beat well.

- Pour the mixture into the prepared tin, sprinkle with the almonds and bake for 20 minutes until firm to the touch.

- Remove from the oven and leave to cool in the tin.

- To serve, dust with the icing sugar and cut into 20 squares.

Hazelnut Plum Dessert Cake with Hazelnut Cream

PLUMS ARE AT their best at Succot and this is a delicious dessert that uses simple ingredients. I am lucky enough to have a plum tree in the garden so I always make two cakes – one for now and one for the freezer.

The many varieties of plum that are available vary in colour, size and shape. The most popular are Victoria, Mirabelle and Santa Rosa. Sweet plums can be eaten raw on their own or added to fruit salads. All varieties can be cooked – they can be stewed, used in pies, puddings and preserves, and, of course, dried or used as below.

This cake is very light and is an ideal dessert after a filling Friday night or Yom Tov meal. It also works well in individual ramekins, which will only need 20 minutes in the oven.

❄ Ⓟ (use soy cream)
Preparation: 30 minutes
Cooking: 40 minutes
Serves 8–10

4 eggs
150 g (5 oz) caster sugar
Grated zest of 1 lemon
150 g (5 oz) plain flour
1 teaspoon baking powder
Pinch of salt
110 g (4 oz) unsalted butter or margarine, melted, plus extra for greasing
575 g (1¼ lb) plums, stoned and sliced
75 g (3 oz) toasted hazelnuts, roughly chopped

To decorate:
I tablespoon vanilla sugar
Zest of I lemon, cut into very fine strips

For the hazelnut cream:
300 ml (½ pint) whipping cream or soy cream
I 10 g (4 oz) toasted hazelnuts, roughly chopped

- Preheat the oven to 180°C/350°F/Gas Mark 4. Grease a 22 cm (9 in) spring-form tin and line it with baking parchment.

- Whisk the eggs, sugar and lemon zest together until the mixture is thick and mousse-like. The whisk should leave a trail.

- Sift the flour, baking powder and salt over the mixture, then fold them in gently. Slowly drizzle in the melted butter or margarine from the side of the bowl and fold in gently with a metal spoon. Carefully stir in the plums and nuts.

- Spoon the mixture into the prepared tin, level the surface and bake for 40 minutes or until firm to the touch.

- Allow the cake to cool for 10 minutes then invert it on to a wire rack. Turn the cake the right way up.

- While the cake is cooling, make the hazelnut cream. Whisk the cream until thick then add the hazelnuts.

- Dust the cake with the vanilla sugar and decorate it with the lemon zest. Cut it into thick slices and serve each portion with a large spoonful of the hazelnut cream.

NOTES: The cake can be made a day in advance. To toast the hazelnuts, place them on a baking sheet and cook in an oven preheated to 200°C/400°F/Gas Mark 6 for 10 minutes until golden.

Cheesecake:
A Shavuot Tradition

SHAVUOT COMMEMORATES THE giving of the Torah and is the time of the year when it is traditional to eat dairy produce and dairy-based meals. There are some interesting reasons for this custom.

When the Jews accepted the Torah they became obligated to the laws of *kashrut*. But until they were familiar with the ones regarding animal slaughter they ate dairy. Receiving the Torah was a form of rebirth for the Children of Israel and drinking milk is a link to this renewal. Shavuot coincided with the time when lambs and calves born in the spring would be suckling. Therefore an abundance of dairy products was available.

In the Torah the Jewish people are promised a 'land flowing with milk and honey' and dairy meals recall this lyrical description of Israel. The Hebrew word for milk, *chalav*, has the numerical value of 40, symbolising the number of days Moses was on Mt Sinai; legend has it that the Jewish people were at Sinai for so long that all their fresh milk soured and turned into cheese.

Cheesecake is a particular favourite during Shavuot – not that we particularly need a religious reason to enjoy it; I can't believe how popular this dish has become, in both the Jewish and wider communities. Frozen and fresh cheesecakes are in every supermarket in every possible flavour. All restaurants seem to feature some version as a dessert and no afternoon tea is complete without a slice of cheesecake. The best recipes are tried, tested, served at room temperature and rich without being heavy.

Vanilla and Lemon Cheesecake

THIS RECIPE CAN be used at Passover if you change the base to *plava*, a Pesach sponge cake, and the cornflour to potato flour. I have used vanilla as the main source of flavour. Vanilla pods are the long, thin, dried, black seed pods of an orchid and are sold whole. Alternatively, you can buy a natural vanilla extract or an essence. To make vanilla sugar, simply leave a pod in a jar of caster sugar. To flavour custards, sweet sauces, ice creams and other creamy desserts, infuse a whole or split pod in the milk or cream. After infusing, it can be rinsed, dried and used again.

Ⓟ (substitute potato flour for cornflour)
Preparation: 20 minutes
Cooking: 30 minutes
Serves 8

50 g (2 oz) soft margarine, plus 1 tablespoon for greasing
10 trifle sponge bases, sliced
675 g (1½ lb) cream cheese
90 g (3¼ oz) caster sugar
1 tablespoon vanilla sugar
Juice and grated zest of 1 lemon
1 teaspoon vanilla essence
2 eggs, separated
1 tablespoon cornflour (potato flour for Passover)
150 ml (¼ pint) double cream
Grated zest of 1 lemon and vanilla sugar, to decorate
**Thick yoghurt and vanilla seeds or ready-made vanilla
  yoghurt, to serve**

- Preheat the oven to 190°C/375°F/Gas Mark 5. Grease a loose-based 22 cm (9 in) cake tin with margarine and line it with baking parchment.

- Arrange the sponge slices on the base of the tin, overlapping them where necessary.

- Put the cheese, all but 1 tablespoon of the caster sugar, and the vanilla sugar, lemon juice and zest, and the vanilla essence into a mixing bowl. Add the margarine, egg yolks, cornflour and, finally, the cream. Whisk together until smooth.

- In a clean, grease-free bowl whisk the egg whites until they form soft peaks. Add the remaining caster sugar. Carefully fold the egg whites into the cheese mixture.

- Pour the mixture over the sponge base and bake for 30 minutes or until the cheesecake is set around the edges and slightly brown.

- Turn off the oven but leave the cheesecake inside it to cool for 2 hours, then transfer to the fridge.

- To serve, remove the cheesecake from the tin and decorate with the lemon zest and vanilla sugar. Serve with yoghurt mixed with vanilla seeds or vanilla yoghurt.

Chocolate Macaroon Cake

CHOCOLATE AND ALMONDS are popular ingredients for Passover, the time when most people bake. Bought cakes and biscuits are rather expensive for the small quantities that you get. This recipe uses store-cupboard ingredients and produces a big cake that keeps well in an airtight container and can be frozen.

Some culinary historians claim that macaroons can be traced to an Italian monastery and came to France in 1533 with the pastry chefs of Catherine de Medici, wife of Henry II. Two Benedictine nuns, Sister Marguerite and Sister Marie-Elisabeth, seeking asylum in the town of Nancy during the French Revolution (1789–99), paid for their housing by baking and selling macaroons, and thus became known as the 'macaroon sisters.'

Italian Jews adopted the macaroon-style biscuit because it contains no flour, uses egg white as a leavening agent and can be enjoyed during the eight-day observation of Passover. It was introduced to other European Jews and became popular as a year-round sweet. Over time, coconut, chocolate and other nuts were added to the ground almonds. Other Pesach biscuits can be used instead of the almond macaroons.

❋ ◈ ◉

Preparation: 25 minutes
Cooking: 40 minutes
Serves 10

200 g (7 oz) margarine, plus extra for greasing
150 g (5 oz) cake meal, plus extra for dusting
150 g (5 oz) almond macaroons
110 g (4 oz) plain chocolate, broken into chunks
200 g (7 oz) caster sugar
1 teaspoon almond essence
5 eggs, separated
200 g (7 oz) toasted sliced almonds
Icing sugar, for dusting
Raspberries and fresh mint leaves, to decorate

- Preheat the oven to 180°C/350°F/Gas Mark 4. Line a 22 cm (9 in) loose-based cake tin with baking parchment and grease with margarine. Dust with cake meal and shake out any excess.

- Put the macaroons in a food processor and whiz to form crumbs. Reserve 3 tablespoons for the topping.

- Place the chocolate in a bowl with 1 tablespoon water and heat over a pan of simmering water, stirring, until melted.

- Cream the margarine with all but 2 tablespoons of the sugar and the almond essence. Add the egg yolks one at a time, followed by the cake meal and macaroon crumbs. Stir in the chocolate and toasted almonds.

- In a clean, grease-free bowl whisk the egg whites until stiff but not dry. Add the 2 tablespoons sugar and whisk again. Fold 1 tablespoon of the egg whites into the chocolate mixture, then fold in the remaining whites.

- Spoon the mixture into the prepared cake tin, sprinkle with the reserved macaroon crumbs and bake for about 40 minutes or until a skewer inserted in the centre comes out clean.

- Allow the cake to cool for 10 minutes, then invert it on to a serving plate and remove the paper.

- To serve, dust with icing sugar and decorate with raspberries and mint leaves.

NOTE: To toast the almonds, place them on a baking sheet and cook in an oven preheated to 200°C/400°F/Gas Mark 6 for 10 minutes until golden.

Glossary

Ashkenazi: Jews from Eastern France, Germany and Eastern Europe, and their descendants. Most Jews in America are Ashkenazi. The word Ashkenazi is derived from the Hebrew word for Germany.

Gemmara: A commentary on the Mishnah (the first written record of the Oral Torah); it forms the second part of the Talmud.

Halachic: The legal part of Talmudic literature; an interpretation of the laws of the Scriptures.

Hassidic: An Orthodox Jewish movement which originated in Eastern Europe (what is now Belarus and Ukraine) in the eighteenth century. Rabbi Israel ben Eliezer (1698–1760), also known as the Ba'al Shem Tov founded Hassidic Judaism. It originated in a time of persecution of the Jewish people, when European Jews had turned inward to Talmud study; many felt that most expressions of Jewish life had become too academic and that they no longer had any emphasis on spirituality or joy.

Kiddush: The Blessing or sanctification made over wine on Friday night, before Shabbat lunch and on festivals. It also refers to the wide range of light sweet and savoury delicacies served buffet style after the synagogue service.

Kishke: Yiddish word for intestine. The Jewish (specifically Ashkenazi) *kishke* is traditionally made from a kosher beef intestine stuffed with *matzah* meal, rendered fat (*schmaltz*) and spices. The cooked *kishke* can range in colour from grey-white to brownish-orange, depending on how much paprika is used. In recent times edible synthetic casings often replace the beef intestines; home cooks also often use kosher poultry neck skin to stand in for the intestines.

Knish: Yiddish word for potato and flour dumpling stuffed with potato and onion, chopped liver or cheese.

Kol Nidre: The evening service of Yom Kippur, and named after the prayer that begins the service.

Kosher: Hebrew word that describes Jewish dietary laws. From a root meaning fit, proper or correct. Jewish dietary laws are the laws of *kashrut* and describe food that is permissible to eat. Kosher can also be used to describe any other ritual that is fit for use according to Jewish law.

Kugel: Yiddish word for pudding. A casserole of grated potatoes, eggs and onion, or a dessert of noodles, fruits and nuts in an egg-based pudding.

Mizrachi: Jews from the Middle East. The word 'Mizrachi' is derived from the Hebrew word for Eastern.

Parev: Yiddish word for neutral. It is used to describe kosher foods that contain neither meat nor dairy and therefore can be eaten with either. Fish, fruit and vegetables are all *parev*.

Pesach: One of the Shalosh R'galim (three pilgrimage festivals), a holiday commemorating the Exodus from Egypt, known in English as Passover. Also marks the beginning of the harvest season.

Pesach Friendly: In the context of *New Flavours Of The Jewish Table* this means that the recipe uses ingredients that are available and appropriate for use over the eight days of Passover.

Plava: Plain sponge cake often flavoured with zest of lemon or almond essence. It is popular over Passover.

Purim: A spring holiday celebrating the rescue of the Jews from extermination at the hands of the chief minister to the king of Persia.

Rosh Hashanah: Jewish New Year, occurring in September or October.

Seder: Yiddish word for order. It refers to the festival meal eaten on the night of Pesach, because what is eaten and the ceremonies performed at this meal follow a precise order.

Sephardi: Jews from Spain, Portugal, North Africa and the Middle East and their descendants. The word Sephardi is derived from the Hebrew word for Spain.

Seudah or Seudah Shlishit: The Hebrew and Yiddish word for the third meal customarily eaten by Sabbath-observing Jews on Shabbat.

Shabbat: The seventh day of the week on which God rested from His creation of the world. A day of rest, spiritual enrichment and good food.

Shavuot: The Jewish Festival when we celebrate the giving of the Ten Commandments to Moses on Mount Sinai. That is why this holiday is called Z' man Matan Torahtenu – the Time of the Giving of Our Law.

Simchat Torah: A joyous holiday celebrating the end and beginning of the annual cycle of weekly Torah readings.

Succah: The temporary dwellings we eat in during the holiday of Succot. In Israel observant Jews also sleep in them.

Succot: One of the three pilgrimage festivals, it commemorates the wandering in the desert and the final harvest. Succot is called the The Time of our Rejoicing and during the festival it is a *mitzvah* (Hebrew for good deed) to sit in a *succah*, and to eat all our meals there. Each day we also wave the Four Species of plants, in celebration of God's gift of the bounty.

Sumac: This spice comes from the berries of a bush that grows wild in all Mediterranean areas, especially in Sicily and southern Italy, and parts of the Middle East, notably Iran. It is an essential ingredient in Arabic cooking, being preferred to lemon for sourness and astringency.

Talmud: The most significant collection of the Jewish oral tradition interpreting the Torah.

Torah: In its narrowest sense, the Torah is the first five books of the Bible: Genesis, Exodus, Leviticus, Numbers and Deuteronomy, sometimes called the Pentateuch. In its broadest sense, Torah is the entire body of Jewish teachings.

Yemenite Jews: The Jews of the Middle Eastern country of Yemen, whose customs and practices are somewhat different than those of Ashkenazi or Sephardi Jews.

Yom Kippur: A day set aside for fasting, depriving oneself of pleasures and repenting from the sins of the previous year. This is always ten days after Rosh Hashanah.

Yom Tov: Yom Tov is used to refer to all major and minor holidays and festivals. Jews greet each other with a 'Good Yom Tov' when they meet at this special time.

Index

Parev index

Pesach-friendly index